Nonformal Education in Latin America
An Annotated Bibliography

UCLA LATIN AMERICAN CENTER PUBLICATIONS

REFERENCE SERIES

Ludwig Lauerhass, Jr.
General Editor
Volume 8

EXECUTIVE EDITORIAL COMMITTEE

Ludwig Lauerhass, Jr.
Johannes Wilbert
James W. Wilkie

Nonformal Education in Latin America

An Annotated Bibliography

by Susan L. Poston

UCLA Latin American Center Publications
University of California, Los Angeles • 1976

UCLA Latin American Center Publications
University of California, Los Angeles
Copyright © 1976 by The Regents of the University of California
All rights reserved
Library of Congress Catalog Card Number: 75-620142
ISBN: 0-87903-108-5
Printed in the United States of America

The cover and title page illustration by Diego Rivera is reproduced
with permission of Carleton Beals. It originally appeared in his
Mexican Maze (New York: Lippincott, 1931).

Contents

FOREWORD ix

ACKNOWLEDGMENTS xi

INTRODUCTION 1

ACRONYMS 7

ARGENTINA 13

Multifaceted Programs, 13   Agricultural Training, 14
Basic Education/Literacy, 14   Cultural Extension, 16
Family Life Education, 17   Vocational Skill Training, 17
Miscellaneous, 19   Conceptualization, 20

BOLIVIA 22

Multifaceted Programs, 22   Agricultural Training, 26
Basic Education/Literacy, 27   Professional/Paraprofessional Training, 28   Vocational Skill Training, 28   Miscellaneous, 28   Conceptualization, 30

BRAZIL 31

Multifaceted Programs, 31   Agricultural Training, 36
Basic Education/Literacy, 36   Cultural Extension, 41
Health, Hygiene, and Nutrition Instruction, 42   Professional/Paraprofessional Training, 43   Vocational Skill Training, 43   Miscellaneous, 51   Conceptualization, 54

CHILE 57

Multifaceted Programs, 57   Agricultural Training, 60
Basic Education/Literacy, 61   Cultural Extension, 62
Health, Hygiene, and Nutrition Instruction, 62   Labor Union Education, 63   Vocational Skill Training, 63
Miscellaneous, 64   Conceptualization, 66

COLOMBIA 68

Multifaceted Programs, 68   Agricultural Training, 73
Basic Education/Literacy, 74   Cultural Extension, 75
Family Life Education, 76   Health, Hygiene, and Nutrition Instruction, 76   Labor Union Education, 77

Professional/Paraprofessional Training, 77   Vocational
Skill Training, 77   Miscellaneous, 80

COSTA RICA   83
Multifaceted Programs, 83   Agricultural Training, 84
Basic Education/Literacy, 85   Cooperative Education, 86
Vocational Skill Training, 86   Conceptualization, 87

CUBA   88
Multifaceted Programs, 88   Basic Education/Literacy, 88
Vocational Skill Training, 90   Miscellaneous, 90

DOMINICAN REPUBLIC   93
Multifaceted Programs, 93   Basic Education/Literacy, 93
Miscellaneous, 93

ECUADOR   94
Multifaceted Programs, 94   Agricultural Training, 97
Basic Education/Literacy, 98   Cooperative Education, 100
Health, Hygiene, and Nutrition Instruction, 100   Profes-
sional/Paraprofessional Training, 100   Vocational Skill
Training, 101   Miscellaneous, 101   Conceptualization,
103

EL SALVADOR   104
Multifaceted Programs, 104   Agricultural Training, 104
Labor Union Education, 105   Miscellaneous, 105

GUATEMALA   107
Multifaceted Programs, 107   Agricultural Training, 108
Basic Education/Literacy, 108   Vocational Skill Training,
109   Miscellaneous, 110

GUYANA   112
Miscellaneous, 112

HAITI   113
Multifaceted Programs, 113   Basic Education/Literacy,
114   Miscellaneous, 115

HONDURAS   116
Multifaceted Programs, 116   Agricultural Training, 116
Basic Education/Literacy, 117

JAMAICA   118
Multifaceted Programs, 118   Agricultural Training, 118

Basic Education/Literacy, 119   Vocational Skill Training, 119

MEXICO   120
Multifaceted Programs, 120   Agricultural Training, 135
Basic Education/Literacy, 137   Health, Hygiene, and
Nutrition Instruction, 141   Professional/Paraprofessional
Training, 142   Vocational Skill Training, 143   Miscel-
laneous, 143   Conceptualization, 149

NICARAGUA   150
Multifaceted Programs, 150   Agricultural Training, 151
Basic Education/Literacy, 151   Professional/Paraprofes-
sional Training, 151

PANAMA   152
Multifaceted Programs, 152   Agricultural Training, 152
Health, Hygiene, and Nutrition Instruction, 152   Vocation-
al Skill Training, 152   Miscellaneous, 153

PARAGUAY   154
Multifaceted Programs, 154   Vocational Skill Training, 154
Miscellaneous, 155

PERU   156
Multifaceted Programs, 156   Agricultural Training, 167
Basic Education/Literacy, 170   Health, Hygiene, and
Nutrition Instruction, 171   Professional/Paraprofessional
Training, 172   Vocational Skill Training, 172   Miscel-
laneous, 173   Conceptualization, 177

PUERTO RICO   179
Multifaceted Programs, 179   Agricultural Training, 180
Basic Education/Literacy, 181   Cooperative Education, 181
Cultural Extension, 181   Health, Hygiene, and Nutrition
Instruction, 182   Professional/Paraprofessional Training,
182   Vocational Skill Training, 182   Miscellaneous,
183   Conceptualization, 184

TRINIDAD AND TOBAGO   185
Health, Hygiene, and Nutrition Instruction, 185   Miscellaneous, 185

URUGUAY   186
Multifaceted Programs, 186   Basic Education/Literacy,

186   Health, Hygiene, and Nutrition Instruction, 187
Conceptualization, 187

VENEZUELA   188
Multifaceted Programs, 188   Agricultural Training, 190
Basic Education/Literacy, 190   Health, Hygiene, and
Nutrition Instruction, 193   Professional/Paraprofessional
Training, 193   Vocational Skill Training, 194   Miscel-
laneous, 195   Conceptualization, 197

CENTRAL AMERICA AND THE CARIBBEAN   199
Multifaceted Programs, 199   Agricultural Training, 199
Basic Education/Literacy, 199   Health, Hygiene, and
Nutrition Instruction, 200   Vocational Skill Training, 200
Miscellaneous, 200   Conceptualization, 204

SOUTH AMERICA   205
Multifaceted Programs, 205   Agricultural Training, 208
Basic Education/Literacy, 209   Health, Hygiene, and
Nutrition Instruction, 210   Vocational Skill Training, 210
Miscellaneous, 212

LATIN AMERICA   216
Agricultural Training, 216   Basic Education/Literacy, 217
Cultural Extension, 219   Health, Hygiene, and Nutrition
Instruction, 219   Labor Union Education, 220   Profes-
sional/Paraprofessional Training, 220   Vocational Skill
Training, 222   Miscellaneous, 223

CONCEPTUALIZATION   235

INDEX   247

Foreword

The UCLA Latin American Center is pleased to include Susan Poston's *Non-formal Education in Latin America: An Annotated Bibliography* in its Reference Series. Published since 1962, this series comprises bibliographies and other reference works of interest to both individual Latin Americanists and libraries. The scope is broad enough to permit the inclusion of any work which will encourage and facilitate research on Latin America, not only in the humanities and social sciences but in any field which may be profitably approached from the area studies point of view. With this volume, the Center hopes to serve the needs of those students and scholars who are concerned with the problems of education and its alternatives in contemporary Latin America.

The Center is especially fortunate to have had Susan L. Poston as a collaborator in the series. Already trained in librarianship, Ms. Poston began this work as a master's degree project in Latin American Studies. In an effort lasting over two years, however, she surpassed the normal requirements for a thesis and brought to bear a sense of dedication, imagination, and diligence which has resulted in a product of professional quality. In fact, she has maintained a standard against which future volumes in this series may be measured.

The author's interest in the topic of nonformal education was stimulated by her involvement in the five-year, multidisciplinary program at UCLA on the theme of alternatives to traditional education in Latin America. This program was made possible by an Agency for International Development (AID) 211(d) grant which was coordinated by Professor Thomas J. La Belle with the assistance of Professors Johannes Wilbert and James Wilkie. Ms. Poston participated in a new graduate seminar and was able to take advantage of other course offerings which were initiated by Professor La Belle, who was also the chairman of her M.A. committee. The grant helped UCLA to develop as an institutional focal point for research and teaching on Latin American education and enabled more than fifty students and faculty members to do field work in Latin America.

The results of much of this research are now being drawn together, and the Latin American Center has begun publication of four anthologies and two bibliographies which treat the problems of formal and nonformal education in Latin America. The first anthology (volume 30 in the Latin American Studies Series) is *Educational Alternatives in Latin America: Social Change and Social Stratification*, edited by Thomas J. La Belle. The present bibliography is the second publication to appear and will be followed by *Education in Latin America: A Bibliography*, compiled by Ludwig Lauerhass, Jr. and Vera A. Haugse. Also in preparation are the three remaining anthologies, the first of which focuses on enculturation in the hinterlands of Latin America and is being edited by Johannes Wilbert.

Ludwig Lauerhass, Jr.

Acknowledgments

I wish to express my gratitude to Thomas J. La Belle of the Graduate School of Education at UCLA for his continuing support throughout the preparation of this bibliography. Particularly, I have appreciated his allowing me to work in a relatively unstructured manner, his enthusiasm about the project from the outset, and his many words of encouragement. He has given me access to documents collected on recent trips to Latin America for inclusion in the bibliography which can only contribute to its usefulness as a research tool. I am also grateful to Ludwig Lauerhass, Latin American Bibliographer in the Research Library at UCLA, for the excellent technical advice he proffered and, reluctant as I am to admit it, for his gentle prodding along the way. His counsel and friendship have been a great support.

The Latin American Center at UCLA has been exceedingly good to me in providing financial assistance throughout, without which the project could not have been completed. The staffs of the UCLA library system and the Library of Congress were no less generous with their time and unfailingly helpful when problems arose. I am especially grateful to Mary Kahler at the Hispanic Foundation of the Library of Congress who arranged access for me both to the authority card catalog and to the stack area, which simplified my task there enormously.

Finally, I owe special thanks to Donald F. Brannan for his patience and loving understanding throughout this endeavor, and for his invaluable assistance in reading and editing the manuscript.

Introduction

As the demands for education and training rise rapidly throughout Latin America, those faced with the task of educational planning find themselves compelled to consider alternatives to formal schooling. Burgeoning populations and shrinking financial resources have placed out of reach the once seemingly attainable goal of formal education for all. Yet nothing less than the economic survival of most Latin American nations demands that a work force be trained sufficient to the needs of societies growing ever more modern and industrialized. Undoubtedly, it is this imperative that most centrally explains the exponential expansion of educational alternatives in Latin America—a portion of which is recorded in the entries of this bibliography.

The marked contrast between urban and rural areas throughout Latin America is both a symptom and a cause of the region's pervasive educational troubles. Even in those countries where significant accomplishments have been made in providing a decent primary education, city children have benefited most. Indeed, educational facilities for the rural young in many Latin American countries are skimpy at best and virtually nonexistent at worst. Seeking a better life, multitudes of country people over the past decades have migrated to the cities, only to find their hopes dashed as they inexorably sink into the masses of uneducated and unskilled urban poor—thus exacerbating the enormous array of problems created by unchecked urban expansion. And so the familiar picture darkens.

Many of the programs reported in the succeeding pages were conceived precisely with the problems of rural population drain and consequent urban crunch in mind. To slow down the rural exodus an extensive range of programs has been implemented as an incentive to remain in the country. On the urban side, the trend has been toward training a presently idle potential labor force for jobs in industry. Training programs initiated in the cities during recent years, however, have not been as varied as those in the country, owing mostly to the earlier emergence into the modern world of urban areas, where an array of social services has existed for some time—which has not been the case in most rural areas of Latin America.

1

Organization

As the principle of inclusion in this bibliography, "nonformal education" was defined as any structured and relatively brief learning activity which takes place outside the formal, diploma- and degree-granting school system. The most cursory glance at the following pages will indicate the broad compass of publications this working definition admitted. On the one side of the spectrum are programs aimed at meeting a particular educational need (e.g., industrial skill training); numerous others are more broadly based but include an instructional component (e.g., the Peru-Cornell Project); while on the other side are theoretical discussions of nonformal education as a preliminary to implementation. So long as the educational activity under discussion satisfied these three requirements—that it occurred or was to occur outside the school system, that the activity was in some fashion or another structured, to distinguish it from so-called informal learning, and that it was of short duration, usually less than a year—the discussion was included. Thus, any publication describing a program which appeared merely to be an extension of the formal school system no matter how "innovative"—for instance, night school programs—was excluded, as were, for example, accounts of community improvement projects such as construction of a road or a school. Nor have I included courses for the handicapped, since they are considered to be in the category of "special education" and usually are an extension of the formal school system; or laws, since their intention of producing concrete programs is often not realized; or manuals and other textual materials, since they are in effect lesson plans and do not say anything about a program in theory or practice.

The bibliography is organized first by Latin American (or Caribbean) country and, within each country, by subject. Because many publications discuss programs from more than one country, I have next made separate regional groupings—Central America and the Caribbean, South America, and Latin America. For the purposes of this bibliography, I consider Latin America as that territory encompassing all independent countries in the western hemisphere south of the United States. Materials from and about Puerto Rico are the single exception which merit inclusion because of that country's Spanish cultural heritage and its orientation toward Latin American affairs.

The subject divisions are based on a program's content. Publications on multifaceted programs compose the first subject division. These are programs designed to instruct in more than one subject matter concurrently—vocational or artisan training, modern agricultural techniques, and nutrition, for example. This category also contains items on what are known as community development programs which aim to influence social change on a broad scale and which involve, but are not limited to, some structured learning activity.

Following this broadly inclusive category, I have grouped the publications according to the specific subject areas around which the programs they describe revolve. Thus the entries in "Agricultural Training" offer information on up-to-date farming techniques as well as on specific agricultural skills, such as tractor operation and repair. "Basic Education/Literacy Programs" contains material on literacy programs, the usual approach of which is to impart fundamentals of such disciplines as mathematics, history and civics in the course of teaching reading and writing. "Cooperative Education" covers precisely what the title states: education on the theory and practice of cooperatives, usually provided by cooperatives for their members. "Cultural Extension" is more of a catchall; it includes entries on library and museum programs, as well as on radio programs devoted to artistic programming such as music appreciation and instruction in literature and the arts. Publications in "Family Life Education" embrace such matters as birth control clinics and family planning campaigns. "Health, Hygiene, and Nutrition Instruction" is an extensive yet interrelated category which includes entries on such educational endeavors as home extension programs in health and nutrition and programs of instruction by local health clinics. The publications listed under "Labor Union Education" deal with theoretical and practical aspects of labor union affairs, and as in the case of the cooperatives, are organized by the leadership for their members.

"Professional and Paraprofessional Training" is a separate division inasmuch as its aim seems to differ widely from the other types of educational activities presented here. This tends to be training for further professional advancement, but outside the formal system, or training for paraprofessionals who in turn will instruct others in a nonformal setting. "Vocational Skill Training" contains items on training for any skilled occupation, artisan as well as industrial. Agricultural training, it should be remembered, is treated in its own section.

The division entitled "Miscellaneous" contains, as one might expect, publications which describe programs that simply will not properly fit in any of the above divisions. Here are found overviews of nonformal programs for a particular country or for a region as a whole and accounts of different types of educational projects, as distinguished from a multipronged single program, which would appear in "Multifaceted Programs."

The final category, "Conceptualization," contains entries which consider nonformal education from a theoretical point of view or in the interest of presenting ideas for a new program or revamping an old one.

A few further remarks on the subject breakdown. First, the material on regional programs (e.g., the Andean Mission) will be found both under the general regional category when the program as a whole is being discussed, and under the specific country involved when an entry is dealing with the program's particular national projects. Second, when an individual project in one of the multifaceted programs is discussed, as is occasionally the case, the publication will be found in the subject category to which it pertains, not in the multifaceted division. My reason for this choice is simple: since this is a subject bibliography, subject must be the primary concern in classifying. Third, it was frequently difficult to determine whether a program in vocational skills training (often called technical training in the literature) was formal or nonformal. When there were any doubts, I excluded the item, on the rationale that technical training offered in the Latin American nations is typically a part of the formal school system, usually at the secondary level.

Scope

The main practical problem confronting the compiler of a bibliography in a newly defined area of interest is to design the best system for uncovering the maximum of relevant materials. My approach was to search a wide variety of sources under an array of subject headings within existing bibliographies, document listings, periodical indexes, collection catalogs, and abstracts. Because of their long-standing interest in education and development programs in the Third World, I began by checking major international agency document listings (UN, UNESCO, FAO, WHO, OAS, PAU). These agencies have actively participated in or, at the very least, have provided the necessary funds for, programs which would fall under the purview of this bibliography. Within most of them there are committees or councils responsible for educational programs—a fact which luckily eliminated the necessity of a page-by-page scan of the document listings.

From my own reading and from checking the various periodical indexes, abstracting services, and collection catalogs, I generated a rather lengthy subject list, the purpose of which was to insure the discovery of as many entries in the field as possible. The broad range of these headings is indicated above. My primary sources were the *Index to Latin American Periodical Literature*, the *Index to Latin American Periodicals, Education Index, Public Affairs Information Service Bulletin, Dissertation Abstracts,* and the *Catalog of the Latin American Collection*, University of Texas.[1] An additional refer-

[1]Pan American Union, Columbus Memorial Library, *Index to Latin American Periodical Literature, 1929-1960* (Boston: G. K. Hall, 1962), 8 vols. and supplement; *Index to Latin American Periodicals: Humanities and Social Sciences* (Washington: Columbus Memorial Library, Pan American Union, 1961-1970), vols. 1-10; *Education Index* (New York: H. W. Wilson, 1940-1974), vols. 5-24; *Public Affairs Information Service Bulletin* (New York: Public

ence work which proved to be most valuable was the *Handbook of Latin American Studies,*[2] which I searched for er.tries in the sections on anthropology, economics, education, and sociology.

In general, I have limited myself to publications from the United States and the Latin American countries in question, and to those written in English, Spanish, and Portuguese, though a few European journals which publish in English with some regularity on the subject are listed. And, as the user will note, the bibliography includes even the briefest of articles, since, despite their length, these often provide the only mention of a program or add information not available elsewhere. I decided on a time frame from 1940—the date when nonformal programs began to appear and be written about in earnest—to the present (1975). Again there are exceptions, notably the Cultural Mission program in Mexico and a few scattered literacy programs. I have included entries on these programs published earlier than 1940 whenever my searching process turned them up, but I did not make a special effort to seek them out.

A full citation appears for all material wherever possible. Also, the reader will find a list of acronyms immediately preceding the text—a virtual necessity in light of their constant use throughout the literature. The index lists authors—corporate and personal—international and government agencies, private organizations, names of programs, and monograph series. It does not include article or monograph titles or names of periodicals.

The decision to annotate was based on my judgment that a bibliography is always helpful when it presents more than citations and subject headings, since inferences about the content of an entry drawn from its title and subject division placement are not infrequently misleading and the occasion of countless wasted steps. The user of this bibliography should note, however, that I have been unable to review every item firsthand, and in some instances I have had to rely on annotations from the reference sources I consulted. These were nonetheless included whenever they appeared germane to the subject but are distinguished by an asterisk (*).

My checking was conducted at three major institutions. I began work in the

---

Affairs Information Service, 1940-1974), vols. 26-60; *Dissertation Abstracts* (Ann Arbor, Mich.: University Microfilms, 1938-1966), vols. 1-26; *Dissertation Abstracts: Section A, Humanities and Social Sciences* (Ann Arbor, Mich.: University Microfilms, 1966-1969), vols. 27-29; *Dissertation Abstracts International: Section A, Humanities and Social Sciences* (Ann Arbor, Mich.: University Microfilms, 1969-1974), vols. 30-34; University of Texas, Austin, Library, *Catalog of the Latin American Collection* (Boston: G. K. Hall, 1969), 31 vols. and supplement.

[2]*Handbook of Latin American Studies* (Gainesville: University of Florida Press, 1940-1974), vols. 6-36.

library system of the University of California, Los Angeles, and continued at the Pan American Union's Columbus Memorial Library and the Library of Congress in Washington, D.C.

Limitations

The bibliography is not, of course, without its problems and limitations. Most importantly, it cannot be emphasized enough that the following is no more than a preliminary effort in this expanding field.[3] As is all too well known by scholars in Latin American studies, information flow from Latin America to the United States is often insufficient. Finding a citation on educational alternatives was one thing, obtaining the materials was quite another—particularly Latin American government documents and international agency publications (notably, the FAO). Either there is little interest in such concerns in this country, or the various governments have, for several reasons, been remiss in distributing their reports and publications; a combination of the two is most likely. The results are the same: these publications are hard to come by in U.S. libraries. Even the Library of Congress lacked many of the Latin American government documents I needed, and there were large gaps as well in their collections of international agency publications, particularly the FAO (which apparently has a very poor system of distribution).

This brings me to yet another limitation. Because those documents which find their way to this country travel at a snail's pace, this bibliography is not as current as one might wish. I have been able to include few government documents from this decade, which means that the use of this reference work for contemporary research will doubtless be diminished.

I am optimistic, nonetheless, that this initial effort will not be without value in aiding those wishing to pursue research in this growing area. The bibliography covers in some depth programs begun in the 1950s and 1960s, thus lending itself well to historical studies. I can only hope that the work undertaken here will be improved and expanded by others.

[3]To the best of my knowledge, Rolland G. Paulston's *Non-Formal Education: An Annotated International Bibliography* (New York: Praeger, 1972), is the only bibliography in print on nonformal education. Given the scope of Paulston's work—publications included are limited to the ten years previous to the publication date—the material on Latin America is necessarily limited.

Acronyms

ABCAR	Associação Brasileira de Crédito e Assistência Rural
ACAR	Associação de Crédito e Assistência Rural (Brazil)
ACPH	Acción Cultural Popular Hondureña
ACPO	Acción Cultural Popular (Colombia)
AIA	American International Association for Economic and Social Development
AID	Agency for International Development (United States)
ALPACA	Asociación de Ligas Peruanas Agrarias de Campesinos de Avanzada
ANCAR	Associação Nordestina de Crédito e Assistência Rural (Brazil)
ANPO	Animação Popular (Brazil)
APRA	Alianza Popular Revolucionaria Americana (Peru)
ARMO	Adiestramiento Rápido de la Mano-de-Obra (Mexico)
ASAR	Asociación de Servicios Artesanales y Rurales (Bolivia)
ASCOFAME	Asociación Colombiana de Facultades de Medecina
CAJP	Clubs Agrícolas Juveniles Perú
CAO	Centro de Adiestramiento de Operadores (Mexico)
CBAI	Commissão Brasileira-Americana de Educação Industrial
CBR	Consejo de Bienestar Rural (Venezuela)
CECATI	Centros de Capacitación para el Trabajo Industrial (Mexico)
CEDEN	Centro para el Desarrollo de la Educación No-Formal (Colombia)
CEPAL	Comisión Económica para América Latina
CGT	Confederación General del Trabajo

7

CIAS	Centro de Investigación y Acción Social (Nicaragua)
CIDA	Comité Interamericano de Desarrollo Agrícola
CIDEA	Consejo Informativo de Educación Alimenticia (Venezuela)
CIDOC	Centro Intercultural de Documentación (Mexico)
CIER	Centro Interamericano de Educación Rural
CIMMYT	Centro Internacional de Mejoramiento de Maiz y Trigo
CINTERFOR	Centro Interamericano de Investigación y Documentación sobre Formación Profesional
CLI	Consejo de Lenguas Indígenas
CNAOP	Comisión Nacional de Aprendizaje y Orientación Profesional (Argentina)
CNEA	Campanha Nacional de Erradicação do Analfabetismo (Brazil)
CNER	Campanha Nacional de Educação Rural (Brazil)
CNFI	Centros Nacionales de Formación de Instructores (Colombia)
COLEFI	Confederación Latinoamericana para la Educación Fundamental Integral
CONET	Consejo Nacional de Educación Técnica (Argentina)
CORA	Corporación de Reforma Agraria (Chile)
COSEC	Coordinating Secretariat of National Unions of Students
CRECER	Campaña para la Reforma Eficaz de las Comunidades Escolares de la República (Peru)
CREFAL	Centro Regional de Educación Fundamental para la América Latina
CRUTAC	Centro Rural Universitário de Treinamento e Ação Comunitária (Brazil)
CTM	Confederación de Trabajadores Mexicanos
CUB	Confederación Universitaria Boliviana
DESEC	Centro para el Desarrollo Social y Económico (Bolivia)
DTICA	Department of Inter-American Technical Cooperation in Agriculture

EBL	Educación Básica Laboral (Peru)
ECLA	Economic Commission for Latin America
FAO	Food and Agricultural Organization
FENACOOPAR	Federación Nacional de Cooperativas Arroceras (Ecuador)
FENCAP	Federación Nacional de Campesinos del Perú
FEPEC	Fundación para la Educación Permanente en Colombia
IAIAS	Inter-American Institute of Agricultural Sciences
IBR	Instituto de Bienestar Rural (Paraguay)
IBRD	International Bank for Reconstruction and Development
ICE	Instituto Campesino de Educación (Bolivia)
ICECU	Instituto Centroamericano de Extensión de la Cultura
ICED	International Council for Educational Development
ICFTU	International Confederation of Free Trade Unions
ICIRA	Instituto de Capacitación, Investigación y Reforma Agraria (Chile)
IDB	Inter-American Development Bank
IDEC	International Development Corporation
IDECO	Instituto de Desarrollo Comunitario (Chile)
IEAG	Instituto Ecuatoriano de Antropología y Geografía
IER	Instituto de Educación Rural (Chile)
IER	Instituto de Educación Rural (Peru)
IESCA	Instituto de Estudios Sindicales de Centro América
IIAA	Institute of Inter-American Affairs (United States)
ILO	Internation Labor Organization International Labor Office
IMF	International Metalworkers' Federation
INA	Instituto Nacional de Aprendizaje (Costa Rica)
INACAP	Instituto Nacional de Capacitación (Chile)
INAH	Instituto Nacional de Antropología y Historia (Mexico)
INCE	Instituto Nacional de Cooperación Educativa (Venezuela)
INCORA	Instituto Colombiano de Reforma Agraria

INCUPO	Instituto de Cultura Popular (Argentina)
INDAP	Instituto de Desarrollo Agropecuario (Chile)
INI	Instituto Nacional Indigenista (Mexico)
INTECAP	Instituto de Capacitación y Productividad (Guatemala)
ISC	International Student Conference
IVAC	Instituto Venezolano de Acción Comunitaria
JAC	Juventud de Acción Católica Cubana
JYC	Jamaica Youth Corps
LBA	Legião Brasileira de Assistência
LEA	Liga de Enseñanza de Analfabetos, Liga de Enseñanza de Alfabetización (Ecuador)
MEB	Movimento de Educação de Base (Brazil)
MOBRAL	Movimento Brasileiro de Alfabetização
MUDES	Movimento Universitário de Desenvolvimento Económico e Social (Brazil)
NEC	Núcleo Educativo Comunal (Peru)
OAS	Organization of American States
ODEA	Oficina de Educación de Adultos (Venezuela)
OEA	Organización de Estados Americanos
OECD	Organization for Economic Cooperation and Development
OEE	Oficina de Estudios Especiales (Mexico)
OIT	Organización Internacional de Trabajo
ORIT	Organización Regional Interamericana de Trabajadores
ORT	Organization for Rehabilitation Through Training (Brazil)
OXFAM	Oxford Committee for Famine Relief (England)
PAEN	Programa de Alimentación y Educación Nutricional (Paraguay)
PAU	Pan American Union
PINA	Programa Integrado de Nutrición Aplicada
PIPMO	Programa Intensivo de Preparação da Mão-de-Obra (Brazil)

PNIPA	Plan Nacional de la Integración de la Población Aborigen (Peru)
PPEA	Agricultural Enterprise Promotion Program (Ecuador)
PROFAMILIA	Asociación Pro-Bienestar de la Familia Colombiana
PRRA	Puerto Rico Reconstruction Administration
SAI	Servicio Agricultura Interamericano
SAPS	Serviço de Alimentação da Previdência Social (Brazil)
SAR	Serviço de Assistência Rural (Brazil)
SAREC	Servicio Ambulante Rural de Extensión Cultural (Ecuador)
SCIA	Servicio Cooperativo Interamericano de Agricultura (Ecuador)
SCIDE	Servicio Cooperativo Interamericano de Educación
SCIPA	Servicio Cooperativo Interamericano de Producción de Alimientos
SCISP	Servicio Cooperativo Interamericano de Salud Pública
SCT	Servicio de Cooperación Técnica (Chile)
SEA	Serviço de Educação de Adultos (Brazil)
SECAP	Servicio Ecuatoriano de Capacitación Profesional
SECPANE	Servicio Cooperativo Peruano Norteamericano de Educación
SENA	Servicio Nacional de Aprendizaje (Colombia)
SENAC	Serviço Nacional de Aprendizagem Comercial (Brazil)
SENAI	Serviço Nacional de Aprendizagem Industrial (Brazil)
SENATI	Servicio Nacional de Aprendizaje y Trabajo Industrial (Peru)
SESC	Serviço Social do Comércio (Brazil)
SESI	Serviço Social da Indústria (Brazil)
SESP	Serviço Especial de Saúde Pública (Brazil)
SFEI	Servicio do Fomento de la Economía Indígena (Guatemala)
SIL	Summer Institute of Linguistics
SIPA	Servicio de Investigación y Promoción Agraria (Peru)

SRI	Stanford Research Institute
STACA	Servicio Técnico Agrícola Colombiano Americano
STICA	Servicio Técnico Interamericano de Cooperación Agrícola
SUDENE	Superintendência do Desenvolvimento do Nordeste (Brazil)
TAA	Technical Assistance Administration (United Nations)
TEPA	Telescuela Popular Americana (Peru)
UFUCH	Unión de Federaciones Universitarias de Chile
UN	United Nations
UNDP	United Nations Development Program
UNESCO	United Nations Educational, Scientific and Cultural Organization
UNICEF	United Nations Children's Fund
UNP	Unión Nacional de Periodistas (Ecuador)
UNRISD	United Nations Research Institute for Social Development
UT	Universidad de Trabajo (Uruguay)
UTC	Unión de Trabajadores de Colombia
WHO	World Health Organization
YMCA	Young Men's Christian Association
YWCA	Young Women's Christian Association

Argentina

MULTIFACETED PROGRAMS

1. "The Activities of the Schools for Adults in Argentina," *Argentine News*, 22 (August 1, 1940), 19.

    A brief article emphasizing the library materials used to supplement the courses in the adult schools established for immigrants which are designed to help them assimilate into Argentine culture. Courses run from technical to agricultural to domestic skill training.

2. CHARTIER, R. A., L. NIILUS, and C. M. SABANES. "Missionary Structures and Training for Missions: The River Plate Area," *International Review of Missions*, 57:226 (April, 1968), 217-228.

    Briefly discusses the Urban Centre project (social service/community development oriented) created in 1963 in the Villa Ilasa section of Lanús, near Buenos Aires. It later came to be known as the Centro Urbano–Nueva Parroquia project (1967)—a united effort of several religious denominations.

3. INTERNATIONAL LABOR OFFICE. "Pilot Farm School for European Agricultural Immigrants to Argentina," *Industry and Labour,* 11:7 (April 1, 1954), 283.

    Reports on the Santa Catalina Center at Llavallol in the province of Buenos Aires. The six-month practical training course is divided into two segments: (1) language, institutions, and customs; and (2) farming methods practiced in Argentina.

4. ORGANIZATION OF AMERICAN STATES. CONSEJO INTERAMERICANO ECONÓMICO Y SOCIAL. COMISIÓN ESPECIAL X: COMISIÓN INTERAMERICANA DE TELECOMUNICACIONES. QUINTA REUNIÓN, BOGOTÁ, COLOMBIA, 22-29 DE JULIO DE 1970. *Plan radio-pedagógico argentino educación popular 1970.* Document OEA/Ser.H/XIII (CIES/Com.X/407). Washington: 1970. 75 pp.

    Presents the plan of the Secretaría de Estado de Comunicaciones, Servicio Oficial de Radiodifusión for 1967. The three broad areas of programming are the adult literacy course, cultural extension and the secondary level support course. Provides a detailed description of literacy and cultural programs (history, folklore, health, music, drama, vocational counseling, etc.) with examples of the written material

13

distributed. The document also describes the proposed adult education program for television (slated for 1971) which is to be composed of literacy and popular culture aspects.

AGRICULTURAL TRAINING

*5. FORNI, FLOREAL H., and ADRIANO GROENEWEGEN. *Metodología para el desarrollo de las comunidades rurales*. Publicaciones, 4. Resistencia, Argentina: Estación Experimental Agropecuaria Sáenz Peña, 1968. 36 pp.
Also published in: *A & P: Revista de Arquitectura y Planeamiento*, 3/4 (1964), 102-114.

*6. PERGAMINO, ARGENTINE REPUBLIC. ESTACIÓN EXPERIMENTAL. *Estación Experimental Agropecuaria Pergamino: 50 años al servicio del productor agropecuario, 1912-1962*. Boletín de Divulgación, 21. Pergamino: 1962. 68 pp.

BASIC EDUCATION/LITERACY

7. ARGENTINE REPUBLIC. COMISIÓN NACIONAL DE ALFABETIZACIÓN Y EDIFICACIÓN ESCOLAR. PROGRAMA NACIONAL INTENSIVO DE ALFABETIZACIÓN Y EDUCACIÓN DE ADULTOS. *Memoria anual 1965*. Serie Informativa, 2. N.p.: 1966. 21 pp.
Report of the literacy program for 1965, its organization and accomplishments.

8. ARGENTINE REPUBLIC. COMISIÓN NACIONAL DE ALFABETIZACIÓN Y EDUCACIÓN DE ADULTOS. PROGRAMA NACIONAL INTENSIVO DE ALFABETIZACIÓN Y EDUCACIÓN DE ADULTOS. *Niveles, objetivos y contenidos mínimos del programa de alfabetización y educación de adultos*. Serie Didáctica, 1. Buenos Aires: 1965. 12 pp.
Description of objectives and programs of study (including foldout chart giving diagrammatic explication) which depend upon individual levels of achievement already attained by students. Percentages of time to be devoted to various subjects and activities given. Stresses the importance of simultaneous cultural and community activities.

*An asterisk indicates that the reference was not consulted firsthand.

9. ARGENTINE REPUBLIC. CONSEJO NACIONAL DE EDUCACIÓN. *Plan de estudios y programas de las escuelas para adultos y escuelas primarias anexas a las unidades del ejército y la armada.* Buenos Aires: Tall. Graf. del Consejo Nacional de Educación, 1942. 259 pp.

> While the adult education program appears to be within the formal school system, the programs offered by the Armed Forces are primarily literacy training for illiterate conscripts.

*10. ARGENTINE REPUBLIC. CONSEJO NACIONAL DE EDUCACIÓN. *Programa Nacional Intensivo de Alfabetización y Educación de Adultos, 1964-1968.* Buenos Aires: 1964. No pagination.

11. ARGENTINE REPUBLIC. JUNTA NACIONAL DE ADMINISTRACIÓN. PROGRAMA NACIONAL INTENSIVO DE ALFABETIZACIÓN Y EDUCACIÓN DE ADULTOS. *Para divulgación pública del Programa Nacional Intensivo de Alfabetización y Educación de Adultos.* Serie Informativa, 3. Buenos Aires: Talleres Gráficos, 1966. 10 pp.

> Description of the national literacy and adult education campaign: objectives, administration, educational centers, study plan, personnel, equipment, and execution.

12. ARGENTINE REPUBLIC. MINISTERIO DE EDUCACIÓN Y JUSTICIA. *Informe de la República Argentina al Congreso Mundial de Ministros de Educación para la Liquidación del Analfabetismo en Teherán, 8-19 de septiembre de 1965.* Buenos Aires: Centro Nacional de Documentación e Información Educativa, 1965. 133 pp.

> Detailed report of the national literacy campaign (May-October, 1965) as presented to the international congress for the eradication of illiteracy, describing goals, official and private cooperation, financing, organization and administration, local centers, and the plan of action.

*13. FORNACIARI, DORA. *El campesino tucumano, educación y cultura.* Serie Estudios y Documentos, 4. Tucumán, Argentina: Centro de Documentación e Información Educativa, 1971. 93 pp.

> Student project (1969-1970) in the interior of Tucumán using the Paulo Freire method. (Annotation from: "Education for Rural Life," *Educational Documentation and Information: Bulletin of the International Bureau of Education*, 46:183 [2d quarter, 1972], 107)

14. GENOVESI, LUIS JOSÉ. *Analfabetismo y alfabetización en la Argentina actual.* Buenos Aires: Editorial Albacara, 1966. 101 pp.

> Discusses the problem of illiteracy in Argentina and briefly describes the national literacy campaign, special courses in the Armed Forces, and special courses for the 14-18 age group.

15. JESSEL, CAMILLA. "Pilot Literacy Campaign in South America," *Times Educational Supplement*, 2700 (February 17, 1967), 532-533.

> Describes the criteria for selection of the areas in which the program was initiated, the creation of learning centers, and the results of the first programs of the literacy campaign in Mendoza. The program includes instruction in topics ranging from hygiene to labor organization as well as in language.

16. *¿Qué es INCUPO?* [Buenos Aires?: Editorial 'Rio Parana,' 1975]. No pagination.

> Describes the work of the Instituto de Cultura Popular, a private organization in northern Argentina, which focuses on literacy training and basic education, primarily by radio.

17. TIDONE, JORGE FEDERICO. "Audición: Escuela del Aire, Consejo Nacional de Educación," *El Monitor de la Educación Común*, 70:931 (July, 1960), 52-59.

> Text of a program used on the *Escuela del Aire* entitled *"Los Personajes de la Oración,"* dealing with parts of speech.

CULTURAL EXTENSION

18. AMALFI, DELIA CECILIA. "Una biblioteca al servicio de la escuela y de la comunidad: Ideal que quiere realizar la Biblioteca 'Almafuerte' de la Escuela Experimental no. 24, de La Matanza," *Revista de Educación*, La Plata, 19 (1968), 116-119.

> Brief mention of community services offered by the library: conferences, courses, theater, films.

19. "Argentina's School of the Air," *World Education*, 5:5 (September, 1940), 464.

> Brief mention of the new radio school program.

20. "La escuela argentina del aire," *La Revista Castellana*, Long Beach, California (May, 1940), 5-6, 12.

> Provides background information on the creation and organization of the radio school network. The first programs consisted of instruction in Spanish, French, English, and Italian.

21. HALL, ROBERT KING. "Argentina's School of the Air," *Education*, Boston, 60:10 (June, 1940), 649-653.

> Good description of early programming, its format and drawbacks.

22. ORGANIZATION OF AMERICAN STATES. CONSEJO INTERAMERICANO ECONÓMICO Y SOCIAL. COMISIÓN ESPECIAL X: COMISIÓN INTER-AMERICANA DE TELECOMUNICACIONES. TERCERA REUNIÓN, RIO DE JANEIRO, 29 DE JULIO AL 9 DE AGOSTO DE 1968. *Argentina— actualización del informe nacional.* Document OEÅ/Ser.H/XIII (CIES/Com.X/141). Washington: 1968. 30 pp.

     Part II of the report covers educational television and radio broadcasting. It includes a brief description of programs in Buenos Aires and several provincial capitals.

23. "People's Libraries in Argentina," *World Education,* 6 (March, 1941), 192.

     Describes the widely distributed system of community libraries (1,450 in 1939), the rapid growth of the system, and the educational activities organized by the libraries.

24. SALGADO, ALVARO. "A radiodifusão educativa na Argentina," *Cultura Política,* 5:48 (January, 1945), 58-74.

     Radio cultural extension programming first began in Argentina in 1925; the *Escuela del Aire* began in the late 1930s. This article describes the goals of the radio programs and offers a detailed discussion of the organization and content of the programming.

FAMILY LIFE EDUCATION

25. GIORDANO, LUIS. "Escuelas para padres: Curso de pedagogía familiar," *El Monitor de la Educación Común,* 64:864 (December, 1944), 54-72.

     Courses are designed to promote understanding of educative functions of parents vis-à-vis their children in the home and emphasize the importance of creating an atmosphere condusive to healthy growth. Pilot project took place in Buenos Aires in 1944. Includes organization plan, course outlines, and content of discussions.

VOCATIONAL SKILL TRAINING

*26. ARGENTINE REPUBLIC. MINISTERIO DE EDUCACIÓN Y JUSTICIA. COMISIÓN NACIONAL DE APRENDIZAJE Y ORIENTACIÓN PROFESIONAL. *La preparación de mano de obra calificada para la industria.* Buenos Aires: 1956. 63 pp.

27. CATTANEO DÍAZ, M. "Los cursos de perfeccionamiento obrero en la República Argentina," *Historium*, 8:86 (July, 1946), 426-428.
    New vocational training program under the direction of the *Dirección General de Aprendizaje* initiated in 1944 offering a wide variety of courses, open to anyone, without requirements for completing the primary education cycle. Also provides special schools and courses for women.

28. "Establishment of Textile Trade Schools in Argentina, 1942," *Monthly Labor Review*, 58:1 (January, 1944), 111.
    Describes the six textile trade schools to be established in Argentina in late 1942 to advance the interests of hand weaving and weavers.

29. ESTRELLA GUTIÉRREZ, FERMÍN. "Las escuelas de adultos en la República Argentina," Pan American Union, *Bulletin*, 70:3 (March, 1936), 281-285.
    While reflecting the popular negative attitude toward education for women, the article does give a fairly clear description of course work available through the special adult night schools. Courses are divided in two groups: primary education and technical training.

30. GARCÍA VIEYRA, ALBERTO. *Política educativa*. Buenos Aires: Librería Huemul, 1967. 315 pp.
    Brief mention of apprenticeship and technical-vocational training available (pp. 259-260).

31. MANTOVANI, JUAN. "La enseñanza técnica industrial," *Nueva Era*, 14 (1945), 85-88.
    Mentions programs of night school vocational training for workers in Buenos Aires and La Plata.

*32. NOGUES, ANDRÉ. *El taller y las disciplinas afines: La formación profesional*. Buenos Aires: Comisión Nacional de Aprendizaje y Orientación Profesional, 1957. 25 pp.

33. "Número extraordinario dedicado a las escuelas para adultos," *El Monitor de la Educación Común*, 67:911 (November, 1948), 1-138.
    Sections include: history of adult schools in Argentina; various approaches used for study plans; organization of schools; initiatives; current status of the schools; projections for the future. Generally two plans have been followed over the years: (1) courses directed toward completing primary education; (2) special individual courses in vocational training for men and women. Deals primarily with the system in Buenos Aires.

34. PAN AMERICAN UNION. "La enseñanza técnica industrial en la Argentina," Pan American Union, *Boletín*, 80 (June, 1946), 355-357.
Part of the technical school program is directed toward workers who want to improve their skills while continuing to work. Courses are usually offered at night.

35. QUIRNO COSTA, JOSÉ A. "Problems of Adult Education in the Argentine Republic," in *Educational Yearbook, 1940*. New York: International Institute, Teachers College, Columbia University, 1940, pp. 5-15.
Mentions system of "people's universities" throughout the country that provides skill training for adults without previous educational requirements.

36. ROBLES, OPTULIO DE. "Escuela de aprendices operarios de Puerto Belgrano," *Infancia y Juventud*, 18 (January/March, 1941), 85-95.
Apprentice skill training offered by the Argentine Navy.

37. "Vocational Education in Argentina," *International Labour Review*, 57:6 (June, 1948), 652-654.
Outlines the new training courses at the Juan Domingo Perón Textile Apprenticeship School and the special training courses for girls and young women sponsored by the National Apprenticeship and Vocational Guidance Committee.

*38. YGOBONE, AQUILES D. *El problema educacional en la Patagonia: Contribución al estudio y solución de las cuestiones vitales del sur argentino*. Buenos Aires: El Ateneo, 1948. 647 pp.
Covers technical schools of arts and crafts, apprenticeship programs, and technical missions. (From: United Nations Educational, Scientific, and Cultural Organization. *An International Bibliography of Technical and Vocational Education*. Educational Studies and Documents, 31. Paris: 1959. p. 14)

MISCELLANEOUS

39. OLIVÉ, RODOLFO. "Volver a estudiar: ¿Trabajan los sindicatos para elevar la calidad del obrero?" *Estudios*, 586 (September/October, 1967), 15-17.
Article describes the structured educational efforts of three labor unions. La Primera Escuela Sindical Argentina was created by the Federación Argentina del Personal de Gas del Estado. "ABC" (literacy) courses—short term and at night—are offered by the CGT. The

Sindicato de Luz y Fuerza offers: literacy training courses; basic skill training; labor union education courses; library services. Courses deal with labor theory, rights, and problems as well as a range of subjects from human relations to history to economics.

40. ORGANIZATION FOR ECONOMIC COOPERATION AND DEVELOPMENT. *Education, Human Resources and Development in Argentina.* Paris: 1967. 465 pp.

The discussion in Chapter 8 ("Para-Scholastic and Informal Education") touches on a wide range of nonformal educational programs, from vocational training to agricultural training to literacy programs to courses in the arts and crafts. It offers an analysis of the contribution of nonformal programs to education as a whole. Chapter 27 talks about the need for complementary formal and nonformal educational systems.

41. TAYLOR, CARL CLEVELAND. *Rural Life in Argentina.* Baton Rouge, Louisiana State University Press, 1948. 464 pp.

Chapter 15 provides an analysis of agricultural extension services, experiment stations, and other agencies involved in agricultural education. Also briefly describes the activities of the Museo Social Argentino which has programs directed toward improving rural life. Chapter 16 mentions the educational activities of the youth organizations of the Federación Agraria Argentina.

CONCEPTUALIZATION

42. ALVAREZ AHUMADA, ZELANDA. *Desarrollo social y reforma agraria: Bases para un programa de desarrollo integral de la comunidad rural.* Colección Agramante. Buenos Aires: Editorial Palestra, 1963. 176 pp.

Presents a detailed plan for a community development program for Argentina which would revolve around cultural missions and educational radio and film services sent out to the countryside, providing fundamental education, technical assistance, and supervised credit programs. Included is an organization scheme for the proposed Dirección de Desarrollo Comunal. The ideas presented are based on the author's work in northern Argentina and her observations of other community development programs.

43. ANDREANI, JUAN. "La educación del araucano," *El Monitor de la Educación Común*, 65:885/886 (September/October, 1946), 24-35.

Calls for the creation of an Instituto Educacional del Indio with the functions of providing: infant care; education of children of school age; education of adults (in formal classroom setting, in the home, in the fields, and in church). Educational programs are to relate to the needs of the Araucano—crop cultivation, livestock raising, health, and sanitation, among others.

44. ARGENTINE REPUBLIC. COMISIÓN NACIONAL DE ALFABETIZACIÓN Y EDIFICACIÓN ESCOLAR. PROGRAMA NACIONAL INTENSIVO DE ALFABETIZACIÓN Y EDUCACIÓN DE ADULTOS. *Función y desarrollo de las bibliotecas escolares y populares y su relación con el Programa Nacional Intensivo de Alfabetización y Educación de Adultos*. Serie Didáctica, 2. Buenos Aires: 1965. 30 pp.

Emphasizes the importance of popular libraries as centers for continuing education, as community cultural centers. Libraries must initiate intensive programs geared to adult education, particularly in semiurban and rural areas where the library is the only institutional source of further education. Recommends a broad expansion of existing services.

45. DAVIE, ALBERTO G. "La enseñanza técnica en la República Argentina," *Universidad*, Santa Fé, Argentina, 39 (January/March, 1959), 157-169.

Proposes three levels of technical education, the first of which is to be established in *"talleres o escuelas fábrica"* and is called *"aprendizaje laboral (obrero calificado)."* This is to be distinct from technical instruction on the secondary and university levels of the formal school system.

46. POZZI, JORGE TOMÁS. "Problemas de la escuela rural en la provincia de Corrientes," *Cursos y Conferencias*, 11:21:125/126 (August/September, 1942), 297-450.

Chapter 4 (*extensión escolar*) suggests the formation of Clubs de Campesinos Cooperadores to meet the need of extending the benefits of the school to the community as a whole by organizing lectures to be held in the school facility after regular hours. The emphasis is on combining educational with social activities. Recommends that the school library become a community resource. Part of a larger study of and plan for education in Corrientes.

Bolivia

MULTIFACETED PROGRAMS

47. BAIRON, MAX A. "La educación del indio en Bolivia," *América Indígena*, 2:3 (July, 1942), 7-10.
    Includes brief description of *núcleos escolares* system and provides chart showing its current organization.

48. BJÖRNBERG, ARNE. *Las poblaciones indígenas y el cooperativismo: Observaciones y experiencias del desarrollo del programa en Bolivia*. Stockholm, Sweden: 1959. 15 pp.
    Activities of the ILO-administered Andean Mission in Bolivia, 1957-1959. Describes the training programs and their results, both practical and social.

49. BOLIVIA. CONSEJO NACIONAL DE EDUCACIÓN. *El estado actual de la educación en Bolivia: Informe a la Misión Magruder*. La Paz: Edit. del Estado, 1943. 15 pp.
    Educational work (literacy training and some vocational training) undertaken by the Army.

50. BOLIVIA. CONSEJO NACIONAL DE EDUCACIÓN. *El estado actual de la educación indigenal en el pais*. La Paz: Edit. Renacimiento, 1940. 142 pp.
    Poorly presented, but some indication given of nonformal aspects of programs of *núcleos escolares campesinos*. Conclusion from the reading is that efforts at the time were haphazard at best.

51. BOLIVIA. MINISTERIO DE SALUD PÚBLICA. *Desarrollo rural*. La Paz: Departamento Nacional de Educación Sanitaria, n.d. 57 pp.
    Detailed description of rural development programs coordinated on an interministerial level and administered through the various rural development centers in Bolivia. Includes sanitation and nutrition programs and local handicraft training.

52. BRAVO, RAÚL, and ERNEST E. MAES. "El programa educacional cooperativo y la educación rural en Bolivia," *El Nuevo Educador*, 4:7 (September, 1948), 12-13.
    Briefly describes the Programa Educacional Cooperativo and the system of *núcleos escolares campesinos* which commenced in 1946. The

latter were designed to be community information centers rather than schools in the traditional sense.

53. CLAURO MONTAÑO, TORIBIO. "¿Seguimos en Bolivia los principios de la educación fundamental?" *América Indígena*, 13:1 (January, 1953), 65-72.
    Elements of rural education of interest here: hygiene and health education and home extension work as part of the rural school program.

54. CUÉLLAR, HERNÁN. "Bolivia: educación fundamental en el Beni," *Boletín Indigenista*, 16:2/3 (August, 1956), 136-141.
    Focuses on the Núcleo Selvícola de Moré, its literacy and agricultural training center. Also describes several other educational activities which were considered unsuccessful, though the author does not mention reasons for their failure.

55. ETLING, ARLEN. "Chapare—a Team Approach to the Educational Challenge in Bolivia's Jungles," *Agricultural Education*, 45:7 (January, 1973), 160, 166.
    Work of community development sponsored by OXFAM (British fundraising organization for development projects), United Methodist Committee for Overseas Relief, and United States missionary and service organizations.

56. HART, THOMAS A. "The Bolivian Nucleos," in U.S. Office of Education, *Education for Better Living*. Bulletin 1956, no. 9. Washington: 1957, pp. 7-23.
    Part of the Warisata Normal School program is directed toward active assistance to the community in the form of instruction and home visits. Several examples are given. Explains the role of the Servicio Cooperativo Interamericano de Educación (SCIDE), a joint United States—Bolivian agency.

57. HUGHES, LLOYD H. "Rural Education in the Andes," *Agriculture in the Americas*, 7:10/11 (October/November, 1947), 131-134.
    Reorganization of rural education on the model of the *núcleos escolares*. One aspect of the program is the Rural Cultural Service—mobile units including a traveling theater for presenting educational plays on health, child care, agriculture, and civics, and educational films. Program was initiated by the Inter-American Education Foundation.

58. HUGHES, LLOYD H. "Rural Education Program in Bolivia," Pan American Union, *Bulletin*, 80:5 (May, 1946), 267-271.
    Mentions the Rural Cultural Service organized by the Department of Culture of the Ministry of Education. The Service prepares educational material for presentation on radio. (See entry 57.)

59. MAUCK, WILFRED. "More than ABC's," *Americas*, 1:8 (October, 1949), 12-15, 46.
    Describes, in part, community work being done by a rural school in the Lake Titicaca region.

60. MAUCK, WILFRED. "SCIDE—an Answer for Bolivia," *Pan American*, 10:2 (May, 1949), 43-46.
    General description of the system of *núcleos escolares campesinos*, sponsored jointly by the U.S. Institute of Inter-American Affairs and the Bolivian government.

61. MENDOZA, ANGÉLICA. "La experiencia de Huarizata," *Sur*, 9:71 (August, 1940), 51-59.
    Emotional description of the meaning of the Warisata school in terms of local support and community cultural incorporation.

62. MONTOYA MEDINACELY, VÍCTOR. "Informe del proyecto 'Coipasi' de educación fundamental: 1953," *Boletín Indigenista*, 14:1 (March, 1954), 14-25.
    Joint program undertaken by the Schools of Christ and the Inter-American Cooperative Public Health Service (Escuelas de Cristo and Servicio Cooperativo Interamericano de Salud Pública). Activities revolve around basic education in health, economics, literacy, and the home. Projects include: education of peasant women; communal library; recreational activities; social center for adults; sanitary post; literacy course; establishment of consumers' cooperative (part of whose function is to serve as an educational institution); home improvement.

63. MONTOYA MEDINACELY, VÍCTOR. "The Teacher's Function in Community Work, Bolivia," *Fundamental and Adult Education*, 9:2 (April, 1957), 85-89.
    Community development and fundamental education work of the *núcleos escolares*. The teacher goes beyond the classroom to instruct the community in literacy, agricultural techniques, health and hygiene, and home improvement.

64. O'HARA, HAZEL. "Bolivia's Adventure in Learning," *Natural History*, 63:10 (December, 1954), 440-447.
    Describes the work of the Servicio Cooperativo Interamericano de Educación (SCIDE) in Bolivia, and particularly at Warisata. Local people are trained in various crafts or agricultural techniques at the Warisata Normal School in order to take these skills back to the villages. An adult education program in home improvement is also offered at the school.

65. RUBIO ORBE, GONZALO. "Equipos especializados de educación fundamental en Bolivia," *Revista Ecuatoriana de Educación*, 8:32 (July/August, 1954), 102-148.

Report on the Equipos de Educación Fundamental, the organization and functions of the program to reach rural areas. Talks about various projects undertaken in localities affected: health; home improvement; agricultural extension; vocational training; literacy; basic education. Brief summaries at the end of the article about the programs in Cochabamba, Portachuelo, and the Altiplano.

66. SCHWENG, LORAND D. "An Indian Community Development Project in Bolivia," *América Indígena*, 22:2 (April, 1962), 155-168.
Description of the Andean Mission program of the International Labor Organization begun in March, 1954, in Pillapi, giving historical background and an analysis of accomplishments to 1956. Among the many activities were the creation of cooperatives, an industrial vocational training center, and a health program.

67. SERVICIO COOPERATIVO INTERAMERICANO DE EDUCACIÓN, BOLIVIA. *Annual Report, 1953/1954-1955/1956*. La Paz: 1955-1956. 3 vols.
Describes community education projects under the auspices of SCIDE and the *núcleos escolares*. Also includes a brief description of the Maryknoll-operated radio school on the Altiplano.

68. SERVICIO COOPERATIVO INTERAMERICANO DE EDUCACIÓN, BOLIVIA. *EL SCIDE informa a Bolivia*. La Paz: 1954. 40 pp.
Brief description of the community educational activities included in the *núcleos escolares* system.

69. "El Servicio Cultural Rural," *Bolivia Rural*, 1:1 (1947), 6-7.
Mobile rural cultural missions whose teams of experts disseminate information on health, agriculture techniques, and so forth. Use film and theater as part of the educational process.

70. TARDÍO MAIDA, ALBERTO. "ABC's on the Air," *Americas*, 10:7 (July, 1958), 26-29.
The Maryknoll radio school in San Gabriel de Peñas concentrates on literacy and basic education work. The Maryknolls are also involved in home and agricultural extension activities in cooperation with the Servicio Agricultura Interamericano (SAI), and they offer a training program in radio operation to selected rural leaders.

71. U.S. INSTITUTE OF INTER-AMERICAN AFFAIRS. *Rural Education in Bolivia: A Study in Technical Co-operation*. La Paz: 1955. 62 pp.
Describes work of the Servicio Cooperativo Interamericano de Educación (SCIDE) with the *núcleos escolares* and particularly with the Warisata Normal School, the latter actively involved in a program of extension education in the community.

72. VELASCO, ADOLFO. *La escuela indigenal de Warisata, Bolivia*. Inter-American Conference on Indian Life, 1st, Pátzcuaro, Mexico,

1940. Mexico: Departamento de Asuntos Indígenas, 1940. 91 pp. Focuses on the community involvement aspect, particularly in agricultural activities. Sectional schools attached to Warisata are charged in effect with being community information centers. Notes development of community library.

AGRICULTURAL TRAINING

*73. BALLESTAEDT G., ALFREDO. "An Evaluation of the Agricultural Extension Service in a Bolivian Province." Unpublished thesis. Cornell University, 1964. 79 numb. leaves.

*74. CALDERÓN CUENTAS, JUAN DE LA C. *Evaluación de la influencia de extensión agrícola en la provincia Ingavi, departamento de La Paz.* La Paz: Instituto Indigenista Boliviano, 1964. 36 pp.

75. DENNISON, EDWARD S. "Bolivia," *National Geographic Magazine,* 126:3 (September, 1964), 315-319.
> Peace Corps projects in Tocoalla concerned primarily with improving agricultural techniques.

*76. FOOD AND AGRICULTURAL ORGANIZATION. *Bolivia: Extensión agrícola—proyecto de Misión Andina; informe al gobierno,* by A. Quesada. Document EPTA Report no. 1098. N.p.: 1959. 20 pp.

*77. FOOD AND AGRICULTURAL ORGANIZATION. *Bolivia; las actividades de extensión agrícola de los programas integrados de nutrición aplicada,* by F. Perlaza Saavedra. Document UNDP/TA 2349, TA/67/7. N.p.: 1967. 20 pp.

*78. FOOD AND AGRICULTURAL ORGANIZATION. *Bolivia; las actividades de extensión agrícola y desarrollo agropecuario dentro del plan nacional de desarrollo rural—informe al gobierno,* by J. Castañón Pasquel. Document UNDP/TA 2477, TA/68/6. N.p.: 1968. 26 pp.

*79. GUARDIA M., LUIS. *Un ensayo sobre extensión en Bolivia.* La Paz: Ministerio de Agricultura, 1960. 111 pp.

*80. ZUNA RICO, JORGE, and HENRY K. BOTCH. *Informe de la División de Extensión Agrícola entre 1948-1960.* La Paz: Servicio Agricultura Interamericano, 1960. 106 pp.

BASIC EDUCATION/LITERACY

*81. COORDINATING SECRETARIAT OF NATIONAL UNIONS OF STUDENTS. *Proyecto piloto de alfabetización en Bolivia; informe.* Leiden, Netherlands: 1962. 37 pp.

82. KEY, HAROLD. "Informe del Instituto Lingüístico de Verano en Bolivia: 1958," *Boletín Indigenista*, 19:1 (March, 1959), 18-25. Describes literacy work.

83. MUTAL, SILVIO. "Bolivia Struggles Against Illiteracy: The Anti-Illiteracy Campaign Organized by CUB Bolivia and Supported by the ISC," *The Student*, Leiden, Netherlands, 5:8 (August, 1961), 2-4.
Discussion of the forthcoming pilot literacy project to be sponsored by the Bolivian university student federation and of the reasons for the need for such projects in Latin America.

84. MUTAL, SILVIO. "Bolivian Illiterates Will Soon Be Able to Read . . . and to Write: Thanks to the Joint Efforts of COSEC, UNESCO, CUB, and the Bolivian Student Community," *The Student*, Leiden, Netherlands, 6:1 (January, 1962), 14-18.
Progress report of the literacy campaign sponsored by the Bolivian university students, and a report of a seminar on problems of illiteracy and the teaching of adult illiterates held in La Paz in September/October, 1961. Mentions ongoing project of Jesuits who have been operating radio literacy classes in the Bolivian Andes.

*85. NOGALES CASTRO, FERNANDO. *El programa de alfabetización y su integración en la educación de adultos y en los planes de desarrollo económico y social de Bolivia.* 2d ed. La Paz: Campaña Nacional de Alfabetización, 1963. 105 pp.

86. SPANGEN, BERTHE. "The Struggle against Illiteracy in Latin America: Impressions of a Volunteer Literacy Worker in Bolivia," *The Student*, Leiden, Netherlands, 8:5 (May, 1964), 9-10.
Part of a national literacy campaign sponsored by the Confederación Universitaria Boliviana (CUB). Personal account of a local campaign in Tarija directed by students from the University of Tarija, its problems, goals, and achievements.

87. "Sunday Courses for Bolivian Workers," Pan American Union, *Bulletin*, 81:8 (August, 1947), 463.

> Courses on reading and writing, basic mathematics, Bolivian culture, fundamentals of civil and criminal law and of social legislation sponsored by the Women's Civic League.

PROFESSIONAL/PARAPROFESSIONAL TRAINING

88. Arze Quintanilla, Oscar. "Programa interamericano de adiestramiento en desarrollo de comunidades indígenas," *Anuario Indigenista*, 26 (December, 1966), 97-123.

> Training program for community development workers held from January-September, 1966, in Bolivia. Part of the course was a 15-week session of practical field work applying methods and project ideas learned earlier. Programs undertaken during this period in five villages in Nor-Yungas are described. Included were courses to train local *colonos* in agriculture, domestic animal raising, community development, cooperatives, construction, credit, and public health. The women were taught food preparation, home improvement, mother and child care, sewing, and recreation. An educational film program was used in conjunction with the field work.

VOCATIONAL SKILL TRAINING

89. "A People's University for Bolivia," Pan American Union, *Bulletin*, 82:1 (January, 1948), 55-56.

> New institution to offer, free of charge, extension courses for working people as well as full-time courses for those wishing to supplement their training. Whole range of technical training courses proposed.

*90. Servicio Cooperativo Interamericano de Educación, Bolivia. *Cursos de perfeccionamiento y capacitación para obreros*. La Paz: Ministerio de Educación, 1957. Various pagination.

MISCELLANEOUS

91. Bolivia. Delegación Boliviana al Seminario de Trabajo sobre Desarrollo de la Comunidad. "El programa de desarrollo de la

comunidad en Bolivia,'' *América Indígena*, 23:3 (July, 1963), 233-262.

Program of the United Nations-sponsored seminar held in Quito, Ecuador, December, 1962, outlined. Fairly detailed summarization of the scope, activities, and accomplishments of the Bolivian National Plan of Rural Development at three project sites: Pillapi, Playa Verde, and Otavi. Also describes activities of the Servicio de Educación Fundamental, Escuela Nacional de Servicio Social, and the Inter-American Program for Training Personnel in Indian Community Development.

92. CENTRO PARA EL DESARROLLO SOCIAL Y ECONÓMICO, BOLIVIA. *Informe preparado a solicitud del Banco Interamericano de Desarrollo*. [La Paz?]: 1972. 49 pp.

Focuses on the organizations created by DESEC to further the integration of the popular sector into the socioeconomic development of the country. Working in the area of agricultural extension are the Organizaciones de Base Campesinos; in the area of agricultural and artisan technical assistance is the Asociación de Servicios Artesanales y Rurales (ASAR); and in the area of vocational training and fundamental education is the Instituto Campesino de Educación (ICE).

93. LEONARD, OLEN E. *El cambio económico y social en cuatro comunidades del altiplano de Bolivia*. Serie Antropología Social, 3. Mexico: Instituto Indigenista Interamericano, 1966. 141 pp.

The chapter on agriculture mentions the formation of the Cuerpo de Extensión de Servicios in 1946, designed to educate people in agricultural methods and techniques. Offers some analysis of agricultural programs in the Altiplano. The chapter on communication talks about educational radio programs, and in particular a program on agriculture. It also mentions the early use of schools as community centers where specialists would come to lecture on agriculture, health, and domestic practices. The communities studied are those later chosen by the International Labor Organization in which to implement the Andean Mission program.

94. RUBIO ORBE, GONZALO. *Educación fundamental*. Quito: Casa de la Cultura Ecuatoriana, 1954. 103 pp.

Focuses on the author's work on several projects in Bolivia: the fundamental education program, the literacy campaign, and the program of the Centro de Rehabilitación Campesina del Altiplano de Bolivia.

95. SANGINÉS URIARTE, MARCELO. *Educación rural y desarrollo en Bolivia*. La Paz: Editorial Don Bosco, 1968. 206 pp.

In the section entitled "Etapa de la Reforma Agraria," some attention is given to nonformal educational projects, such as the work done by the Summer Institute of Linguistics and Agency for International Development literacy programs.

CONCEPTUALIZATION

96. EGUINO, CARLOS A. "La organización de bibliotecas populares para obreros mineros," *Protección Social*, 4:40:11/12 (May, 1941). Material should be largely of a technical nature, designed to improve skills and technical knowledge. Such library services should be made available in all mining areas.

Brazil

MULTIFACETED PROGRAMS

97. BOND, D'ESTE. "Brazilian Visitor: ETV in São Paulo," *Times Educational Supplement*, 2731 (September 22, 1967), 564.
Short account of plans for a new educational television station in São Paulo. Envisaged as initially having general cultural content and later working into professional training in various fields, particularly health and agriculture.

*98. BRAZIL. MINISTÉRIO DA EDUCAÇÃO E CULTURA. CAMPANHA NACIONAL DE EDUCAÇÃO RURAL. *Estructuração de um centro regional de educação de base, 1957-1958*. Rio de Janeiro: n.d. 184 pp.
Regional center for fundamental education in Colatina. (From: "Rural Education," United Nations Educational, Scientific, and Cultural Organization, *Education Abstracts*, 14:3 [1962], 6)

99. BRAZIL. SERVIÇO DE INFORMAÇÃO AGRÍCOLA. *Missões rurais de educação: A experiência de Itaperuna; uma tentativa de organização da comunidade*. Série Estudos Brasileiros, 3. Rio de Janeiro: Serviço de Informação Agrícola, Ministério da Agricultura, 1952. 200 pp.
Pilot project of the Rural Social Service in Brazil. Detailed report of the fundamentals, objectives, administration, activities (agricultural extension, home economics, health, fundamental education) of the program and an analysis of its accomplishments.

100. BRAZIL. SUPERINTENDÊNCIA DO DESENVOLVIMENTO DO NORDESTE. *Sudene dez anos*. Recife: 1969. 205 pp.
In sections on human resources and agriculture, several educational programs on the nonformal level are mentioned: SUDENE cooperation with SENAI in vocational training; rural agricultural extension efforts; health education programs.

101. "Brazilian Industrial Social Service (SESI)," *International Labour Review*, 56:4 (October, 1947), 452.
Brief resume of the intent of the legislation which created SESI (Industrial Social Service) in June, 1946.

102. "A Campanha Nacional de Educação Rural (CNER): Suas origens, sua vida e seus trabalhos desde 1950 ao 1º semestre de 1959," *Revista da Campanha Nacional de Educação Rural,* 6:8 (1st Quarter, 1959), 14-317.

> Entire issue devoted to a description of the rural education campaign from its inception in 1950 through 1959. Local programs, importance of audio-visual material, activities of the national administration, background information, and course descriptions are all discussed.

*103. "Como trabalha uma equipe de missão rural da C.N.E.R.," *Revista da Campanha Nacional de Educação Rural,* 2:2 (1956), 98-119.

104. CONCEIÇÃO, DIAMANTINA COSTA. "La campaña de educación rural," *La Educación,* Washington, 3:9 (January/March, 1958), 8-11.

> Objectives and organization of the Campanha Nacional de Educação Rural (CNER), the work of its mobile missions, and its system of centers for training local leaders and rural auxiliary teachers, with training in, among other things, cooperative methods.

105. FREITAS, HONORATO DE. "Educação rural: Base para uma reforma agrária," *O Observador Econômico e Financeiro,* 16:188 (September, 1951), 59-65.

> Describes the concept behind and the efforts of the first rural education mission in Itaperuna. Activities (agricultural training, domestic arts courses, health instruction) in the community revolve around the rural social center.

106. HERZOG, WILLIAM A., JR. "Adult Education in Northeast Brazil: Does Literacy Training Make People More Modern?" in Thomas J. La Belle, ed., *Educational Alternatives in Latin America: Social Change and Social Stratification.* Latin American Studies Series, 30. Los Angeles: Latin American Center, University of California, 1975, pp. 185-208.

> Studies the effectiveness of the Cruzada ABC by testing the hypothesis that participation in a literacy – adult education program is associated with increasing modernization as indexed by selected variables.

107. LEWIS, ALFRED E. "Road to Social Peace," *Brazil,* 24:8 (August, 1950), 7-9.

> Comments on the work of the Serviço Social da Indústria (SESI) which is paid for by employers and is geared toward the welfare of the workers. Describes the program in nutrition for workers' families and the courses conducted in basic education, literacy, cooking, sewing,

and crafts. The Serviço uses mobile units and educational films to reach the people.

*108. "Libros à vontade para o trabalhador em São Paulo," *Lar, Revista da Família,* 51 (September, 1948), 32-34.
Describes the work of SESI. (From: Connor, John M. *Bibliografía de la literatura sobre educación de adultos en la América Latina.* Bibliographic Series, 37. Washington: Departamento de Asuntos Culturales, Unión Panamericana, 1952. 88 pp.)

109. LIMA, VICENTE FERRER CORREIA. "A educação de base ou fundamental: conceito e objetivos—instantáneo do Brasil," *Revista do Serviço Público,* 18:4:2 (November, 1954), 64-66.
Discourse on the concept of basic or fundamental education and measures taken by the Campanha Nacional de Educação Rural to implement it, including: programs of instruction and demonstration of agricultural techniques and rural industry; introduction to cooperative methods; instruction in hygiene and budgeting; organization of special interest groups and libraries.

110. LYON, NORMAN. "The ABC of Literacy," *New York State Education,* 55:6 (March, 1968), 10-11, 40-41.
Organization and work of the Cruzada ABC volunteer program directed by the Agnes Erskine College in Recife. The program's five levels of instruction consist of: basic literacy training; basic education (two levels of arithmetic, science, social studies, hygiene); basic vocational skills for men and basic domestic skills for women.

111. MARY LORETTA, SISTER. *Amazonia: A Study of People and Progress in the Amazon Jungle.* New York: Pageant Press, 1963. 212 pp.
Discusses some adult education efforts by missionaries in the states of Amazonas and Pará in northern Brazil. Professional courses and instruction in home economics and crafts were offered in the night school which was initiated in 1950. Also worked with the Serviço Especial de Saúde Pública (SESP) to educate people in matters of health and sanitation.

112. MOSHER, ARTHUR T. *Case Study of the Agricultural Program of ACAR in Brazil.* Technical Cooperation in Latin America Series. Washington: National Planning Association, 1955. 63 pp.
Detailed description of the Associação de Crédito e Assistência Rural (ACAR) program of related services: farm and home extension education; supervised credit; medical care and health education; distribution of material. Chapter 2 is devoted to organization and administration on

regional and local levels (including statement of finances). Chapter 3 discusses "the program in operation." Chapter 4 deals with the accomplishments of the program over a six-year period.

*113. *O que é a C.N.E.R.* Rio de Janeiro: Ministério de Educação e Cultura, 1958. 15 pp.

114. ORGANIZATION OF AMERICAN STATES. CONSEJO INTERAMERICANO ECONÓMICO Y SOCIAL. COMISIÓN ESPECIAL X: COMISIÓN INTER- AMERICANA DE TELECOMUNICACIONES. QUINTA REUNIÓN, BOGOTÁ, COLOMBIA, 22-29 DE JULIO DE 1970. *Actualización de informe brasilero sobre radio y televisión educativas.* Document OEA/Ser.H/XIII (CIES/Com.X/362). Washington: 1970. 8 pp.
Reviews programs of the Ministério da Educação e Cultura's Serviço de Rádiodifusão Educativa, including agriculture, health advice, and literacy. Lists programs by locality—Distrito Federal, Rondónia, Pará, Rio Grande do Norte, Paraíba, Pernambuco, Sergipe, Bahia, Espírito Santo, São Paulo, and Rio Grande do Sul.

115. PELLEGRINI, MARIA, and MARIA REGINA LÔBO. "Programa experi- mental para organização e desenvolvimento de comunidades indí- genas," *Revista Brasileira de Estudos Pedagógicos*, 49:109 (January/March, 1968), 108-133.
Detailed report of experimental community development program directed toward indigenous population whose basic aims were to further the process of acculturation primarily through self-directed activities in a climate of respect for indigenous culture and values. Pro- gram activities include health education, leadership training, and tech- nical training. Report discusses various phases of the program, tech- niques and methods used, and concludes with an overall evaluation and an accounting of expenditures.

116. RICHTER, WILLI. "Pindorama—an Example of Development Aid," *Free Labour World*, 205/206 (July/August, 1967), 12-15.
Educational Center established in this agricultural settlers' cooperative is intended to reach the entire community by offering instruction in agricultural techniques and crafts, such as woodwork, ironwork, and textile work, to existing settlers and new applicants. The Center is funded by both Swiss and German donations (government and private).

117. RÍOS, JOSÉ ARTHUR. "Co-operation and Integration in Community Development: Brazilian Experience," *Fundamental and Adult Edu- cation*, 9:2 (April, 1957), 66-71.
Calls for development of new forms of "informal [i.e., nonformal] education, such as rural missions and social centers." Discusses the organization, in 1952, of the Campanha Nacional de Educação

Rural (CNER), recruitment and training of staff, operation of the program, and problems encountered. Work is largely carried out through a system of rural missions patterned after Mexico's Cultural Missions.

118. "Rural Welfare Service in Brazil," *Industry and Labor*, 15:10 (May 15, 1956), 426-427.
    Organization of the newly created (September, 1955) Rural Welfare Service whose objectives are both practical and educational.

119. SAMPAIO, ROGERIO. "Dois anos de actividade," *Revista Industrial de São Paulo*, 4:43 (June, 1948), 27-40.
    Lengthy article describing activities of the Serviço Social da Indústria (SESI), an employer-financed social service that includes medical, educational, and social work services in Brazilian industry. Educational activities range from literacy programs to technical training.

*120. SERVIÇO SOCIAL DA INDÚSTRIA. *O que é o SESI: Serviço Social da Indústria; Confederação Nacional da Indústria; "pela paz social no Brasil."* São Paulo: 1948. 31 pp.

121. SERVIÇO SOCIAL DA INDÚSTRIA. DEPARTAMENTO REGIONAL DA BAHIA. *O SESI na Bahia, 1948-1950.* Salvador: 1950. 75 pp.
    Bulk of the report is devoted to a detailed evaluation of programs in Bahia for the two-year period. Section on *"educação social"* is of particular interest: discusses the literacy course, sewing classes, educational film series, and theater projects. The appendix lists SESI activities throughout Brazil by department.

122. SERVIÇO SOCIAL DA INDÚSTRIA. DEPARTAMENTO REGIONAL DE SÃO PAULO. *Bibliotecas do SESI ao alcance de todos.* São Paulo: 1969. 20 pp.
    Describes SESI circulating mobile library services.

*123. SERVIÇO SOCIAL DA INDÚSTRIA. DEPARTAMENTO REGIONAL DE SÃO PAULO. BIBLIOTECA AMBULANTE. *O carro-biblioteca das bibliotecas ambulantes do SESI.* São Paulo: 1956. 18 pp.

*124. SERVIÇO SOCIAL DA INDÚSTRIA. DEPARTAMENTO REGIONAL DE SÃO PAULO. DIVISÃO DE EDUCAÇÃO FUNDAMENTAL. *Diretrizes e bases da educação fundamental supletiva do SESI, autores: Equipe da Divisão de Educação Fundamental.* Coleção SESI, 22. São Paulo: 1968. 31 pp.

*125. UNIVERSIDADE CATÓLICA DE PERNAMBUCO, RECIFE, BRAZIL. SERVIÇO DE AÇÃO COMUNITÁRIA. "Cruzada de educação: Filosofia e

dinâmica do plano," Universidade Católica de Pernambuco, *Symposium*, 12:2 (1970), 97-106.
Describes the University's literacy and community action campaign.
(From: *Handbook of Latin American Studies*, 33 [1971], 301).

AGRICULTURAL TRAINING

*126. ASSOCIAÇÃO BRASILEIRA DE CRÉDITO E ASSISTÊNCIA RURAL (ABCAR). *Plano nacional de extensão rural: Programação 1970*. Rio de Janeiro: 1970. 229 pp.

*127. BARBER, FRED W. *The Origin and Development of Brazil's Cooperative Agricultural Extension Service*. Rio de Janeiro: U.S. Agency for International Development, 1965. 184 pp.

*128. BECHARA, MIGUEL. *Extensão agrícola*. São Paulo: Secretaria de Agricultura, 1954. 531 pp.

*129. FOOD AND AGRICULTURAL ORGANIZATION. *Brasil: Los servicios agrícolas como instrumento para el desarrollo del nordeste; informe al gobierno*, by M. A. Castro Rivas. Document UNDP/TA 3056. N.p.: 1972. 24 p.

*130. FOOD AND AGRICULTURAL ORGANIZATION. TECHNICAL WORKING PARTY ON COCOA PRODUCTION AND PROTECTION. *Papers. Second Session, 19-23 September 1966*. "Programa de extensión agrícola en la región cacaotera de Bahia," by A. Matos, et al. Rome: 1967. 15 pp.

131. SMITH, THOMAS LYNN. *Brazil: People and Institutions*. 4th ed. Baton Rouge, Louisiana: Louisiana State University Press, 1972. 778 pp.
The final chapter includes a section on the development of agricultural extension services during the 1960s. Focuses on the program of the Associação Brasileira de Crédito e Assistência Rural (ABCAR) combining credit with educational efforts.

BASIC EDUCATION/LITERACY

132. "Adult Education Campaign in Brazil for the Year 1950: A Detailed

Report,'' *Foreign Education Digest*, 17:3 (January/March, 1953), 283-284.
Focuses on some aspects of the adult education campaign begun in 1947: (1) rural missions, comprised of mobile units of education material (films, museum, library, laboratory), and (2) personnel (specialists in agronomy, social welfare, veterinary medicine, nursing).

133. "Atividades da TV2 Cultura de São Paulo," *Revista Brasileira de Estudos Pedagógicos*, 52:116 (October/December, 1969), 377-386.
Background of TV2 Cultura and description of programs, including basic education–adult literacy courses.

134. BANDEIRA, MARINA. "Movimento de educação de base," *Síntese Política Económica Social*, 10:39/40 (July/December, 1968), 72-80.
The author first discusses problems facing formal education in Brazil—rapid population growth, dispersion of rural population to urban areas, competition between school and work. She then goes on to describe the origins, objectives, organization, and various projects of the Movimento de Educação de Base (MEB), directed by the Catholic church, which was designed to tackle educational problems in new ways. The article emphasizes the network of radio schools and also describes the "*animação popular*" method of organizing communities to discover their own solutions to their particular problems, needs, and desires.

135. BEISIEGEL, CELSO DE RUI. "Uma campanha de alfabetização de adultos no Brasil," *Pesquisa e Planejamento*, 9 (June, 1965), 29-39.
Presents the events of the effective though short-lived program of the Campanha Nacional de Alfabetização de Adultos from 1963-1964. Offers an analysis of the Freire method and reasons for its demise in the Brazilian context.

*136. BRAZIL. FUNDAÇÃO MOVIMENTO BRASILEIRO DE ALFABETIZAÇÃO (MOBRAL). *Literacy: A Brazilian Program*. Rio de Janeiro: 1972. 17 pp.

*137. BRAZIL. MINISTÉRIO DA EDUCAÇÃO E CULTURA. *Plano piloto do erradicação de analfabetismo*. Rio de Janeiro: 1958. 10 pp.

138. BRAZIL. MINISTÉRIO DA EDUCAÇÃO E SAÚDE. DEPARTAMENTO NACIONAL DE EDUCAÇÃO. *Campanha de educação de adultos*. Rio de Janeiro: 1949. No pagination.
Illustrated booklet describing the adult education–literacy campaign.

139. BRAZIL. MINISTÉRIO DA EDUCAÇÃO E SAÚDE. DEPARTAMENTO NA-

CIONAL DE EDUCAÇÃO. *Planejamento geral da campanha*. Campanha de Educação de Adultos, Publicação 2. Rio de Janeiro: 1947. 30 pp.

Brief outline of adult education campaign followed by charts showing distribution of resources by municipality.

*140. BRAZIL. MINISTÉRIO EXTRAORDINÁRIO PARA A COORDENAÇÃO DOS ORGANISMOS REGIONAIS AND SUPERINTENDÊNCIA DO DESENVOLVIMENTO DO NORDESTE. SEMINÁRIO DE EDUCAÇÃO E DESENVOLVIMENTO, RECIFE, 1967. *Educação de adultos: Documento básico* Recife: 1966. 63 pp.

Description of the basic education and literacy programs in the Northeast. (From: *Handbook of Latin American Studies*, 31 [1969], 341).

*141. BRAZIL. MOVIMENTO BRASILEIRO DE ALFABETIZAÇÃO (MOBRAL). *The Mobral System/le système Mobral*. Rio de Janeiro: 1973. 40 pp.

*142. CAMARINHA, JOSÉ. "Programas e métodos na alfabetização e educação de adultos," *Educação de Adultos* (June, 1954), 18-27.

*143. "Campaign against Illiteracy in Brazil," Pan American Union, *Bulletin*, 69:12 (December, 1935), 958.

*144. CORREA, ARLINDO LÓPEZ. *Permanent Education and Adult Education in Brazil*. Rio de Janeiro: Fundação Movimento Brasileiro de Alfabetização, 1973. 56 pp.

145. DE KADT, EMANUEL. *Catholic Radicals in Brazil*. London: Oxford University Press, 1970. 304 pp.

Chapters 7-10 offer a careful and thorough reconstruction of the formation and activities of the Movimento de Educação de Base (MEB), from its inception in 1958 through the military takeover period in 1964. Following that are several chapters describing the programs of Animação Popular (AnPo) and *conscientização*, techniques used and developed by MEB.

146. DEMARTINI, PEDRO PAULO, and JOSÉ CARLOS N. DA SILVA. "Educação de base para adolescentes e adultos na rádio e televisão cultura," *Educação Hoje*, 11 (1970), 24-32.

Reviews various efforts around the country of the Movimento de Educação de Base (MEB), with emphasis on the proposed basic education project of the Padre Anchieta Foundation in São Paulo.

147. DEMARTINI, PEDRO PAULO, et al. "Projeto de educação de base para adolescentes e adultos," *Educação Hoje*, 12 (1970), 60-103.

Detailed report of the proposed radio/television basic education project of the Padre Anchieta Foundation of São Paulo, primarily describing courses but also providing information on equipment, monitors, forms of evaluation, and so forth.

148. "Fundamental Education and Broadcasting," International Bureau of Education, *Bulletin*, 35:141 (4th Quarter, 1961), 205.
Brief report of the newly created Fundamental Education Movement and its rural education broadcasting center at Natal.

149. LOURENÇO, MANOEL BERGSTRÖM. "Adult Education Campaign in Brazil," *Education Digest*, 16:5 (January, 1951), 51-53.
Discusses the adult education campaign begun in 1947 in general terms.

150. LOURENÇO, MANOEL BERGSTRÖM. "The Adult Education Campaign in Brazil," *Fundamental Education*, 2:2 (April, 1950), 3-9.
Describes the campaign initiated in 1947: its organization, types of teaching material used, results to date, and an account of private cooperation.

151. LOURENÇO, MANOEL BERGSTRÖM. "O problema da educação de adultos," *Revista Brasileira de Estudos Pedagógicos*, 5:14 (August, 1945), 169-185.
The author discusses concepts and fundamentals of adult education— its functions (supplemental, professional, civic, and cultural), definition of the term, methodology, and limitations. Gives examples of programs in this century, some active, some defunct, noting particularly those of Rio de Janeiro.

152. MELO, ALMERI BEZERRA DE. "Método 'Paulo Freire' de alfabetización en Brasil," *Comunidad*, 2:6 (April, 1967), 137-142.
Describes Freire's program under the auspices of the Serviço de Extensão Cultural at the University of Recife. Freire was concerned with the larger aspects of adult education, of which literacy work was only a part. Comments on the significance of Freire's system in political, social, and economic terms.

153. MOREIRA, JOÃO ROBERTO. *Uma experiência de educação: O projeto pilôto de erradicação do analfabetismo do Ministério da Educação e Cultura*. Rio de Janeiro: 1960. 102 pp.
Work encompasses an historical account of the problem of illiteracy in Brazil, the feasibility study conducted by the author to back up his proposal for an experimental program, and a step-by-step account of the implementation of the pilot project of the Campanha Nacional de Erradicação do Analfabetismo (CNEA). Discusses problems encountered in various parts of the country and in rural versus urban areas. An outline of the organization and administration of the campaign on

the national level is followed by a description of one of the pilot centers, Leopoldina, and its operation. Campaign activities in Leopoldina include the Parque Complementar where vocational skills were taught. There is also a briefer description of the pilot project in the municipality of Caraguatatuba.

154. MOVIMENTO DE EDUCAÇÃO DE BASE, BRAZIL. "MEB: Prêmio Reza Pahlavi de Alfabetização," *Revista Brasileira de Estudos Pedagógicos*, 51:113 (January/March, 1969), 104-110.

Paper presented to UNESCO for consideration for the Mohammed Reza Pahlavi Award for efforts in the eradication of illiteracy. Discusses the origin, objectives, definition of the basic concept, organization, functions, area of activity, activities (including radio schools, popular animation programs, training of leaders, and organization of community centers), and evaluation of the Movimento de Educação de Base (MEB) which was created by the Catholic church in northeastern Brazil.

*155. OFICINA REGIONAL DE EDUCACIÓN DE LA UNESCO PARA AMÉRICA LATINA Y EL CARIBE. *La experiencia brasileña de alfabetización de adultos: El MOBRAL*. Estudios y Documentos de Educación, 15. Paris: United Nations Educational, Scientific, and Cultural Organization, 1974. 67 pp.

156. RIO DE JANEIRO. INSTITUTO NACIONAL DE ESTUDOS PEDAGÓGICOS. "Campanha de educação de adultos," *Revista Brasileira de Estudos Pedagógicos*, 5:14 (August, 1945), 270-277.

Organization of the adult education campaign directed by the Instituto Brasileiro de Estudos Pedagógicos on regional and local levels, and the proposed methodology and approaches for establishing local programs.

157. SALBADO, DILKE. "Campanha de educação dos adultos," *Revista do Serviço Público*, 10:3:1/2 (September/October, 1947), 90-101.

Ambitious national program of adult education begun in 1947. Emphasis is on literacy and basic education. System of night schools created to serve the program. Courses also held in offices, industrial plants, jails, hospitals, agricultural service centers, and Indian protection agencies. Article accounts for the history of the campaign, its organization and administration, goals and objectives.

158. SOUZA, FERNANDO TUDE DE. "Radio in the Service of Fundamental Education," *Fundamental Education*, 2:2 (April, 1950), 17-21.

Work of the Ministério da Educação e Saúde's Serviço de Radiodifusão Educativa and the Instituto Nacional de Cinema Educativo. Stresses their importance as adjuncts to the literacy campaign.

Describes several radio courses which have been offered and proven successful. Special programs are directed toward women and rural areas.

159. SUMMER INSTITUTE OF LINGUISTICS. "Levantamento lingüístico de Leopoldina," *Educação e Ciências Sociais*, 3:9 (December, 1958), 31-56.
   Work of the Summer Institute of Linguistics in the literacy campaign in Minas Gerais. Diagrams and charts of the alphabet and vocabulary used are included.

160. TABBUSH, YVONNE. "La 'loca de la escuela': Guerra contra el analfabetismo en el Brasil," *Tegucigalpa*, 34:1188 (April 22, 1951), 20.
   Work of Zilma Coelho Pinto in Espírito Santo primarily in literacy training but also in health education as part of the adult education campaign which began in 1947.

*161. TAVARES, JOSÉ NILO. *A educação de adultos e o SESC*. Rio de Janeiro: Serviço Social do Comércio, 1970. 79 pp.

*162. TIRADO BENEDI, DOMINGO. "La campaña de alfabetización en el Brasil," *Revista del Instituto Nacional de Pedagogía*, 2:6 (April, 1948), 1-11.

CULTURAL EXTENSION

163. BARDI, P. M. "An Educational Experiment at the Museu de Arte, São Paulo," *Museum*, 1:3/4 (December, 1948), 142, 212.
   Mentions the museum training program, initiated during the first months of the museum's operation, which trains young people to become assistants. The museum also offers courses on a variety of levels serving a diversity of interests: art club for children; course on history of art for secondary students; university level art course; courses for teachers; course on the history of music; life drawing classes; traveling exhibitions.

164. MACEDO, LUIZ ANTÓNIO. "ETV in Brazil," *Educational Television International*, 5:2 (June, 1971), 126-127.
   Describes a large number of educational television stations already in existence and the wide variety of programs ranging from those of cultural interest to university level instruction. Map shows the locations of existing and projected stations.

165. NEVES E SILVA, MARIA HELENA. "O papel dos museus na vida

moderna," *Formação*, 3:28 (November, 1940) 15-29.
> Museums should be thought of as educational institutions, not as display quarters. The author describes some educational activities in Brazilian museums.

166. SALGADO, ALVARO DE FARIA. *A radiodifusão educativo no Brasil: Notas*. Rio de Janeiro: Serviço de Documentação, Ministério de Educação e Saúde, 1946. 119 pp.
> Describes early educational radio efforts in Rio de Janeiro, São Paulo, and Pernambuco.

HEALTH, HYGIENE, AND NUTRITION INSTRUCTION

167. "Adult Education Campaign in Brazil," Pan American Union, *Bulletin*, 82:8 (August, 1948), 474.
> Achievements of the first year of the adult education campaign (1947) which focused on health, nutrition, and child care education.

168. HOLLANDA, HORTENSIA DE, MANOEL JOSÉ FERREIRA, and HOWARD W. LUNDY. "Two Experiments in Brazil," *Fundamental Education*, 4:2 (April, 1952), 35-39.
> One experiment initiated by the Serviço Especial de Saúde Pública (SESP) in Minas Gerais is directly educational: health centers were established in Chonin with the principal task of educating the local population by means of adult education courses offered in the centers. This project was designed as a model for other areas.

169. *Program of the Rio Doce Valley: A Serviço in Action*. Building a Better Hemisphere Series, 4. Washington: Technical Cooperation Administration, Inter-American Regional Office, Institute of Inter-American Affairs, 1951. 7 pp.
> Part of the services of the Serviço Especial de Saúde Pública (SESP) are the local health education programs carried out both by formal instruction in the health centers and by individual instruction in the home by auxiliary nurses.

170. RIBEIRO, ADALBERTO MÁRIO. "O problema nacional da alimentação; Feição prática de duas campanhas de grande expressão social," *Revista do Serviço Público*, 4:2:1 (April, 1941), 189-205.
> Discussion of the creation of the Serviço de Alimentação da Previdência Social (SAPS) and its nutrition education programs.

171. WHITE, JOHN W. *Miracle on the Amazon.* Washington: Technical Cooperation Administration, Inter-American Regional Office, Institute of Inter-American Affairs, 1952. 7 pp.

    Describes educational activities of the health clinic in Cametá, near Belém, which include providing instruction in health and child care to the local population.

172. YAHN, MARIO. *Preparación para el matrimonio: Cursos para novias.* Cuadernos de Asistencia Social, 3. Buenos Aires: Editorial Humanitas, 1963. 37 pp.

    Annual course given in health centers throughout São Paulo which include instruction in hygiene, sex and reproduction, mental health, physical education for children, child education, common illnesses, and domestic arts. The course is available for women only. Detailed course outline included.

PROFESSIONAL/PARAPROFESSIONAL TRAINING

173. NORDIN, JUNE LEITH. "For Better Living in Brazil," *Agriculture in the Americas*, 4:8 (August, 1944), 148-150, 156.

    Brief mention of the new Home Demonstration Service program under the direction of the Serviço de Alimentação da Previdência Social (SAPS) which trains women for practical nutrition work.

VOCATIONAL SKILL TRAINING

174. ABREU, JAYME. "Craft and Industrial Training in Brazil: A Socio-Historical Study," in Joseph A. Lauwerys, and David G. Scanlon, eds. *World Year Book of Education: Education Within Industry.* London: Evans Brothers, 1968, pp. 210-225.

    Historical account of vocational training from colonial times to the present. Discusses public and private initiatives and legislation, and culminates in a portrayal of the national organization for industrial training—SENAI.

*175. "A aprendizagem industrial no Brasil," *Revista Paulista de Indústria*, 2:10 (September/October, 1952), 7-87.

*176. BOLOGNA, ITALO. "A atuação do Serviço Nacional de Aprendizagem

Industrial na formação de mão-de-obra nacional," *Ensino Industrial*, 4:11 (April, 1965), 2-6.

*177. BOLOGNA, ITALO. *Formação profissional na indústria, o SENAI.* Rio de Janeiro: Diretoria do Ensino Industrial, Ministério da Educação e Cultura, 1969. 112 pp.

*178. BRAZIL. SERVIÇO NACIONAL DE APRENDIZAGEM COMERCIAL. *SENAC, 1946-1956; 10 anos.* Rio de Janeiro: 1958. No pagination.

*179. BRAZIL. SERVIÇO NACIONAL DE APRENDIZAGEM INDUSTRIAL. *Organización del Servicio Nacional de Aprendizaje Industrial en el Brazil.* Rio de Janeiro: n.d. 13 pp.

180. BRAZIL. SERVIÇO NACIONAL DE APRENDIZAGEM INDUSTRIAL. *Relatório 1964.* Rio de Janeiro: 1965. 110 pp.
Briefly describes activities of regional departments and of national headquarters.

*181. BRAZIL. SERVIÇO NACIONAL DE APRENDIZAGEM INDUSTRIAL. *Relatório 1966.* Rio de Janeiro: [1967?]. 100 pp.

182. BRAZIL. SERVIÇO NACIONAL DE APRENDIZAGEM INDUSTRIAL. ADMINISTRAÇÃO REGIONAL NO ESTADO DA GUANABARA. *Relatório das atividades.* Rio de Janeiro: 1970-1971. 2 vols.
Provides general information and description of schools and special programs, followed by charts illustrating courses and other activities.

*183. BRAZIL. SERVIÇO NACIONAL DE APRENDIZAGEM INDUSTRIAL. DEPARTAMENTO NACIONAL. *SENAI, 1961: Escolas, cursos, matrículas.* Rio de Janeiro: 1961. 17 pp.

*184. BRAZIL. SERVIÇO NACIONAL DE APRENDIZAGEM INDUSTRIAL. DEPARTAMENTO REGIONAL DO ESPÍRITO SANTO. *Cursos e programas.* Vitória: 1968. 32 pp.

185. BRAZIL. SERVIÇO NACIONAL DE APRENDIZAGEM INDUSTRIAL. DEPARTAMENTO REGIONAL DO RIO GRANDE DO SUL. *Relatório das atividades.* Pôrto Alegre: 1970-1972. 3 vols.
Detailed and lengthy report of courses offered, costs, etc., prepared by each administrative division for the fifteen schools and centers in the state of Rio Grande do Sul. Complete with charts and diagrams.

186. BRAZIL. SERVIÇO NACIONAL DE APRENDIZAGEM INDUSTRIAL. DEPARTAMENTO REGIONAL DO RIO GRANDE DO SUL. *O SENAI no Rio Grande do Sul.* Pôrto Alegre: 1968. 64 pp.
Reports on each of the fourteen SENAI schools and centers in Rio

Grande do Sul, describing courses, equipment, and students in rather general terms.

187. BRAZIL. SERVIÇO NACIONAL DE APRENDIZAGEM INDUSTRIAL. DE-PARTAMENTO REGIONAL DE SÃO PAULO. *Relatório dos trabalhos realizados.* São Paulo: 1945. Various pagination.
Describes organization, courses offered, and different programs and activities of SENAI/São Paulo.

188. BRAZIL. SERVIÇO NACIONAL DE APRENDIZAGEM INDUSTRIAL. DE-PARTAMENTO REGIONAL DE SÃO PAULO. *Relatório dos trabalhos realizados.* São Paulo: 1955. Various pagination.
See entry 187.

189. BRAZIL. SERVIÇO NACIONAL DE APRENDIZAGEM INDUSTRIAL. DE-PARTAMENTO REGIONAL DE SÃO PAULO. *Relatório dos trabalhos realizados.* São Paulo: 1971. Various pagination.
See entry 187.

190. BRAZIL. SERVIÇO NACIONAL DE APRENDIZAGEM INDUSTRIAL. DE-PARTAMENTO REGIONAL DE SÃO PAULO. *O SENAI em São Paulo, 1942-1967: Ed. comemorativa do jubileu de prata.* São Paulo: 1968. 109 pp.
Briefly describes SENAI activities, school by school (for 32 schools), in the São Paulo region.

191. BRAZIL. SERVIÇO NACIONAL DE APRENDIZAGEM INDUSTRIAL. DE-PARTAMENTO REGIONAL DE SÃO PAULO. DIVISÃO DE SELEÇÃO E DIVISÃO DE ENSINO. *Cursos vocacionais e orientação profissional no SENAI.* Monografias SENAI, 6. São Paulo: 1947. 54 pp.
Organization and methodology of courses at SENAI in São Paulo.

192. BRAZIL. SERVIÇO NACIONAL DE APRENDIZAGEM INDUSTRIAL. DE-PARTAMENTO REGIONAL DE SERGIPE. *Relatório dos trabalhos realizados.* Aracajú: 1970. 39 pp.
Relates efforts and expenditures for 1970 for SENAI in Sergipe.

193. BRAZIL. SUPERINTENDÊNCIA DO DESENVOLVIMENTO DO NORDESTE. *A formação dos recursos humanos para um novo nordeste.* N.p.: 1969. 7 pp.
Briefly outlines vocational and artisan training programs of SUDENE in the Northeast.

194. "Brazilian Industrial Apprenticeship Service," Pan American Union, *Bulletin,* 80:2 (February, 1946), 111-112.
Brief summary of SENAI organization.

195. CARDOSO, FERNANDO HENRIQUE, and OTÁVIO IANNI. "As exigências educacionais do processo de industrialização," *Revista Brasiliense*, 26 (November/December, 1959), 141-168.
   Deals with SENAI programs as one avenue of attack in efforts to cope with the problems of rapid industrialization and the lack of trained people.

196. CARVALHO, MANUEL MARQUES DE. "Situação atual e tendências do ensino técnico comercial no Brasil," *Revista Brasileira de Estudos Pedagógicos*, 44:99 (July/September, 1965), 72-98.
   Notes contributions of the Serviço Nacional de Aprendizagem Comercial (SENAC) to the area of commercial training, and provides description of its organization and detailed listing of its courses.

197. CONCEIÇÃO, DIÓGENES. "Brazil's Workers Earn as They Learn," *Brazil*, 20:6 (June, 1946), 12-14.
   Describes administration and operation of SENAI in general terms. The training program is supplemented with medical and dental care, dietary instruction, and recreational activities.

198. DANNEMANN, ROBERT N. "Problems of Human Resources in Brazil," *International Labour Review*, 94:6 (December, 1966), 570-589.
   Section on SENAI and SENAC relates their roles in attempting to deal with the problems of utilization of human resources and meeting educational needs in Brazil.

199. DÁVILA, CARLOS. "School of Many Skills, Quito, Ecuador," *Industrial Arts and Vocational Education*, 43:9 (November, 1954), 305-307.
   Report on a special training course offered by SENAI and sponsored by SENAI and the International Labor Organization to worker-students from eighteen Latin American countries.

200. "Economic Mobilisation and Man-Power Problems in Brazil," *International Labour Review*, 47:6 (June, 1943), 721-730.
   Section devoted to new measures undertaken in the field of vocational training mainly discusses SENAI, its formation and organization in responding to wartime needs.

*201. *Educação técnica e industrialização: Conferências*. Coleção Forum Roberto Simonsen. São Paulo: Centro e Federação das Indústrias do Estado de São Paulo, [1964?]. 111 pp.
   Paper on SENAI included. (From: *Handbook of Latin American Studies*, 29 [1967], 383)

202. "Enseñanza industrial del Brasil," *Revista Interamericana de Educación*, 9:36/37 (May/June, 1950), 170-171
Brief article describing efforts made by the Brazilian government to provide training in vocational skills for the working class, namely through SENAI.

203. FISCHLOWITZ, ESTANISLAU. "Manpower Problems in Brazil," *International Labour Review*, 79:4 (April, 1959), 398-417.
Programs of SESI, SENAI, and SENAC discussed in the section on improving the manpower situation.

204. FONSECA, CELSO SUCKOW DA. *História do ensino industrial no Brasil*. Rio de Janeiro: 1961-1962. 2 vols.
Chapter 3 (volume 1) talks about the antecedents (colonial period) of the apprenticeship system. The Lei Orgânica do Ensino Industrial of 1942 and its effect on the system of industrial training, including SENAI, is covered in chapter 8, with a full chapter (12) devoted to SENAI, its antecedents and organization. Chapter 9 deals with the leading role of the army in vocational training through its apprenticeship training programs, and chapter 10 focuses on Navy training efforts. Volume 2 deals with industrial training in each individual state, with a separate chapter devoted to each.

205. FURTADO, JORGE ALBERTO. *Porque se realizou o programa intensivo de preparação da mão-de-obra industrial*. Rio de Janeiro: Diretoria do Ensino Industrial, Ministério da Educação e Cultura, 1968. 30 pp.
Explains objectives and administration of the Programa Intensivo de Preparação da Mão-de-Obra Industrial which began in 1964 and attempted to coordinate and utilize all possible resources in the country. Outlines courses given and results obtained to date in various regions of the country.

206. GERBRACHT, CARL. "Alliance for Progress and Industrial Education in Brazil," *School Shop*, 26:2 (October, 1966), 54-56.
Describes Brazil's system of industrial education, explains SENAI's role within that system, and briefly describes several training programs undertaken by SENAI to meet various specific needs.

*207. GOES, JOAQUIM FARIA. "Diretrizes atuais de aprendizagem industrial." Centro de Estudos 'Roberto Mange,' *Boletim*, 1:2 (1956), 5-24.

208. GOES, JOAQUIM FARIA. *Produtividade, aspecto educacional*. Cader-

nos de Ciências Sociais, 3. Rio de Janeiro: Instituto de Ciências Sociais, Universidade do Brasil, 1960. 73 pp.

> Includes a description of SENAI courses and various aspects of its organization. The appendix includes comments by others regarding SENAI and SENAC.

209. GOES, JOAQUIM FARIA. "Technological Development and Education in Brazil," in Robert King Hall, N. Hans, and J. A. Lauwerys, eds., *Year Book of Education 1954*. London: Evans Brothers, [1954?], pp. 332-343.

> Includes a brief account of SENAI and its part in the larger scope of technical training.

210. GROSSMAN, WILLIAM L. "Industrial Education in Brazil," *Brazil*, 25:1 (1951), 18-20.

> General description of SENAI's purposes and activities within the broader context of vocational education in Brazil.

211. HALL, ROBERT KING. "Industrial Education in Brazil," Pan American Union, *Bulletin*, 82:9 (September, 1948), 497-505.

> Organization and accomplishments of SENAI since its inception in 1942.

212. HALL, ROBERT KING. "El servicio nacional de aprendizaje industrial del Brasil," *Nueva Era*, 19 (1950), 232-236.

> Offers a brief description of SENAI's organization.

213. "Intensified Vocational Training," *International Bureau of Education Bulletin*, 17:69 (4th Quarter, 1943), 123.

> Reorganization of vocational training to meet wartime demands briefly commented upon.

214. INTERNATIONAL LABOR ORGANIZATION. "International Technical Assistance in Vocational Training," *International Labour Review*, 75:6 (June, 1957), 514-529.

> Includes discussion of International Labor Organization assistance to SENAI in improving facilities, devising curricula, and supplying instructors.

215. LIMA, FRANCISCO DA GAMA. "O estado atual do ensino comercial e o SENAC," *Revista SENAC*, 2 (January, 1953), 28-38.

> Talks about SENAC and its relation to the area of commercial instruction in general in Brazil.

*216. LOPES, STÊNIO. "Panorama educacional de Campina Grande," *Revista*

Campinense de Cultura, 2:3 (March, 1965), 49-57.
Includes description of the local SENAI program. (From: *Handbook of Latin American Studies,* 31 [1969], 348).

217. MONTOJOS, FRANCISCO. "Brazil—Where Education Keeps Pace with Industry," *American Vocational Journal,* 21:2 (February, 1946), 14-15, 36-37.
General discussion of industrial education which includes apprenticeship training (administered by SENAI), basic vocational instruction, and extension courses. Lists courses available through SENAI facilities and mentions other apprenticeship programs of the departments and ministries of the federal government.

218. MORALES DE LOS RIOS, ADOLFO. "Evolução do ensino técnico-industrial no Brasil," *Revista Brasileira de Estudos Pedagógicos,* 5:14 (August, 1945), 210-235.
Historical account of vocational training from the colonial era to the present. Section on nonformal apprenticeship programs comments on the differences between formal vocational education and the apprenticeship system. Focuses only on programs for men.

219. "The Organization of Commercial Apprenticeship in Brazil," *International Labour Review,* 53:5/6 (May/June, 1946), 410-411.
Outline of the organization of SENAC as provided by the legislation of January, 1946.

220. PASQUALE, CARLOS. "SENAI: emprêsa a serviço do bem comum," *Revista Brasileira de Estudos Pedagógicos,* 47:105 (January/March, 1967), 162-164.
Philosophy underlying the existence of SENAI, and its educational contribution to the community at large.

221. "Programas dos cursos técnicos para adultos," *Revista de Educação Pública,* 2:8 (October/December, 1944), 784-806.
Course content of the adult education campaign established in Rio de Janeiro in 1943.

*222. *Revista SENAI,* 22:86/87 (January/June, 1967).
Commemorative issue discussing activities from 1942-1966. (From: *Handbook of Latin American Studies,* 31 [1969], 353)

223. ROBBINS, JERRY H. "SENAI: Model for Latin America," *American Vocational Journal,* 47:9 (December, 1972), 40.
Brief description of the organization of SENAI and its current objectives (in apprenticeship, training, research, and scholarships). De-

scribes joint efforts with international agencies, foreign governments, and international corporations, and discusses its importance in meeting the demand for skilled workers.

224. SEMINÁRIO INTERNACIONAL SÔBRE 'RESISTÊNCIAS À MUNDANÇA— FATÔRES QUE IMPEDEM OU DIFICULTAM O DESENVOLVIMENTO', RIO DE JANEIRO, 1959. *Resistências à mudança: fatôres que impedem ou dificultam o desenvolvimento; anais do seminário internacional reunido no Rio de Janeiro, em outubro de 1959.* Rio de Janeiro: Centro Latino-Americano de Pesquisas em Ciências Sociais, 1960. 349 pp.
    Section entitled "Education, Instruction, and Social Change," briefly treats SENAI and SENAC as examples of alternatives to the formal school system.

*225. "O SENAI de São Paulo no decênio 1950-1960," *Informativo do Serviço Nacional de Aprendizagem Industrial*, 15:184 (July, 1961), 3-5.

*226. "SENAI treina imigrantes em Ponta Grossa," *Revista SENAI*, 21:85 (October/December, 1966), 2-3.

227. SILVEIRA, HORÁCIO. "O ensino industrial em São Paulo," *Revista Brasileira de Estudos Pedagógicos*, 3:8 (February, 1945), 208-222.
    Report of a conference organized by SENAI in São Paulo. Relates the history of technical-vocational instruction in São Paulo, including comments on the work of SENAI and its contribution in producing skilled workers.

228. "Vocational Education in Brazil," *International Labour Review*, 42:6 (December, 1940), 406.
    Discusses ramifications of the legislative decree of May 2, 1939, requiring employers of more than 500 persons to organize vocational training courses for adults and young people.

229. "Vocational Education in Brazil," *International Labour Review*, 46:1 (July, 1942), 75-77.
    Further description of the newly created national apprenticeship service (SENAI), outlining organization of courses, establishment of schools, and general provisions of the enabling legislation.

230. "Vocational Training in Brazil," *International Labour Review*, 52:4 (October, 1945), 401.
    Brief account of the development of SENAI from its inception in July, 1942, to May, 1945.

231. WRIGHT, J. C. *Industrial Education in Brazil.* Building a Better

Hemisphere Series, 6. Washington: Technical Cooperation Administration, Inter-American Regional Office, Institute of Inter-American Affairs, 1952. 3 pp.

Describes work of SENAI and the Commissão Brasileira-Americana de Educação Industrial (CBAI) in vocational training.

MISCELLANEOUS

232. BRAZIL. MINISTÉRIO DO PLANEJAMENTO E COORDENAÇÃO GERAL. *Programa estratégico de desenvolvimento 1968-1970: Area estratégica IX—infraestrutura social.* Rio de Janeiro: 1969. 2 vols.

Volume 2 deals with plans for vocational training programs, such as the Programa Intensivo de Preparação de Mão-de-Obra and the program of the Diretoria do Ensino Agrícola—Preparação de Tratoristas.

233. CONGRESSO BRASILEIRO DE EDUCAÇÃO. 8TH, GOIÂNA, 1942. *Anais.* Rio de Janeiro: Serviço Gráfico do I.B.G.E., 1944. 626 pp.

Part 8 deals with cultural missions in the rural areas and their role in the educational process. Part 9 covers the *colônias-escolas*—institutions providing agricultural and technical training and advice in areas of colonization.

234. "Congresso Nacional de Educação de Adultos, II," *Educação*, 61 (3rd Quarter, 1958), 1-44.

Record of sessions and discussions of the second congress on adult education in Brazil. Efforts to date discussed as well, with particular reference to activities of SENAI and SENAC. Historical survey of adult education included, dating back to 1834.

235. CORNELY, SENO A. "Desenvolvimento de comunidade," *Revista de Administração Municipal*, 15:88 (May/June, 1968), 296-306.

Though not describing any particular program, of usefulness is a list of government agencies and departments and private organizations active in community development projects in Brazil. Many of these programs are directly educational.

236. EDFELT, RALPH. "Occupational Education and Training: The Role of Large Private Industry in Brazil," in Thomas J. La Belle, ed., *Educational Alternatives in Latin America: Social Change and Social Stratification*, Latin American Studies Series, 30. Los Angeles: Latin American Center, University of California, 1975, pp. 384-413.

Discusses the contribution of private industry to nonformal education on all levels of instruction. Included are educational programs of the Serviço Social da Indústria (SESI), corporate efforts in the MOBRAL literacy campaign, training services of SENAI, PIPMO, and FORMO, as well as a number of in-house programs.

237. FAUST, AUGUSTUS F. *Brazil: Education in an Expanding Economy.* U.S. Office of Education, Bulletin 1959, no. 13. Washington: Government Printing Office, 1959. 142 pp.

Includes sections on SENAI, SENAC, and the adult education campaign organized in 1947. Very general presentation.

238. GODFREY, ERWINA E. " 'Foreign Aid' to Brazil from Private U.S. Sources," *Journal of Inter-American Studies*, 5 (April, 1963), 257-265.

Discusses private assistance ventures which include several that are directly educational. The Rockefeller-funded Associação de Crédito e Assistência Rural (ACAR) administers rural extension programs. Among denominationally-backed programs are the Instituto Rural Evangélico at Itapinga (basic education for illiterate teenagers combined with agricultural instruction) and the Jewish-sponsored Organization for Rehabilitation through Training (ORT), which combines primary education with vocational training.

239. HAVIGHURST, ROBERT J., and JOÃO ROBERTO MOREIRA. *Society and Education in Brazil.* Studies in Comparative Education, 4. Pittsburgh: University of Pittsburgh Press, 1965. 263 pp.

Chapter 8 on primary and fundamental education deals with educational efforts in rural areas outside the school system, such as the Associação Nordestina de Crédito e Assistência Rural (ANCAR) which combines credit with agricultural and home extension services, the Campanha de Educação de Adultos, and MEB and CNEA pilot projects.

240. LOURENÇO, MANOEL BERGSTRÖM. *Education in Brazil.* Translated by John Knox. Rio de Janeiro: Service of Publications, Cultural Division, Ministry of Foreign Relations, 1951. 39 pp.

Brief section on adult education campaign, followed by a description of the rural missions and the methods and techniques used, such as circulating libraries and filmstrips dealing with such subjects as hygiene, rural work, and civic education. Also discusses work of SENAI and SENAC.

241. MOREIRA, JOÃO ROBERTO. "Rural Education and Socioeconomic Development in Brazil," *Rural Sociology*, 25:1 (March, 1960), 38-50.

Describes two rural educational efforts which were initiated because it was felt that schools were inadequate for the task. The first is the fundamental education pilot project in the states of Minas Gerais, Pernambuco, and Goiás. The second is the supervised credit program of the Associação Nordestina de Crédito e Assistência Rural (ANCAR).

242. ORGANIZATION OF AMERICAN STATES. CONSEJO INTERAMERICANO ECONÓMICO Y SOCIAL. COMISIÓN ESPECIAL X: COMISIÓN INTERAMERICANA DE TELECOMUNICACIONES. TERCERA REUNIÓN, ASUNCIÓN, PARAGUAY, 8-12 DE SETIEMBRE DE 1969. *Actualización del informe del Brasil para la cuarta reunión de la CITEL sobre radio y televisión educativas.* Document OEA/Ser. H/XIII (CIES/Com. X/204); OEA/Ser. H/XIII (CIES/Com. X/246). Washington: 1969. 7 pp.

> Report covers the educational programming of radio and television stations throughout the country for the period 1968-1969. Mentions the literacy program on television sponsored by the Movimento Brasileiro de Alfabetização (MOBRAL), activities of the Movimento de Educação de Base (MEB), and seminars on educational television held in major cities during the year. Includes a list of educational radio and television programs by locality (Ceará, Rio Grande do Norte, Paraíba, Pernambuco, Bahia, Minas Gerais, Rio de Janeiro, São Paulo, Paraná, and Rio Grande do Sul).

243. "Política social do Brasil," *O Observador Económico e Financeiro*, 13:151 (August, 1948), 163-191.

> Lengthy discussion of SENAI and SESI (Serviço Social da Indústria) programs. Also mentions work of the Serviço Social do Comércio (SESC), the Legião Brasileira de Assistência (LBA) and SENAC. Among activities are literacy programs, health and sanitation courses, and educational films. Offers a detailed description of SESI's Rio de Janeiro division.

244. SALLES, EUGENIO DE ARAUJO. "A Survey of the Development of Rural and Urban Communities in the Brazilian Northeast," in International Conference of Social Work, XI, Petrópolis, 1962, *Proceedings: Urban and Rural Community Development*. Rio de Janeiro: Brazilian Committee of the International Conference of Social Work, 1963, pp. 93-101.

> Discusses a number of projects in general terms: the Campanha Nacional de Educação Rural (CNER); the Movimento de Educação de Base (MEB); and in some detail about the Serviço de Assistência Rural (SAR).

245. U.S. AGENCY FOR INTERNATIONAL DEVELOPMENT. HUMAN RESOURCES OFFICE, BRAZIL. *Brazil: Education Sector Analysis.* N.p.: 1972. 112 pp.

> Part D on higher education includes a section on its relation to devel-

opment. Briefly discusses the program of the Federal University of Rio Grande do Norte called the Centro Rural Universitário de Treinamento e Ação Comunitária (CRUTAC), which trains university students to provide technical assistance to rural communities. Also notes the Movimento Universitário de Desenvolvimento Econômico e Social (MUDES), a private foundation sponsoring a wide range of programs in community development—a particularly noteworthy effort being the "Projeto Rondon" pilot program in the São Francisco River Valley. Mentioned as well are the Campi Avançados which send students and professors to rural areas to work on development projects and to train local personnel in community development skills.

Part E, entitled "Non-Formal Education," includes sections on literacy training, professional training, and community organization and development. The major responsibility for such programs now falls to the Departamento de Ensino Complementar of the Ministério da Educação e Cultura. Provides an historical survey of all aforementioned areas of activity. Active in literacy training have been the Serviço de Educação de Adultos (SEA), the Movimento de Educaçao de Base (MEB), the João Baptista do Amaral Foundation, the Método Dom Bosco, the Cruzada ABC sponsored by the Agnes Erskine Foundation in Recife, and, most recently, the Movimento Brasileiro de Alfabetização (MOBRAL). In the area of professional training are descriptions of SENAI, SENAC, and the Programa Intensivo de Preparação de Mão-de-Obra (PIPMO). Under community development and organization are such multifaceted programs as ABCAR, MEB, and Ação Comunitária do Brasil (in Rio de Janeiro and São Paulo).

CONCEPTUALIZATION

246. Ação Popular, Brazil. "Cultura popular," *Verbum*, 21:1/2 (March/June, 1964), 96-112.
    Philosophical discussion of the need to awaken popular culture as a means of politicizing, raising consciousness (*conscientização*) of, and organizing the masses. Among the instruments for accomplishing these objectives are literacy training, organization of *"núcleos populares"* (medium for educational activities such as films and courses), theater, "praça de cultura," and festivals.

247. Dannemann, Robert N. *Formação profissional: Conceituação problemática social brasileira*. Rio de Janeiro: Divisão de Estudos

e Pesquisas Sociais, Serviço Nacional de Aprendizagem Comercial, 1967. 36 pp.

Discusses the need for nonformal technical training services in developing countries and the functions (social and economic) that training should serve.

248. FONSECA, EDSON NERY DA. "Importância da biblioteca nos programas de alfabetização e educação de base," *Revista do Serviço Público*, 25:94:3 (July/September, 1962), 99-108.

Calls for libraries to take an active role in literacy, adult, and fundamental education programs.

249. FONTOURA, AMARAL. *Aspectos da vida rural brasileira: Seus problemas e soluções*. Rio de Janeiro: Guarany, 1952. 285 pp.

Proposes (as part of the solution) the creation of rural social centers which would in effect be coordinators of all social services in a community, including the library, museum, radio programs, meetings, and adult education. Its function would be to administer a wide variety of educational programs, ranging from child care to instruction in agricultural techniques. The author sees the need for centers to go beyond the scope of schools in order to reach the whole community and provide the kinds of information and services needed by all.

250. FREITAS, M. A. TEIXEIRA DE. "O exército e a educação nacional," *Revista Brasileira de Estatística*, 8:32 (October/December, 1947), 920-937.

Lengthy discussion of the educational role that the military could play in Brazilian society. Proposes the formation of military education missions (*missões militares de educação*) which are viewed, at least in part, as organizations for civic improvement.

251. HSIN-PAO, YANG. "A educação de adultos nas comunidades rurais," *Formação*, 13:155 (June, 1951), 39-48; 13:156 (July, 1951), 7-16.

Discusses the need for rural adult education and the forms it should take.

252. ORLANDÍ, J. "As 'missões culturais'," *Revista Brasileira de Estudos Pedagógicos*, 3:8 (February, 1945), 185-190.

Discussion of the concept of and the elements necessary for a successful cultural mission program. Scores the importance of drama, film, museums, and libraries as elements of cultural missions.

253. PAN AMERICAN UNION. DIVISION OF EDUCATION. *La educación fundamental del adulto americano: OEA, UNESCO, Brasil*. Semi-

narios Interamericanos de Educación, 7. Washington: 1951. 232 pp.

Section on literacy and adult education recognizes the need for out-of-school educational programs and offers a detailed proposal for the content, methodology, and cooperating institutions (labor unions, cooperatives, press, radio, libraries, health services, agricultural extension services, cultural missions, armed forces, church) which should comprise such programs.

Chile

MULTIFACETED PROGRAMS

254. CALM, LILLIAN. "El canal 13 y la televisión educativa," *Finis Terrae*, 13:58 (November/December, 1966), 16-20.

Describes programming of the educational television station begun in Santiago in 1965. The three types of programs are: (1) entertainment; (2) directly educational; (3) cultural enrichment. Educational programs include carpentry, *cestería*, and the role of women in society.

255. CHILE. DIRECCIÓN DE ASUNTOS INDÍGENAS. *Labor actual de la Dirección de Asuntos Indígenas (Chile) y proyectos elaborados por ésta, en favor de la población indígena.* Santiago: 1966. 19 pp.

Indicates activities undertaken (by locality), such as: course for women; vocational training in textile weaving; courses in painting and design; family life education; cooperative theory and practice; community development techniques; literacy training.

256. CORTÉS CARABANTES, WALDEMAR. "Los planes extraordinarios de educación de adultos," *Revista de Educación*, Santiago, 7 (June, 1968), 28-35.

Outlines the principles of adult education. Literacy training forms the basis for all programs. Explains the program of the Instituto de Desarrollo Comunitario (IDECO), which is directed toward women and the home.

*257. *Escuela experimental de cultura popular 'Pedro Aguirre Cerda.'* Santiago: Comuna de Quinta Normal, 1949. 26 pp.

Adult and community education experiment in Santiago. (From: United Nations Educational, Scientific, and Cultural Organization. *Education for Community Development: A Selected Bibliography.* Educational Studies and Documents, 7. Paris: 1954. 49 pp.)

258. GAETE PEQUEÑO, DORA. "El Instituto del Inquilino," *Revista de Educación*, Santiago, 8:51 (November/December, 1948), 285-288.

Through publications and missions, the Institute has carried its educational work to the campesino. Efforts focus on basic agricultural and home extension, but the Institute serves as a center for information dissemination on a whole range of subjects.

259. GILLETTE, ARTHUR. "Servicio voluntario de estudiantes en Chile," *Educación de Adultos y de Jóvenes: Boletín Trimestral*, 15:4 (1963), 219-227.

> Voluntary rural community development program of Chilean university student union, Unión de Federaciones Universitarias de Chile (UFUCh). Provides a brief history of the program and a discussion of problems encountered and activities undertaken, which include literacy work and instruction in agricultural techniques.

260. GILLETTE, ARTHUR. "Student Voluntary Service in Chile," *International Journal of Adult and Youth Education*, 15:4 (1963), 193-200.

> Unión de Federaciones Universitarias de Chile (UFUCh) volunteer student groups working as literacy, home, and agricultural extension agents and instructing in vocational skills and principles of agricultural cooperatives.

261. GONZÁLEZ M., GUILLERMO. "Labor social y educadora del Instituto del Inquilino," *Acción Social*, 14:115/116 (August/September, 1947), 31-33.

> Efforts of the Institute to educate the campesino in areas of health, livestock, and agriculture. Talks about publications directed toward the campesino for improving living conditions.

262. INSTITUTO DE EDUCACIÓN RURAL. *20 años sirviendo a los campesinos*. Santiago: [1974?]. No pagination.

> Celebrating twenty years of service, this booklet outlines activities of IER over the years. Efforts are concentrated in vocational and agricultural training, as well as offering one-year training courses for community *promotores*.

263. LEVY, GUSTAVO. "Lo Valledor, una provechosa experiencia estudiantil en el desarrollo de una comunidad," Universidad de Chile, *Boletín*, 23 (1961), 54-58.

> Work in a Santiago slum undertaken by students from the Departamento de Extensión Social of the Federación de Estudiantes de Chile. Activities include instruction for working mothers, *teatro obrero*, and health education.

264. MAUNA, NELSO SEVERINO. "El Centro de Educación Fundamental de Ancud, Chile," Instituto Interamericano del Niño, *Boletín,* 34:4 (December, 1960), 372-390.

> Relates the organization and activities of the fundamental education center established in Ancud in 1956 by recent graduates of CREFAL in Mexico. Carries the account up to 1960.

265. MOLL BRIONES, LUIS. "Bibliotecas y talleres de costura ambulantes,"

Revista de Educación, Santiago, 8:50 (October, 1948), 261-263.
Article about mobile libraries and sewing classes (complete with machines) which are part of the work of the Cuerpos Cívicos de Alfabetización Popular.

266. MOLL BRIONES, LUIS. "Cuerpo Cívico de Alfabetización Popular," *Revista de Educación*, Santiago, 5:28 (May, 1945), 93-96.
Account of the organization of the literacy corps.

267. PARRA PRADENAS, ORTELIO. "Evolución de la enseñanza rural en los últimos 25 años," *Revista de Educación*, Santiago, 5:30 (August, 1945), 249-254, 259.
Experimental integrated education program in San Carlos discussed. One new aspect is the Departamento de Extensión Cultural under whose jurisdiction fall most nonformal educational projects, such as home improvement courses, vocational education, and literacy training.

268. ROSSI, ADRIANO. "Cooperativa de viviendas José Cardijn, de Chile," in *Las cooperativas como método de desarrollo de regiones y comunidades*. Estudios y Monografías, 14. Washington: Department of Social Affairs, Pan American Union, 1964, pp. 3-43.
Includes description of the Comité de Educación, and, in particular, its Comité Femenino, which has organized courses on home economics, general culture, child care, and cooperative methods. The committee has also arranged training courses, such as hair styling.

269. SALAS S., IRMA, and ENRIQUE SAAVEDRA E. *La educación en una comuna de Santiago*. Universidad de Chile, Instituto de Educación, Estudios de Comunidades y Regiones, 1. Santiago: Editorial Universitaria, 1962. 2 vols.
Describes the entire educational system of the community. Nonformal aspects include the health education courses and community development projects conducted by the Centro Experimental de Salud San Joaquín.

270. "Ten Years of Rural Education in Chile," *ILO News*, New Series, 9 (June, 1964), 18-23.
Describes ten years of effort of the Institute of Rural Education: rural centers; vocational training; educational radio programs; mobile units equipped with libraries and projection equipment; training for cooperatives.

271. URTUBIA L., OLGA. "La escuela experimental de cultura popular 'Pedro Aguirre Cerda'," *Revista de Educación*, Santiago, 4:22 (June/July, 1944), 163-166.
Cultural center established in a working class section of Santiago which

conducts a variety of education programs for the community: health instruction; domestic skill training; theater; radio school.

AGRICULTURAL TRAINING

272. BROWN, MARION R. "Agricultural 'Extension' in Chile: A Study of Institutional Transplantation," *Journal of Developing Areas*, 4:2 (January, 1970), 197-210.

   Extension is defined as disseminating agricultural technology. The article offers a program-by-program discussion and an analysis of recent and ongoing programs designed to improve techniques of farming and farm workers. Programs under discussion include the Department of Agricultural Extension of the Ministry of Agriculture, in conjunction with the Rockefeller Foundation and the National Health Service, and the Department of Inter-American Technical Cooperation in Agriculture (DTICA).

*273. FOOD AND AGRICULTURAL ORGANIZATION. *Chile: Organización e intensificación del servicio nacional de extensión agrícola; informe al gobierno*, by N. T. Theodorou. Document EPTA Report, 1185. N.p.: 1960. 25 pp.

*274. GALECIO G., JUAN. *Informe del Servicio de Extensión Agrícola de Chile*. Santiago: Ministerio de Agricultura, 1959. No pagination.

275. HALL, ROBERT KING, and MARGARET GWENLLIAN STANTON. "Educating the Chilean *Huaso*: An Experiment in Rural Education," Pan American Union, *Bulletin*, 75:4 (April, 1941), 216-224.

   Work of the Instituto de Información Campesina of the Junta de Exportación Agrícola which revolves around the dissemination of information among the *huasos* (cowboys), *inquilinos* (tenant farmers), and small landholders. Their aim is to improve and modernize work on farms. Examples of literature disseminated include: care and pruning of trees; plant diseases; raising chickens; social legislation. The Institute sends out mobile units of agricultural experts.

276. TARSO SANTOS, PAULO DE. "Training Agricultural Workers by Television: Aspects of a Project Being Implemented in Chile," *Educational Broadcasting International*, 5:1 (March, 1971), 8-11.

   Program developed by the Instituto de Capacitación, Investigación y Reforma Agraria (ICIRA) and the FAO to aid agrarian reform. The experimental program is carried out in Santiago province. Describes content and methodology.

BASIC EDUCATION/LITERACY

*277. BARRIENTOS SALAS, ROBINSÓN. *Educación de adultos y alfabetización.* Santiago: Escuela de Verano, Universidad de Chile, 1951. 149 pp.

*278. "A Campaign Against Illiteracy," *South Pacific Mail*, (March 7, 1929), 1.

279. CHACÓN NARDI, RAFAELA. "Chile y la lucha contra el analfabetismo," Cuba, Comisión Nacional de la UNESCO, *Boletín*, 3:8 (August, 1954), 13-14.
    Description of the activities under the direction of the Sección de Alfabetización y Educación de Adultos of the Ministerio de Educación: adult schools; mobile units; libraries.

*280. CHILE. DIRECCIÓN GENERAL DE EDUCACIÓN PRIMARIA. SECCIÓN EDUCACIÓN DE ADULTOS. *Cuerpo Cívico de Alfabetización Popular, institución nacional al servicio de la cultura del pueblo.* Santiago: 1945. 10 pp.

281. CORTÉS, WALDEMAR, and JAVIER HERRERA. "El programa nacional de alfabetización en 1967/1968," *Revista de Educación*, Santiago, 20 (September, 1969), 64-68.
    Detailed report, complete with schematics, describing financing, legislation, structure, organization, methods, and personnel of the literacy campaign.

282. FREIRE, PAULO. "To the Coordinator of a Cultural Circle," *Convergence*, 4:1 (1971), 61-62.
    Circular sent to coordinators of study groups by Freire. Deals with methods that should be employed and basic tenets behind the concept of "cultural circles."

283. "Literacy Campaign: Chile," Pan American Union, *Bulletin*, 64:7 (July, 1930), 752.
    Announcement of the organization of a new literacy campaign.

*284. MOLL BRIONES, LUIS. "Brigada cívica de alfabetização popular no Chile," Pan American Union, *Boletím*, 48:4 (April, 1946), 187-189.

*285. SANDERS, THOMAS GRIFFIN. *Literacy Training and Conscientización: the Paulo Freire Method.* Santiago: Institute of World Affairs, 1968. 14 pp.

286. SANDERS, THOMAS GRIFFIN. "The Paulo Freire Method: Literacy Training and *Conscientización*," American Universities Field Staff, Report Service, *West Coast South America Series*, 15:1 (1968), 18 pp.
    Critiques and describes the Freire method and Chile's literacy program incorporating it.

287. ZÚÑIGA, EDUARDO. "A Start in the Battle Against Cultural Poverty in Chile: An Account of the First National Student Literacy Seminar," *The Student*, Leiden, Netherlands, 7:4 (1963), 2-4, 27.
    Description of the literacy campaign undertaken by student members of the Unión de Federaciones Universitarias de Chile (UFUCh). The seminar was held in February, 1963, in Valparaíso, Chile.

CULTURAL EXTENSION

288. CHILE. DIRECCIÓN GENERAL DE EDUCACIÓN PRIMARIA. SECCIÓN PEDAGÓGICA. *Radio escuela experimental.* Santiago: 1943. 22 pp.
    Details daily programming of the radio school. Concentrates on Chilean history and culture.

289. DONOSO LOERO, TERESA. "El campesino chileno y la televisión," *Finis Terrae*, 12:50 (July/August, 1965), 54-56.
    Analysis of educational television in Chile. Describes the system of *teleclubes* sponsored by the Fundación de Vida Rural of the Catholic University of Chile as a means of reaching more people and of using programming more effectively.

290. "Inauguración de los servicios de radiodifusión educativa," *Revista de Educación*, Santiago, 9:52 (June, 1949), 85-87.
    The first programs were language and cultural instruction. Discusses programming to date (1943-1949).

HEALTH, HYGIENE, AND NUTRITION INSTRUCTION

291. BAEZA GOÑI, ARTURO. "Programas de bienestar social y su influencia sobre la nutrición," Instituto Americano del Niño, *Boletín*, 33:2: 129 (June, 1959), 177-185.
    General description of the community development project in the

barrio San Joaquín in Santiago undertaken by the Centro Experimental de Asistencia Médico Social. Emphasis is on health and nutrition education, but they also organize home economics classes for women.

292. "Chile: Nutrition Campaign," Pan American Union, *Bulletin*, 64:1 (January, 1930), 104.

Notes efforts on the part of the Department of Social Welfare to educate people about proper diet through use of posters, public meetings, radio programs, and motion pictures.

293. Ríos Castro, Rigoberto. "Organization of Health Education in Chile," in Pacific Science Association, *Proceedings of the Sixth Pacific Science Congress, 1939*. Berkeley: University of California Press, 1943, pp. 711-719.

Detailed organization plan of the National Health Service, department by department. Activities include: educational films; radio programs; lectures; poster campaigns; publications; magic lantern slides. Also deals with principal defects of health education to the time of the writing. Makes suggestions for a plan of health education for 1939 (directed toward educational institutions, labor unions, parent associations, and radio stations).

LABOR UNION EDUCATION

294. Martins Pereira, José. "Chile: Union Training in Rural Areas," *Labour Education*, 19 (June, 1970), 7-11.

Training of potential union leaders by the national agricultural trade union federation, "Libertad." Offers some critical analysis of the program content.

VOCATIONAL SKILL TRAINING

295. Alberti S., Agustín. "Vocational Training in Chile," *International Labour Review*, 95:5 (May, 1967), 452-464.

Description of apprenticeship and adult vocational training programs of the Instituto Nacional de Capacitación (INACAP). Includes an account of activities: courses; vocational training centers; programs; methodology; cooperation with other institutions, e.g., the army.

296. EDWARDS, AGUSTÍN. "Technical Education in Chile," *Inter-American Quarterly*, 2:2 (April, 1940), 30-35.

> Organization of Santa María University in Valparaíso (vocational school), open to men only, but no previous formal education is necessary and training is provided free of charge. Apprentice and night schools are directed toward those with little or no previous education and toward those who must work during the day. The school is privately funded from the personal estate of the founder.

MISCELLANEOUS

297. "Adult Education Activities," *International Bureau of Education Bulletin*, 20:79 (2nd Quarter, 1946), 53.

> Mentions efforts undertaken by the Ministry of Education in 1943 in literacy and technical education for adults, as well as describing its "popular culture" teams and library activities.

298. CARRASCO, ROSA, et al. "El desarrollo de la comunidad rural y urbana," *Servicio Social*, 37:3 (December, 1963), 32-47.

> Community development work of the National Health Service, Fundación de Viviendas y Asistencia Social, Corporación de Vivienda, Ministry of Education, Institute of Rural Education, and the Misión de Educación Rural of the Catholic University of Chile.

299. CORTÉS, WALDEMAR, and ALVARO VIEIRA. "Perspectivas actuales de la educación de adultos en Chile," *Revista de Educación*, Santiago, 2 (November, 1967), 25-29.

> First part of the article is devoted to the philosophy underlying adult education in Chile. Discussion follows of a number of adult education programs, such as the Instituto de Desarrollo Comunitario (IDECO) and the Instituto Nacional de Capacitación (INACAP).

300. EBAUGH, CAMERON D. *Education in Chile*. U.S. Office of Education, Bulletin 1945, no. 10. Washington: Government Printing Office, 1945. 123 pp.

> Gives the history of adult education dating back to the first efforts of the army in 1840. Also includes information on the mobile teams of popular culture, circulating library program, literacy campaign, and the Instituto del Inquilino programs.

301. FREEBURGER, ADELA R., and CHARLES C. HAUCH. *Education in Chile*. U.S. Office of Education, Bulletin 1964, no. 10; Studies in

Comparative Education. Washington: Government Printing Office, 1964. 42 pp.

Section on adult and continuing education describes work of the Ministry of Education and the Instituto de Educación Rural.

302. LATORRE SALAMANCA, GONZALO. "La experimentación educacional en Chile," *Revista de Educación*, Santiago, 15:27 (April, 1945), 39-44.

Mentions three experiments in nonformal education—La Escuela Experimental de Cultura Popular, Radio Escuela Experimental, and the Cuerpo Cívico de Alfabetización—all initiated under the Aguirre Cerda regime.

303. MARDONES GUÍÑEZ, IRENE. "Papel de los asistentes sociales en programas de educación fundamental y desarrollo de la comunidad," *Servicio Social*, 36:1 (January/April, 1962), 21-33.

After defining "fundamental education" and "community development," the author describes the role of social workers in fundamental education and community development projects and actual projects in which social workers are involved, through the Ministry of Education, National Health Service, Ministry of Agriculture, Institute of Rural Education, and private programs.

304. NAVEA ACEVEDO, DANIEL. "Por una educación al servicio del pueblo," *Revista de Educación*, Santiago, 2:12 (October/November, 1942), 65-71.

Notes several nonformal programs (Instituto de Orientación Campesina and the Misiones de Cultura Campesina) in addition to the literacy campaign.

305. ORGANIZATION OF AMERICAN STATES. PRIMERA CONFERENCIA INTERAMERICANA SOBRE DESARROLLO DE LA COMUNIDAD, SANTIAGO, CHILE, 20-26 DE JULIO DE 1970. *Informe de Chile*. Document OEA/Ser.K/XVII/1.1 (Doc.20). Washington: 1970. 73 pp.

One of the basic tenets of Ministry of Education policy is that education is a lifelong process and therefore must have both formal and nonformal aspects. Paper describes some nonformal programs, including the activities of the Consejería de Promoción Popular and the Instituto de Desarrollo Agropecuario (INDAP) in the areas of rural adult education and vocational training. Also describes the work of the Ministerio de Trabajo y Previsión Social in union organization and education (which has included literacy training). Appendix provides a description of the structure of the Consejería Nacional de Promoción Popular. Information in this report covers the period of the Frei government only.

306. PLATT, WILLIAM JAMES. *Chile's Search for Educational-Economic Consistency.* Paper presented at the Comparative Education Conference, University of California, Berkeley, 25-27 March 1966. Menlo Park, California: Stanford Research Institute, 1966. 42 pp.
    Describes vocational training and apprenticeship programs of the joint United States–Chile Servicio de Cooperación Técnica which began in 1952. Section on agriculture and agrarian reform discusses the work of the Instituto de Educación Rural, the Agrarian Reform Corporation (CORA), and the Institute for Agricultural Development (INDAP) in the area of dissemination of technical agricultural information. Raises the question of formal versus nonformal education.

307. PLATT, WILLIAM JAMES, et al. *Training and Educational Needs in Chile's Agricultural Development.* Stanford Research Institute, SRI Project XI-9245. Sacramento: Chile-California Program of Technical Assistance, 1965. 86 pp.
    Proposes two types of educational programs: (1) accelerated skill training (short-term); (2) formal education (long-term). Discusses various short-term training projects which have been undertaken by the Servicio de Cooperación Técnica and the Instituto de Educación Rural, in addition to community development projects, radio school programs, and audio-visual units of the Instituto de Educación Rural (IER). A detailed evaluation of IER programs is found in Appendix A. A section of the paper is devoted to outlining "alternative strategies for agricultural training and education," and chapter 3 deals with recommendations for adult education and agricultural skill training. Appendix C discusses efforts in nonformal education (extension programs, television program, mobile units) by the Fundaciones de Vida Rural, a private organization.

CONCEPTUALIZATION

308. AVALOS DAVIDSON, BEATRICE. "La educación en Chile: Perspectivas," *Cuadernos de Economía*, 7:22 (December, 1970), 3-13.
    Raises question of the validity of formal schooling for all and says that alternatives of some sort will have to be considered.

309. BUNSTER, MARTIN. "Un nuevo departamento del Ministerio de Educación Pública: Labor que realizará la Sección Cultura y Publicaciones," *Revista de Educación*, Santiago, 3:13 (April, 1943), 36-38.
    Recognizes the limitations of formal schooling. The Sección Cultura

y Publicaciones was created to coordinate out-of-school educational activities. Provides a long list of proposed activities from cultural programs to technical training.

310. CHONCHOL CHAIT, JACQUES. "From Isolation to Unity: The Achievement of the Chilean Farmer," *CERES: FAO Review*, 1:3 (May/June, 1968), 41-45.

The vice-president of the Chilean National Institute for Livestock Development argues that special emphasis must be given to ways and means of organizing, motivating, mobilizing, and training the broad farm masses. Perceives the need for large scale training programs within farm labor organizations and discusses a number of possible approaches.

311. JORNADAS BIBLIOTECARIAS CHILENAS, 4TH, ANTOFAGASTA, 1966. *La biblioteca y la comunidad: Informe final*. N.p.: Asociación de Bibliotecarios de Chile, 1966. 156 pp.

Section on *"bibliotecas populares; función social, función docente y responsabilidad de las autoridades"* talks about the need to establish popular libraries as one aspect of community development. Discusses proposals for mobile units and the incorporation of a library in a proposed pilot project of community development.

312. SALAS S., IRMA, and ENRIQUE SAAVEDRA E. "La educación en una comuna de Santiago," Universidad de Chile, *Boletín*, 31 (July, 1962), 16-26.

Calls for the extension of on-the-job training and vocational training centers as part of adult education. Section on adult education sees the need for expansion of all levels of adult education: basic education; training centers; libraries; museums; cultural centers.

Colombia

MULTIFACETED PROGRAMS

313. Acción Cultural Popular. *Agencia de desarrollo*. Bogotá: Editorial Andes, 1968. 30 pp.
     Describes history, function, and activities of Acción Cultural Popular focusing on Radio Sutatenza educational programs.

314. Amaya, Susana. "Radio Helps Eradicate Mass Illiteracy in Rural Colombia," *Gazette*, Leiden, Netherlands, 5:4 (1959), 403-408.
     History, organization of the radio schools, objectives, and programs of Radio Sutatenza. Educational programs include literacy training, arithmetic, history, civics, agriculture, and home economics by radio. Special training courses for assistants at the Rural Institutes of Sutatenza headquarters have been created which include fundamentals of radio equipment operation, practical farming, and home improvement.

315. Behrman, Daniel. "Don Quixote of the Radio," *Courier*, 7:12 (May, 1955), 18-23.
     Work of Father Salcedo and Radio Sutatenza/Acción Cultural Popular. Describes programming and past and future activities.

316. Brownstone, Paul L. "International Understanding Through Communication: One Plan, One Plea," *Journal of Communication, 20:2 (June, 1970), 142-152*.
     Includes account of early UNESCO assistance to help establish Radio Sutatenza. Began basically as a literacy campaign.

317. Burnet, Mary. *ABC of Literacy*. Paris: United Nations Educational, Scientific, and Cultural Organization, 1965. 64 pp.
     Section on radio literacy programs includes brief description of Radio Sutatenza programs.

318. Capó, Carmelina. *A Family Living Programme in Viani, February-July 1950*. Occasional Papers in Education, 9; Document UNESCO/ED/Occ./9. Paris: Education Clearing House, United Nations Educational, Scientific, and Cultural Organization, 1951. 28 pp.
     Report of practical training in family living of the fundamental education project at Vianí. On a nonformal level, this included home visits, adult classes, organization of neighborhood groups, and the home problem clinic of the Health Service station.

319. CONSIDINE, JOHN J. "Radio Reaches the Illiterates," *Catholic School Journal*, 62:6 (June, 1962), 61.
Discusses Salcedo's work with Radio Sutatenza and Acción Cultural Popular. Focuses on literacy programs.

320. Cullell, Inés. "Problemas actuales de la educación de adultos," *Universidad*, Santa Fe, 47 (January/March, 1961), 299-316.
Philosophical tract on what is meant by adult education, what methods of instruction should be employed, and the environment that should be created. There is a section devoted to cultural missions, what they should be like, and how they should operate. Talks about both urban and rural missions. Final section discusses the work of Radio Sutatenza as illustrative of concepts presented earlier.

321. "La educación en América," *Educación*, Washington, 7:25/26 (January/June, 1962), 239-249.
Section for Colombia is devoted to a brief description of Radio Sutatenza programming and the work of Acción Cultural Popular.

322. EGGINTON, EVERETT, and J. MARK RUHL. "Nonformal Education and the Colombian Agrarian Reform," in Thomas J. La Belle, ed., *Educational Alternatives in Latin America: Social Change and Social Stratification*. Latin American Studies Series, 30. Los Angeles: Latin American Center, University of California, 1975, pp. 102-148.
Reports on a study to ascertain the effectiveness of the Instituto Colombiano de Reforma Agraria (INCORA) program and its technical assistance, supervised credit, and social development components as a type of nonformal education.

*323. FERRER MARTÍN, S. *Estudio y evaluación de las escuelas radiofónicas rurales*. N.p.: Escuelas Radiofónicas de Sutatenza, Acción Cultural Popular, 1959. 103 pp.

*324. HOUTART, FRANÇOIS. *Acción Cultural Popular: Sus principios y medios de acción; consideraciones teológicas y sociológicas*. Bogotá: 1960. 69 pp.

325. INSTITUTO COLOMBIANO DE BIENESTAR FAMILIAR. DIRECCIÓN GENERAL. OFICINA DE PLANEACIÓN. *Políticas y programas*. Bogotá: 1973. 109 pp.
Detailed report focusing on programs and policies of the Instituto de Bienestar Familiar. Educational activities are concentrated in the areas of nutrition and family life education.

326. INSTITUTO COLOMBIANO DE BIENESTAR FAMILIAR. DIVISIÓN PROMOCIÓN SOCIAL DEL MENOR Y LA FAMILIA. *Programa I: 'Promoción*

del Menor y la Familia'; área prioritaria: atención del menor de siete años y la familia. Bogotá: 1973. 19 pp.

Reports on a special program for problem children and their families. Among the educational services provided for the families are instruction in interpersonal relations, family planning, home economics and nutrition, and civic education.

327. INSTITUTO COLOMBIANO DE BIENESTAR FAMILIAR. OFICINA DE RECURSOS HUMANOS. *Capacitación de la comunidad: Justificación, objetivos, programas.* [Bogota?]: 1972. 29 pp.

Describes an intensive program of family life, health, and nutrition education mounted in an effort to deal with problems of juvenile delinquency and family relations.

328. KELLEY, JOSEPH B. "Community Organization in Colombia, S.A.," *Catholic Charities Review*, 48:3 (March, 1964), 13-16.

Briefly describes a program called Acción Comunal, a community self-help project for which the federal government provides technical and financial assistance. Local projects have included adult and health education classes.

329. MOHR, HERMANN J. "Oportunidades de educación en las zonas rurales de Colombia," *Revista Javeriana*, 66:330 (November/December, 1966), 571-578.

Recognizes that schools are not adequate in Colombia to fulfill the task of education and thus calls for initiation and expansion of other programs, such as radio schools and agricultural extension. Describes activities of Acción Cultural Popular.

330. NANNETTI, GUILLERMO. "Model Town," *Americas*, 1:6 (August, 1949), 16-19, 47.

Describes the UNESCO fundamental education project at Vianí and the experts who are participating in it, mostly in the areas of agriculture and health.

331. "New Out-of-School Education Center in Colombia," *Adult Education Information Notes*, 4 (October/November, 1973), 5.

Reports on a recent agreement between the governments of Colombia and West Germany for the establishment of an out-of-school education center for young people and adults in Cali.

332. NITSCH, MANFRED. "Fundamental Integral Education: Radio Schools in Latin America," *Comparative Education Review*, 8:3 (December, 1964), 340-343.

Within the context of the report of the Latin American Congress of Radiophonic Schools held in Bogotá, 13-19 September 1963, there is some discussion of the concrete work of Radio Sutatenza and Acción Cultural Popular. One major outcome of the congress was the creation of the Confederación Latinoamericana para la Educación Fundamental Integral (COLEFI).

333. ORGANIZATION OF AMÉRICAN STATES. CONSEJO INTERAMERICANO ECONÓMICO Y SOCIAL. COMISIÓN ESPECIAL X: COMISIÓN INTERAMERICANA DE TELECOMUNICACIONES. QUINTA REUNIÓN, BOGOTÁ, COLOMBIA, 22-29 DE JULIO DE 1970. *Programas teleducativos de Acción Cultural Popular (informe de Colombia).* Document OEA/Ser.H/XIII (CIES/Com.X/301). Washington: 1970. 10 pp.

Describes educational television programs under the direction of Acción Cultural Popular and Radio Sutatenza—fundamental education directed toward the Colombian peasant. Course content focuses on achieving basic literacy and numerical skills, and providing information on agricultural techniques, health, nutrition, and so forth.

334. OZAETA, PABLO M. "The Radiophonic Schools of Sutatenza, Colombia," in George Z. F. Bereday, and Joseph A. Lauwerys, eds., *Year Book of Education 1960: Communication Media and the School.* New York: Harcourt, Brace and World, 1960, pp. 557-564.

Good account of Radio Sutatenza and Acción Cultural Popular. Describes the training program for local assistants; programming for transmission; services offered by ACPO; the Institutos Campesinos de Sutatenza which are designed to improve rural life; agricultural training and livestock raising courses; and the Radio Sutatenza weekly newspaper.

335. RADIO SUTATENZA. *Programación.* Bogotá: Editorial Andes, 1969. 131 pp.

Noting first the objectives of Radio Sutatenza, the main body of this book is devoted to a thorough description of the station's educational programming.

336. "Radiophonic Schools," *International Bureau of Education Bulletin*, 35:138 (1st Quarter, 1961), 6.

Mentions work of Acción Cultural Popular, the Catholic church-sponsored organization which functions through the medium of Radio Sutatenza to educate the Colombian peasant.

337. SALCEDO, JOSÉ JOAQUÍN. *La educación popular y el problema del desarrollo en América Latina.* Conferencia dictada por Monseñor José Joaquín Salcedo en la Organización de los Estados America-

nos, el día 3 de mayo de 1967. Washington: Organization of American States, 1967. 21 pp.

   Describes the private, church-based organization and program which attempts to reach remote rural areas of Colombia—Acción Cultural Popular and its Escuelas Radiofónicas. Programming deals with practical problems, e.g., health, in an effort to supply the basic education necessary for participation in the national culture.

338. SÁNCHEZ, PATRICIO S. *Activities in the Associated Project of Viani: A Report for 1949.* Occasional Papers in Education, 7; Document UNESCO/ED/Occ./7. Paris: United Nations Educational, Scientific, and Cultural Organization, 1950. 39 pp.

   UNESCO community development project in Colombia. Discusses in part such nonformal educational activities as the conservation project devised by a soil conservation expert to get information into the community.

339. TORRES RESTREPO, CAMILO, and BERTA CORREDOR RODRÍGUEZ. *Las escuelas radiofónicas de Sutatenza, Colombia: Evaluación sociológica de los resultados.* Centro de Investigaciones Sociales, Série Socio-Económica, 2. Bogotá: Oficina Internacional de Investigaciones Sociales de FERES, 1961. 75 pp.

   Brief history of Acción Cultural Popular in Colombia and an analysis of the impact of Radio Sutatenza programs.

340. UNITED NATIONS EDUCATIONAL, SCIENTIFIC, AND CULTURAL ORGANIZATION. DEPARTMENT OF CULTURAL ACTIVITIES. *Report on the Pilot Public Library for Latin America, Medellin: Third Anniversary (October 1954-October 1957)*, by Julio Arroyave. Document CUA/84. Paris: 1957. 5 pp.

   Pilot library offers a library training program, cultural activities (lectures, discussion groups, films), and mobile services.

341. "The Use of Audio-Visual Media in Fundamental and Adult Education," *Fundamental and Adult Education*, 11:1 (1959), 31-49.

   Includes a review of the work of Acción Cultural Popular and Radio Sutatenza.

342. "The Viani Associated Project," *Courier*, 2:8 (September, 1949), 22.

   Describes initial steps taken in the fundamental education project sponsored by UNESCO.

AGRICULTURAL TRAINING

*343. BALLESTAEDT G., ALFREDO. "Evalución del trabajo de extensión agrícola en la provincia de Linares," in Seminario Suramericano de Extensión Agrícola, 1st. *Informe.* Bogotá: STACA and Ministerio de Agricultura, 1961, pp. 68-95.

344. COLOMBIA. MINISTERIO DE EDUCACIÓN NACIONAL. OFICINA DE PLANEACIÓN. *Informe del proyecto para el plan quinquenal.* Volume 3. Bogotá: 1958. No pagination.

Part 2 deals with *campesino* education, one section discussing the program of *campesino* adult education called Cursos para Campesinos Adultos, primarily agricultural training.

345. CHAPARRO G., ALVARO. "Bases de un servicio de extensión agrícola," *Universidad Pontificia Bolivariana*, 12:47 (August/September, 1946), 439-457.

Discussion of the bases for agricultural extension: must do more than disseminate information on the latest equipment or seeds; must also serve the needs of the rural family to help improve life. Describes particular needs and problems of Colombian agricultural extension and reviews existing extension services on national, regional, and local levels. Provides an outline for use in directing an extension program, which includes both field work and home service.

*346. DI FRANCO, JOSEPH, and ROY A. CLIFFORD. *Analytic Study of Five Extension Organizations in Colombia.* Turrialba, Costa Rica: Instituto Interamericano de Ciencias Agrícolas, 1962. 84 pp.

*347. DUQUE VILLEGAS, A. "Formación acelerada de recolectores de algodón," Centro Interamericano de Investigación y Documentación sobre Formación Profesional, *Boletín*, 8 (April, 1970), 37-44.

Vocational training scheme for rural workers on cotton plantations. (From: "Education for Rural Life," *Educational Documentation and Information*, 46:183 [2nd Quarter, 1972], 106).

*348. FOOD AND AGRICULTURAL ORGANIZATION. *Colombia; las actividades de extensión agrícola de los programas integrados de nutrición aplicada—informe al gobierno*, by J. Bolton Caro. Document UNDP/TA 2421. N.p.: 1967. 40 pp.

*349. MONTENEGRO B., RAÚL. "Estudio del sistema educativo de extensión agrícola del Servicio Técnico Agrícola Colombiano Americano en Boyaca." Unpublished thesis. Instituto Tecnológico Agrícola, Universidad de Nariño, 1967. 66 numb. leaves.

350. SERVICIO NACIONAL DE APRENDIZAJE. *SENA: Revolución pacífica en el campo.* Bogotá: 1967. No pagination.
Describes SENA's agricultural training courses.

351. SUÁREZ S., ALBERTO, and EDUARDO ARZE LOUREIRO. *Hacia los grupos de amistad.* Instructivo Interno de Extensión, 1. N.p.: División de Extensión, Departamento de Comunicaciones y Adiestramiento, Federación Nacional de Cafeteros de Colombia, 1971. 19 pp.
Describes agricultural extension work through the formation of local groups by the Federación Nacional de Cafeteros.

BASIC EDUCATION/LITERACY

*352. BOOKS FOR THE PEOPLE FUND. *Report on the Literacy Materials Center and Literacy Programs in Medellin, Colombia.* Status Report, 5. Washington: Pan American Union, 1967. 6 pp.

*353. COLOMBIA. MINISTERIO DE EDUCACIÓN NACIONAL. "Alfabetización y educación fundamental," in *Memoria del Ministro de Educación Nacional.* Bogotá: 1964, pp. 68-73.

354. COLOMBIA. MINISTERIO DE EDUCACIÓN NACIONAL. *Campaña contra el analfabetismo.* Publicación, 1. Bogotá: 1948. 29 pp.
Describes organization, administration, and content of courses of the literacy campaign begun in 1948.

355. COLOMBIA. MINISTERIO DE EDUCACIÓN NACIONAL. DEPARTAMENTO DE EXTENSIÓN CULTURAL Y BELLAS ARTES. *Las escuelas ambulantes.* Bogotá: 1941. 58 pp.
Report on the activities of the mobile school program in Colombia. Units include educational cinema, library, records, and health educators.

356. "Cuban and Colombian Campaigns Against Illiteracy," Pan American Union, *Bulletin*, 71:1 (January, 1937), 74-75.
Notes the creation of the Voluntary School Service, a program for women only to work as literacy instructors in their communities.

357. GALAT NOUMER, JOSÉ. "Colombia, un gigantesco centro educativo," *Revista Javeriana*, 72:358 (September, 1969), 298-307.

Centers on the advantages of teleducation: it is available to those who do not or can not attend school, and it is viewed as relatively inexpensive (in comparison to building and staffing schools) and as an accessible education medium. Calls for basic education courses and some type of "SENA-by-television" programming. Describes early experimental efforts in the area of literacy training in 1968.

358. SHEPARD, MARIETTA DANIELS. "Literacy Programs in Colombia," *Wilson Library Bulletin*, 41:8 (April, 1967), 829-833.

While the emphasis is on literacy teaching material supplied by the Books for the People Fund and Laubach Literacy Inc., there is some discussion of literacy programs themselves, particularly those of the Peace Corps.

359. UNIVERSIDAD NACIONAL DE COLOMBIA. CENTRO DE ESTUDIOS DE TERRITORIOS NACIONALES. "La universidad colombiana tiene una cita con la selva," *Revista Javeriana*, 69:344 (May, 1968), 451-454.

Recommends that universities take an active part in community development by initiating and participating in such programs as literacy training. Comments on a small scale effort already taken in that direction in 1966 by a group of 150 students and faculty who spent a month in the field doing literacy work.

CULTURAL EXTENSION

360. ARROYAVE C., JULIO CÉSAR. "Una biblioteca modelo: La biblioteca pública piloto de Medellín," Dirreción General de Archivos y Bibliotecas, Madrid, *Boletín*, 5:38 (June/August, 1956), 63-64.

Describes the bookmobile program and gives a general idea of regular activities.

361. FORERO NOGUÉS, MARION. "The Cultural Theater of Colombia: How the Ministry of Education Uses Motion Pictures and Educational Films," Pan American Union, *Bulletin*, 71:7 (July, 1937), 527-534.

Educational films shown free of charge usually twice a day, and more often on Sundays and holidays. Each theater will also house a small library. Projects that 825 such facilities will be operational throughout the country within a few years. As of the writing, however, only one existed, in Bogotá.

362. UNITED NATIONS EDUCATIONAL, SCIENTIFIC, AND CULTURAL ORGA-
NIZATION. DEPARTMENT OF CULTURAL ACTIVITIES. *La biblioteca
pública piloto de Medellín, Colombia.* Document CUA/69. Paris:
1955. 4 pp.
> Discusses various library projects, such as radio programs and lecture
> film series.

FAMILY LIFE EDUCATION

363. SANDERS, THOMAS GRIFFIN. "Family Planning in Colombia," American Universities Field Staff, Reports Service, *West Coast South
America Series*, 17:3 (1970), 6 pp.
> Describes family planning activities of three groups who generally
> disseminate information through health centers in municipalities
> around the country: Asociación Colombiana de Facultades de Mede-
> cina (ASCOFAME); La Asociación Pro-Bienestar de la Familia Colom-
> biana (PROFAMILIA); Ministry of Public Health.

HEALTH, HYGIENE, AND NUTRITION INSTRUCTION

364. INSTITUTO NACIONAL DE NUTRICIÓN (COLOMBIA). *Plan de opera-
ciones para un programa integrado de nutrición aplicada (PINA)
en los departamentos de Cauca y Norte de Santander.* Bogotá:
1965. 20 pp.
> Nutrition education plan for Cauca and Santander. Medical services
> (from the Distritos de Salud) and agricultural extension services will
> take part in the educational promotion. Courses to be offered. De-
> scribes the organization (FAO, UNICEF, and WHO are all partici-
> pants) and the financing.

365. VANNOY, JOELLENE. "Nutrition Education Program in Colombia,
South America," *Journal of Home Economics*, 53:1 (January,
1961), 29-31.
> Describes nutrition education efforts of television stations, Radio
> Sutatenza, radio station Nuevo Mundo, newspaper El Espectador,
> home demonstration agents, and traveling nutrition teams.

LABOR UNION EDUCATION

366. "The Colombian Scene," *Labour Education*, 5 (October, 1965), 18.
Outline of regular courses for training trade union leaders and instructors by the Confederation of Colombian Workers and the National Union of Colombian Workers.

367. COLORADO, EUGENIO. *El sindicato y la comunidad rural*. Serie sobre Organización de la Comunidad, 8. Washington: Sección de Servicio Social, División de Trabajo y Asuntos Sociales, Unión Panamericana, 1954. 8 pp.
Mentions leadership training courses of the Unión de Trabajadores de Colombia (UTC) in collaboration with Acción Social Católica.

PROFESSIONAL/PARAPROFESSIONAL TRAINING

368. CARO AGUIRRE, HORACIO. *Programas de adiestramiento en servicio sobre nutrición y alimentación para extensionistas agrícolas*. Bogotá: Instituto Nacional de Nutrición de Colombia, 1966. 7 pp.
Training of nutrition education workers to be part of agricultural extension services.

VOCATIONAL SKILL TRAINING

369. CÉSPEDES, AURELIO. "In Colombia, It's SENA: Industry-Taxed Training System Shows Sturdy Growth," *American Vocational Journal*, 47:9 (December, 1972), 41-43.
Discusses various aspects of the national apprenticeship service established in 1957 and modeled on SENAI in Brazil. Operates training centers throughout the country which offer courses in agricultural, industrial, and commercial skills. Provides a critique and evaluation of the program to date.

370. "Colombia: Se funda una escuela de cerámica autóctona en Malambo," *Boletín Indigenista*, 11:1 (March, 1951), 40-51.
Ceramics school created by the Institute of Ethnological Research of

the University of the Atlantic to reinvigorate the local pottery craft in 1950. Instruction is given about types of clay and their preparation, modeling of clay, use of the lathe, and glazing and baking.

371. HARBISON, FREDERICK, and GEORGE SELTZER. "National Training Schemes," in Cole S. Brembeck, and Timothy J. Thompson, eds., *New Strategies for Educational Development: The Cross-Cultural Search for Nonformal Alternatives.* Lexington, Massachusetts: Heath, 1973, pp. 195-206.
Good analysis of the Servicio Nacional de Aprendizaje (SENA), which is characterized as the most extensive and best financed training organization in the country. Provides information on its financial base, scale of operations, range of activities, and problem areas.

372. INTERNATIONAL LABOR ORGANIZATION. *Colombia: Programa de capacitación en el empleo; informe técnico.* Geneva: 1972. 56 pp.
Relates the activities of the ILO team with SENA over a four-year period (1967-1971) in devising on-the-job training programs.

373. INTERNATIONAL LABOR ORGANIZATION. *Formación profesional en Colombia.* Geneva: 1970. 127 pp.
Carefully written report giving background to the formation of SENA and discussing some of its activities. Creation of the new training centers for industrial and agricultural instructors to staff SENA (Centros Nacionales de Formación de Instructores—CNFI) is discussed in depth. This program was developed by a United Nations technical assistance team. Offers analysis of and recommendations for SENA. Appendixes detail the organization and financing of SENA and CNFI.

374. INTERNATIONAL LABOR ORGANIZATION. *Informe al gobierno de Colombia sobre la creación de una división de mano de obra dentro el Servicio Nacional de Aprendizaje (SENA).* Document OIT/TAP/Colombia/R.7. Geneva: 1959. 49 pp.
The first part includes sections on the organization of SENA and the functions and activities of the manual labor division and its sections (statistical, research and studies, selection of candidates, and occupational analysis). Second part is devoted to conclusions and recommendations.

375. Koenig, Werner. *El aprendizaje contractual y su aplicación en Colombia.* Bogotá: Editorial Pax, 1962. 113 pp.
Good deal of discussion on theories and concepts of contractual apprenticeship. Author also devotes a chapter to SENA and the development of apprenticeship in Colombia.

376. MARTÍNEZ TONO, RODOLFO. "La educación para el desarrollo, al

alcance de todos," *Economía Colombiana*, 8:25:76 (September, 1965), 43-49.

Describes achievements of SENA during the year—including the opening of new training and apprenticeship centers—international assistance, and financing. Also includes chart of matriculations by center.

377. MARTÍNEZ TONO, RODOLFO. *Una nueva ruta: Capacitación para el desarrollo.* Bogotá: Imprenta Nacional de Colombia, 1966. 37 pp.

Written by the national director of SENA, this document describes in general terms the philosophy, organization, financing, objectives, technical training and the apprenticeship system, and achievements to date of SENA.

378. PURYEAR, JEFFREY M. "Recruitment to Industrial Apprenticeship Programs in Colombia: The Case of SENA," in Thomas J. La Belle, ed., *Educational Alternatives in Latin America: Social Change and Social Stratification.* Latin American Studies Series, 30. Los Angeles: Latin American Center, University of California, 1975, pp. 414-433.

Analyzes the recruitment efforts of the Servicio Nacional de Aprendizaje (SENA), suggesting that the program does not reach the most disadvantaged portion of those eligible for admission.

*379. SERVICIO NACIONAL DE APRENDIZAJE. *La formación profesional en Colombia.* Bogotá: 1967. 47 pp.

*380. SERVICIO NACIONAL DE APRENDIZAJE. *Programación de cursos.* Bogotá: 1966. 108 pp.

381. SERVICIO NACIONAL DE APRENDIZAJE. SECCIONAL CUNDINAMARCA. *Una década al servicio de Colombia, 1957-1967.* Cundinamarca: 1967. 28 pp.

Using diagrams, this booklet primarily describes the structural organization of SENA on the national and local levels, its objectives and basic philosophy.

*382. SERVICIO NACIONAL DE APRENDIZAJE. SECCIONAL DE ANTIOQUÍA, MEDELLÍN. *Prospecto 1966.* Medellín: Editorial Bedout, [1965?]. 90 pp.

383. SERVICIO NACIONAL DE APRENDIZAJE. SECCIONAL DE ANTIOQUÍA, MEDELLÍN. *Prospecto 1969.* Antioquía: 1969. 135 pp.

Briefly describes the organization and administration of SENA, accomplishments of the past, and projections for the future. Then goes into detail regarding courses offered by SENA in Antioquía.

384. "Skilled Manpower for Latin America: The Example of SENA,"
ILO News, New Series, 8 (March, 1964), 16-19.
Describes the organization and administration of SENA, which was
established in 1957. Notes ILO assistance.

MISCELLANEOUS

385. COLOMBIA. MINISTERIO DE EDUCACIÓN NACIONAL. *La obra educativa
del gobierno en 1940, tomo 3: La extensión cultural.* Bogotá: 1940.
224 pp.
Enumerates a number of nonformal educational programs, such as
mobile schools, educational theater and film, radio schools, and the
Escuela Complementaria de Especialización Artística (an apprenticeship program aimed at working class youth).

386. "Colombia's Educational Program," *World Education*, 6:3 (May,
1941), 265-268.
General article on the literacy campaign, mobile schools, and educational radio programs.

387. FURBAY, JOHN H. *Education in Colombia.* U.S. Office of Education,
Bulletin 1946, no. 6. Washington: Government Printing Office,
1946. 111 pp.
Section on cultural extension programs of the Ministry of Education
briefly reviews nonformal educational programs, such as the Teatro
Cultural, Centro de Cultura Social (directed toward the working class),
and traveling schools (*escuelas ambulantes*).

388. GALE, LAURENCE. *Education and Development in Latin America:
With Special Reference to Colombia and Some Comparison with
Guyana, South America.* New York: Praeger, 1969. 178 pp.
Section on rural pilot projects discusses Colombia's *núcleo escolar*
program, which combines formal and nonformal aspects. One part of
each *núcleo* is the technical team consisting of an agricultural extension
agent, health and sanitation officer, rural crafts teacher, and literacy
expert whose work lies mainly with adults outside the school. The
chapter on adult education and community development comments
on some nonformal educational efforts: (1) the literacy program and
centers administered by the Literacy and Fundamental Education Section of the Ministry of Education, which includes some 20 fundamental
education teams; (2) schools for rural housewives which offer courses
in home improvement; (3) División de Acción Comunal (now a part

of the Ministry of Home Affairs), a community development program offering technical advice and training; (4) agricultural extension services; (5) educational work of the agricultural commodity federations, such as the Federation of Coffee Growers and the Cotton and Tobacco Development Institutes; (6) bank supervised credit plans (Banco Cafetero, Caja Agraria, Agricultural Credit Bank); (7) Acción Cultural Popular and Radio Sutatenza.

389. INTERNATIONAL LABOR OFFICE. *Towards Full Employment: A Programme for Colombia*. Geneva: 1970. 471 pp.

With regard to rural education, the reporting ILO team calls for the creation of rural education centers which should be staffed by an agricultural extension agent and an adult education teacher (responsible primarily for literacy training), in addition to the formal primary school teacher. The chapter on training talks about SENA's successes and weaknesses, and calls for a network of prevocational agricultural training centers to do actual training and to act as extension outlets. The chapter on health calls for a training program for *promotoras de salud*, who would in turn take their knowledge to their communities in a massive program of rural health education. The chapter on organizations outside the government which have been active in community development programs focuses on Acción Comunal, but also mentions a number of others in passing. Central to the concepts and proposals presented here seems to be the notion of the need to utilize both formal and nonformal education on a wide basis.

390. MISIÓN 'ECONOMÍA Y HUMANISMO'. *Estudio sobre las condiciones del desarrollo de Colombia*. Bogotá: Aedita, Cromos, 1958. 2 vols.

Part 5, entitled "Instruction for Adults," comments on the following: Acción Cultural Popular and Radio Sutatenza; Cursos para Campesinos of the Ministry of Education; agricultural extension services; vocational training. At a later point, the need for an integrated educational policy, particularly in the rural zones, is noted.

391. SAMPER ORTEGA, DANIEL. "Mass Education in Colombia," *Quarterly Journal of Inter-American Relations*, 1:2 (April, 1939), 71-76.

Briefly describes a wide range of out-of-school educational activities undertaken in Colombia: (1) labor union work through the formation of libraries funded by the government; (2) national library programs, including radio campaign, educational film, marionette theater, and village library programs of dissemination of literature on such subjects as child education, health, horticulture, and animal breeding; (3) Ministry of Education's traveling teachers' groups which instruct peasants in modern methods of agriculture.

392. VELANDIA B., WILSON, and EMILY VARGAS DE ADAMS. *Proyecto de*

investigación sobre la educación no-formal en Colombia: Informe preliminar de la investigación. Bogotá: Fundación para la Educación Permanente en Colombia (FEPEC) and Centro para el Desarrollo de la Educación No-Formal (CEDEN), 1973. 16 pp.

Reports the results of a study of nonformal educational projects in four departments (Cundinamarca, Valle, Santander, and Bolivia). Discusses the concept of nonformal education and methods used in this study. Also describes the formation of the Centro para el Desarrollo de la Educación No-Formal (CEDEN), which is conceived of as a research and evaluation body.

Costa Rica

MULTIFACETED PROGRAMS

393. BEHRMAN, DANIEL. "Boom Town on the Pan American Highway," *Courier*, 7:12 (May, 1955), 25-26.

    Comments on the UNESCO fundamental education projects in Valle El General and La Lucha. Focuses attention on the adult education centers.

394. CHAVES ESQUIVEL, O. "The Role of Agricultural Co-operatives and University Extension in the Development of the Rural Community," in Egbert de Vries, ed., *Social Research and Rural Life in Central America, Mexico and the Caribbean Region: Proceedings of a Seminar Organized by UNESCO in Cooperation with the United Nations Economic Commission for Latin America, Mexico City, 17-27 October 1962.* Paris: United Nations Educational, Scientific, and Cultural Organization, 1966, pp. 141-149.

    Provides a brief description of the University of Costa Rica's Extension Centers, local community development projects which work in the areas of health and agricultural education, economic and social questions, and general culture.

395. FURBAY, JOHN H. *Education in Costa Rica.* U.S. Office of Education, Bulletin 1946, no. 4. Washington: Government Printing Office, 1946. 62 pp.

    Chapter 7 on agencies of public and pupil welfare includes a short account of the traveling cultural missions program, which offers instruction in various areas as well as exposure to Costa Rican cultural heritage.

396. GAINES, CAROLYN L. "Point Four Brings 4-S to Costa Rica," *Journal of Home Economics*, 44:4 (April, 1952), 266-268.

    Describes the 4-S club and home demonstration programs of the Servicio Técnico Interamericano de Cooperación Agrícola (STICA), which are directed toward young people.

397. INTER-AMERICAN IINSTITUTE OF AGRICULTURAL SCIENCES, TURRIALBA, COSTA RICA. *Informe del Seminario Interamericano de Líderes*

de Juventudes Rurales: Intercambio internacional de juventudes agrícolas. San José: 1962: 1962. 87 pp.

> Includes a section on the growth of extension services and Clubes 4-S in Costa Rica and a section evaluating the agricultural projects of the clubs in San Ramón. Publication primarily focuses attention, however, on the Inter-American Program for Rural Youth, whose activities revolve around improving rural farms and homes by introducing new methods and offering basic education in health, nutrition, agricultural techniques, and so on. The program concentrates its efforts in four areas: (1) organization of committees to help rural youth clubs; (2) training leaders in rural youth club programs; (3) organization of projects; (4) publicity for rural youth programs.

398. KARSEN, SONJA. *Desenvolvimento educacional de Costa Rica con la asistencia técnica de la UNESCO, 1951-1954*. San José: Ministerio de Educación Pública, 1954. 175 pp.

> Chapter 2 goes to some length in discussing the pilot educational projects developed in La Lucha and the Valle El General. Purposes of the projects were to introduce new agricultural techniques, to provide a program of health education, and to reach beyond the school into the community at large with special programs directed toward the adult population. In chapter 3 there is an evaluation of the projects and a further description of their various program elements.

*399. MIÑANO GARCÍA, MAX H. *El proyecto piloto de educación rural en Costa Rica: Investigación, análisis y realizaciones sobre educación fundamental en el área del proyecto*. San José: Ministerio de Educación Pública and Misión de Asistencia Técnica de la UNESCO, 1954. 139 pp.

400. "STICA: Una institución al servicio y para el bienestar del agricultor costarricense," *Suelo Tico*, 1:1 (August, 1948), 6-20.

> The Departamento de Extensión Agrícola and the Departamento de Economía Doméstica y Extensión Social Rural are the educational arms of the Servicio Técnico Interamericano de Cooperación Agrícola (STICA). Describes the activities and programs of the extension services: farming techniques; home improvement; sewing classes; nutrition education; livestock raising.

AGRICULTURAL TRAINING

401. ALERS MONTALVO, MANUEL. "Cultural Changes in a Costa Rican

Village.'' Unpublished thesis. Michigan State University, 1953. 250 numb. leaves.

In the context of studying cultural change, focuses on three separate instances of the introduction of insecticide by extension students from the Inter-American Institute of Agricultural Sciences (IAIAS). Describes methods used by the students. Gives a good indication of how extension works in the field. Also reports on an unsuccessful extension project in San Juan Norte to get people to cultivate vegetable gardens.

402. DI FRANCO, JOSEPH, and EARL JONES. *Estudio analítico del Servicio de Extensión en Costa Rica.* Turrialba: Instituto Interamericano de Ciencias Agrícolas, 1962. 80 pp.

Appendix 1 describes the organization of agricultural extension in Costa Rica, its philosophy and objectives. Appendix 2 gives a somewhat brief account of 4-S clubs, their organization and objectives.

403. FLEMING, PHILIP B. *A Letter to the President: The Story of the 4-S Clubs in Costa Rica.* Building a Better Hemisphere Series, 15. Washington: Technical Cooperation Administration, Inter-American Regional Office, Institute of Inter-American Affairs, 1952. No pagination.

Work of the 4-S rural youth clubs (comparable to 4-H) and a description of the agricultural extension service.

404. GAINES, CAROLYN L. *Point Four Brings 4-S to Costa Rica.* Building a Better Hemisphere Series, 13. Washington: Technical Cooperation Administration, Inter-American Regional Office, Institute of Inter-American Affairs, 1952. 7 pp.

4-S rural youth club activities, directed by the Servicio Técnico Interamericano de Cooperación Agrícola (STICA).

405. JONES, EARL, ed. *Un ensayo de evaluación de impacto de la agencia de extensión agrícola, Atenas, Costa Rica en las comunidades de San José Sur y Morazan.* Turrialba: Instituto Interamericano de Ciencias Agrícolas, 1963. 97 pp.

Chapter 3 offers a history of the agricultural extension agency in Atenas, its organization, projects undertaken, and methods employed.

BASIC EDUCATION/LITERACY

406. BRENES MESÉN, ROBERTO. ''Costa Rica,'' in *Educational Yearbook,*

1942. New York: International Institute, Teachers College, Columbia University, 1942, pp. 135-150.

Briefly touches on adult education programs: the Escuela Popular de Adultos (for working adults), and the Escuela Vespertina (for young boys who work during the day). Adult education programs are admittedly meager because of the large percentage of people who attend the formal school system.

COOPERATIVE EDUCATION

407. RUIZ, RODRIGO, and ANTONIO VEGA. "Cooperativa de Producción Agrícola Industrial Victoria R. L., de Costa Rica," in *Las cooperativas como método de desarrollo de regiones y comunidades*. Estudios y Monografías, 14. Washington: Department of Social Affairs, Pan American Union, 1964, pp. 89-107.

Brief section on cooperative education explains the educational program of the cooperative, which takes place both in study groups and in courses offered by the Cooperative's Escuela Julio Peña Morúa. The cooperative also began offering leadership training courses in 1960.

VOCATIONAL SKILL TRAINING

408. "Capacitación y aprendizaje," Ministerio de Trabajo y Bienestar Social, *Temas Sociales*, 11:26 (May/August, 1964), 49-52.

Describes the apprenticeship and training program organized in 1960 under the direction of the Oficina de Capacitación y Aprendizaje of the Ministerio de Trabajo. Comments on the types of courses, location of programs, and general organization.

*409. CHANG, L. "Centros móviles de formación profesional en el Instituto Nacional de Aprendizaje," Instituto Nacional de Aprendizaje, División Técnica, *Boletín Mensual de Actividades*, (October, 1969), 1-16.

Organization of the mobile apprenticeship training centers in the rural areas of Costa Rica. (From: "Education for Rural Life," *Educational Documentation and Information*, 46:183 [2nd Quarter, 1972], 105).

*410. COSTA RICA. SECRETARÍA DE TRABAJO Y PREVISIÓN SOCIAL. *Programa de capacitación y aprendizaje*. San José: 1961. 22 pp.

411. INTERNATIONAL LABOR ORGANIZATION. *Costa Rica: Instituto Nacional de Aprendizaje (INA); la estructura funcional de la formación en la empresa en Costa Rica.* Informe Técnico, 2. Geneva: 1972. 30 pp.

Covers additional background information and the organization of training courses and activities from 1967 to 1971 of the Instituto Nacional de Aprendizaje.

412. INTERNATIONAL LABOR ORGANIZATION. *Costa Rica: Instituto Nacional de Aprendizaje (INA); la estructura funcional de la formación profesional industrial en Costa Rica.* Informe Técnico, 1. Geneva: 1971. 58 pp.

Covers background information and administrative organization of the Instituto Nacional de Aprendizaje.

CONCEPTUALIZATION

413. WALSH, THOMAS E. "¿Donde están los trabajadores expertos de Costa Rica?" Ministerio de Trabajo y Bienestar Social, *Temas Sociales,* 5:11/12 (April/September, 1958), 25-26.

Calls for apprenticeship programs to augment the existing vocational school system.

Cuba

MULTIFACETED PROGRAMS

414. ALONSO SÁNCHEZ, HILARIO, comp. *25 años de labor del Club de Cantineros de la República de Cuba: Memoria*. Habana: Compañía Editora de Libros y Folletos, 1951. 715 pp.

Notes several educational efforts on the part of the union, such as training members in bartending and offering language instruction.

415. CASABON SÁNCHEZ, LUIS. "Blueprint for Fundamental Education," *WAY Forum*, 18 (February, 1956), 33-36.

Activities of the Juventud de Acción Católica Cubana (JAC) in the area of fundamental education. Describes the creation of the Missionary and Fundamental Education Plan whose aims include the formation of neighborhood groups for such educational purposes, in part, as literacy training and instruction in hygiene, agricultural techniques, and domestic arts.

416. CUBA. MINISTERIO DE EDUCACIÓN. '. . . *Y toda Cuba es una gran escuela': Fidel Castro, informe 1963-64*. Ciudad Libertad: n.d. 111 pp.

Includes information on the Superación de la Mujer program in the section on adult education.

417. PERERA, HILDA. "Women in a New Social Context in Cuba," *International Journal of Adult and Youth Education*, 14:3 (1962), 144-149.

Discusses educational programs specifically directed toward women: six-month dressmaking course which includes instruction in literacy, hygiene, and community living; courses for women domestic servants; special training for child care center staff.

BASIC EDUCATION/LITERACY

418. CUBA. MINISTERIO DE EDUCACIÓN. *Alfabetización: Nacionalización de la enseñanza*. Habana: 1961. 71 pp.

First part devoted to discussion of the antecedents to, organization, and successes of the national literacy campaign of 1961.

419. FAGEN, RICHARD R. *The Transformation of Political Culture in Cuba.* Stanford: Stanford University Press, 1969. 271 pp.

Chapter 3 focuses on the campaign against illiteracy, describing its foundations, organization, and meaning in the context of the Cuban revolution.

420. JESUALDO. "Cuba territorio libre de analfabetismo," *Casa de las Américas*, 2:9 (November/December, 1961), 38-49.

After an initial discussion of the meaning of the literacy campaign, the author describes the organization and administration of Cuba's effort in 1961 to erradicate illiteracy.

421. "The Literacy Campaign in Cuba," *Foreign Education Digest*, 17:3 (January/March, 1953), 281-282.

Briefly describes the night school programs created in 1950 to combat illiteracy.

422. MANZANO, MATILDE. "Apuntes de una alfabetizadora," *Casa de las Américas*, 3:19 (July/August, 1963), 91-117.

Personal account of experiences as a literacy teacher during the campaign of the Year of Education in 1961. The author lived and worked with a brigade in Cerro.

423. MURILLO, JOSÉ, et al. *5 maestros argentinos alfabetizaron en Cuba.* Buenos Aires: Ediciones Hoy en la Cultura, 1964. 62 pp.

Personal experiences of five Argentines who worked in the Cuban literacy brigades in 1961, describing in some detail the organization and activities of the literacy campaign.

424. PRITT, D. N. "Cuba Travel Notes: Education," *Labour Monthly*, 44 (June, 1962), 282-286.

Goes briefly into the literacy campaign of 1961.

425. ROUCEK, JOSEPH S. "Pro-Communist Revolution in Cuban Education," *Journal of Inter-American Studies*, 6:3 (July, 1964), 323-335.

Some mention of the literacy campaign of 1961.

426. UNITED NATIONS EDUCATIONAL, SCIENTIFIC, AND CULTURAL ORGANIZATION. "Informe sobre los métodos y los medios utilizados en Cuba para eliminar el analfabetismo," *Universidad de la Habana*, 29:175 (September/October, 1965), 53-128.

Lengthy and detailed report made by a UNESCO investigative team of Cuba's literacy campaign of 1961. Report is based on interviews, visits to educational institutions, and study of ministerial documents. The document is broken into three parts: background and antecedents to the campaign; the campaign itself (organization, methods employed, etc.); results of the campaign and postcampaign efforts.

VOCATIONAL SKILL TRAINING

427. KIRBERG, ENRIQUE. "La enseñanza tecnológica en Cuba," Universidad de Chile, *Boletín*, 36 (December, 1962), 18-23.
    Describes the system of technical-vocational education since the revolution, whose facets include training programs of short duration in particular industries—such as the Plan del Mínimo Técnico and the Plan de Escuelas Populares—in addition to formal education at the secondary and university levels.

428. NEGRÍN, JULIO. "The Polyvalent Centre as a Means for Qualifying and Giving Professional Training to Workers," UNESCO National Commissions in the Western Hemisphere, Oficina Regional de Cultura para América Latina y el Caribe, *News Letter*, 5:3 (July/September, 1972), 6-7.
    Analyzes the new educational form designed to meet the needs and demands of a changing Cuban society. Describes the principles and characteristics of polyvalent education for workers: emphasis is on improving skills; structure of courses is flexible, depending on needs; includes long and short-term activities; location varies, but is usually on-the-spot; emphasizes that the Center is *not* a school; designed for working adults. Educational services of Centers include: popular culture clubs; documentation center; training courses. The article focuses in particular on the activities of the Polyvalent Educational Center '5 de Septiembre', Cienfuegos.

MISCELLANEOUS

429. ALEXANDER, ANGELA. "The Year of Education," *Mainstream*, 14:5 (May, 1961), 53-61.
    Describes in personal terms the year-long literacy and basic education program launched in 1961 which trained young people and sent them out over the island. Also talks about "factory schools" and educational programs in cooperatives.

430. CONFERENCE ON EDUCATION AND ECONOMIC AND SOCIAL DEVELOPMENT IN LATIN AMERICA, SANTIAGO DE CHILE, 1962. DELEGATION FROM CUBA. *Cuba y la Conferencia de Educación y Desarrollo Económico y Social, celebrada en Santiago de Chile del 5 al 19*

de marzo de 1962. Habana: Editorial Nacional de Cuba, 1962. 180 pp.

Section in chapter 2 reports in some depth on the literacy campaign and several adult education programs, including the literacy follow-up program, the worker and farmer improvement program, the Mínimo Técnico program of vocational training, and the program for women.

431. CUBA. COMISIÓN NACIONAL CUBANA DE LA UNESCO. *Cuba: Educación y cultura*. Habana: 1963. 81 pp.

Section on raising the educational level of the people includes descriptions of the literacy campaign, the Curso de Seguimiento (literacy follow-up), Superación Obrera and Mínimo Técnico (to train workers on-the-job), and Superación de la Mujer.

432. "Etapas de la educación rural," *Educación*, Washington, 3:9 (January/March, 1958), 18-21.

Historical account of rural educational programs which include the creation of the Servicio de Cultura del Ejército in 1936 to do literacy and agricultural extension work, and the Misiones Educativas, mobile units sent to predominantly rural provinces.

433. FAGEN, RICHARD R. *Cuba: The Political Content of Adult Education*. Hoover Institution Studies, 4. Stanford: Hoover Institution on War, Revolution, and Peace, Stanford University, 1964. 77 pp.

Offers a brief outline of the 1961 literacy campaign, plus a partial translation of two manuals: "Alfabeticemos," a teaching manual used by literacy workers, and "Producir, ahorrar, organizar: segunda parte," an arithmetic workbook used in the Superación Obrera-Campesina classes.

434. GILLETTE, ARTHUR. *Cuba's Educational Revolution*. Fabian Research Series, 302. London: Fabian Society, 1972. 36 pp.

Included in this critique of the post-revolutionary educational system are passages describing nonformal as well as formal programs within the broad context of education.

435. JOLLY, RICHARD. "The Literacy Campaign and Adult Education," in Dudley Seers, ed., *Cuba: The Economic and Social Revolution*. Chapel Hill: University of North Carolina Press, 1964, pp. 190-219.

In chapter 6 the section on adult education is entirely devoted to an explanation of nonformal programs, such as the Mínimo Técnico, people's schools, *seguimiento* program (continuation of study after literacy), and the Superación Obrera-Campesina classes (worker-peasant improvement).

436. MORALES Y DEL CAMPO, OFELIA. "Cuba," in *Educational Yearbook, 1942*. New York: International Institute, Teachers College, Columbia University, 1942, pp. 151-174.
Section on adult education touches on a few public and private programs designed to combat illiteracy and provide some basic and vocational education.

437. PAULSTON, ROLLAND G. "Changes in Cuban Education," in Richard L. Cummings, and Donald A. Lemke, eds., *Educational Innovations in Latin America*. Metuchen, New Jersey: Scarecrow Press, 1973, pp. 150-177.
Discusses post-revolutionary reforms, including new nonformal programs: literacy campaign; "Six by Six" program (six months of work alternated with six months of technical training); Mínimo Técnico program of on-the-job training.

438. TUROSIENSKI, SEVERIN K. *Education in Cuba*. U.S. Office of Education, Bulletin 1943, no. 1. Washington: Government Printing Office, 1943. 90 pp.
In chapter 7 (general cultural and welfare agencies), the section on adult education briefly notes existing programs, including "people's theater-libraries," mobile units whose purpose is to eliminate illiteracy and impart civic values, special courses for farmers, and traveling schools in domestic science conducted by the Ministry of Agriculture.

439. UNITED NATIONS EDUCATIONAL, SCIENTIFIC, AND CULTURAL ORGANIZATION. *Métodos y medios utilizados en Cuba para la supresión del analfabetismo: Informe de la UNESCO*, by Anna Lorenzetto and Karel Neys. Habana: Editora Pedagógica, 1965. 79 pp.
Lengthy discussion of the post-revolution literacy campaign, worker-*campesino* educational program (cultural and technical), and the special education program for women.

Dominican Republic

MULTIFACETED PROGRAMS

440. BAEZ SOLER, OSVALDO. *Realidades dominicanas modernas*. Ciudad Trujillo: Luis Sánchez Andújar, 1948. 42 pp.
    Describes the literacy campaign and its *escuelas de emergencia,* the vehicle created for literacy training. The activities of the campaign include basic education in arithmetic, skill training, and civic education.

BASIC EDUCATION/LITERACY

441. "Anti-Illiteracy Campaign in the Dominican Republic," Pan American Union, *Bulletin,* 76:3 (March, 1942), 176-177.
    Discusses the literacy campaign, rural emergency schools, and the special summer program requiring all teachers to teach a group of 15 to 25 people to read and write.

442. POU DE MEJIA, MARGARITA. "Escuelas de alfabetización nocturnas para adultos," *Previsión Social,* 5 (September, 1948), 24.
    Briefly describes the evening adult literacy courses begun in 1942.

MISCELLANEOUS

443. "Rural Education in the Dominican Republic," Pan American Union, *Bulletin,* 81:3 (March, 1947), 174-175.
    Emergency schools in the rural areas were designed for formal schooling for children during the day and used for adult literacy classes in the evening. Article also discusses the agricultural clubs and experimental farms for young people administered by the Department of Agriculture.

Ecuador

MULTIFACETED PROGRAMS

444. CENTRO DE MOTIVACIÓN Y ASESORIA, ECUADOR. *Informe final de la evaluación del proyecto de educación no formal.* Quito: 1972. 63 pp.

> Report on the pilot program, begun in 1971, which focused on literacy training and community development projects. An additional aspect is the five-week program to train community leaders as facilitators. The report provides an evaluation of the first year of operation, as well as a description of the activities and historical background. The program takes place in selected communities of the provinces of Chimborazo and Tungurahua.

445. CLARK, JOHN M. "Curtain-Raiser in Rehabilitation," *Survey Graphic,* 32:6 (June, 1943), 245-249, 267.

> Report on the rehabilitation efforts in El Oro, giving details on the programs to teach agricultural fundamentals and paramedical instruction. Work is being directed by the Ecuadoran Development Corporation.

446. CLARK, JOHN M. "Revival in El Oro," *Foreign Commerce Weekly,* 12:8 (August 21, 1943), 5-8.

> Touches on nonformal educational aspects of the Ecuadoran Development Corporation program underway as part of the rehabilitation of an area which had suffered during the Peru-Ecuador border dispute. Efforts include demonstration farms and training in fiber weaving.

*447. COMAS, JUAN. "La Misión Andina y la aculturación indígena," *América Indígena,* 19:3 (July, 1959), 169-177.

448. ECUADOR. MINISTERIO DEL TRABAJO Y BIENESTAR SOCIAL. *Servicio Ecuatoriano de Capacitación Profesional 'SECAP': Informe anual de actividades 1974.* Quito: 1975. 5 pp. and appendices.
> Résumé of vocational and agricultural training programs offered by the Servicio in 1974.

*449. ECUADOR. MISIÓN ANDINA. *Informe sobre la encuesta: Evaluación de actividades.* Quito: 1964. 83 pp.

450. ECUADOR. MISIÓN ANDINA. *Seis años de trabajo de la Misión Andina en el Ecuador: Una campaña nacional de integración del campesino indígena.* N.p.: Impreso Misión Andina, 1964. 59 pp.
Report divided into two sections: general information (antecedents, goals, administration, programming of activities, etc.) and résumé of activities (agricultural extension, vocational training, artisan training, home improvement, health education).

451. ESTUPIÑAN TELLO, JULIO. *La educación fundamental.* Quito: Editorial Casa de la Cultura Ecuatoriana, 1957. 199 pp.
Basic tenets of fundamental education discussed. Section devoted to the organization and activities of the Misiones Sociales (modeled on the Mexican Cultural Missions).

452. EVANS, DAVID R. "An Approach to Nonschool Rural Education in Ecuador," in Thomas J. La Belle, ed., *Educational Alternatives in Latin America: Social Change and Social Stratification.* Latin American Studies Series, 30. Los Angeles: Latin American Center, University of California, 1975, pp. 169-184.
Describes an experimental project to introduce new types of educational materials to reach rural out-of-school populations. Materials, which are introduced by trained facilitators, include games (fluency and simulation), media-based materials (booklets and radio-disseminated material), and expressive materials (drama, puppets, community newspapers).

453. FUNDACIONES DE DESARROLLO RURAL BRETHREN & UNIDA. *Memoria general de actividades: Período 1970-1974.* Quito: 1974. 25 pp.
Work of the Misiones Evangélicas Brethren & Unida Andina Indígena since 1953 in the province of Pichincha. Focus is on literacy and basic education, vocational skill training, and agricultural and cooperative education. Provides background information and an outline of current activities by zone, as well as financial figures and an organization chart.

454. JIMÉNEZ CASTELLANOS, JUAN. "Misión de ayuda técnica de la UNESCO-OIT en el Ecuador," *Revista Ecuatoriana de Educación,* 6:21 (May/June, 1952), 128-184.
Outlines in detail the plan for and content of the permanent rural cultural missions to work in conjunction with the Servicio Ambulante Rural de Extensión Cultural (SAREC). Designed as multipurpose units, covering health, nutrition, agricultural, vocational, cultural, and crafts education.

455. MATHIAS, R. "Literacy and Ecuador's National Development Plan,"

School and Society, 95:2287 (February 4, 1967), 84-86.
Describes the literacy program originated by the Unión Nacional de Periodistas, now taken over and expanded by the government. Pilot projects were established in three areas: (1) Cuenca, where literacy work is part of a larger program which includes a vocational training center; (2) Milagro, where literacy is coupled with rural agricultural development by means of a model farm; (3) Pesillo, where the literacy program is coupled with technical agricultural assistance. The expanded program will also include home economics training for village women and an area demonstration school oriented toward agriculture and handicrafts for adults and young people.

456. MENCÍAS CHÁVEZ, JORGE. *Riobamba (Ecuador): Estudio de la elevación socio-cultural y religiosa del indio.* Estudios Sociológicos Latino-Americanos, 16. Fribourg, Swtizerland: Oficina Internacional e Investigaciones Sociales de FERES, 1962. 154 pp.
Part 2 is devoted to an examination of the Andean Mission program, with chapters on its antecedents, legal formation, history and future projections, organization, activities and programs, financing, and an evaluation of work accomplished. The section on church activities in part 3 relates efforts in literacy and skill training in conjunction with the Andean Mission program.

457. O'HARA, HAZEL. "The Voice of the Andes: Station Reaches Four Corners of Ecuador as World Listens In," *Americas,* 13:9 (September, 1961), 27-30.
Work of the radio station "La Voz de los Andes," which includes a number of educational programs, such as "El Agricultor Progresista."

458. OSPINA RESTREPO, GABRIEL, and ALICIA CASERES ARANDI. *'¡Pelileo en marcha! ¡Adelante!'* Serie sobre Organización de la Comunidad, 7. Washington: Sección de Servicio Social, División de Trabajo y Asuntos Sociales, Unión Panamericana, 1954. 13 pp.
Brief report of the Organization of American States (OAS) technical mission team which directed the reorganization of communities destroyed during the 1949 earthquake. In several instances remarks are made of vocational training extended to local workers as part of the reconstruction program and of training given to selected community leaders.

459. "Plan nacional de alfabetización y educación de adultos," *Revista Ecuatoriana de Educación,* 17:53 (January/June, 1964), 133-187.
Detailed report of the plan for adult literacy and education programs, an outgrowth of the first national seminar on adult education held in 1963. Includes proposals for different levels of education and budget estimations.

460. RAVNDAL, CHRIṢTIAN M. "Journey into the Jungle," *Foreign Service Journal*, 36:3 (March, 1959), 28-31.
Touches on activities of the Summer Institute of Linguistics (SIL) in Limoncocha which include literacy work and agricultural training.

*461. SALAZAR, SEGUNDO MIGUEL. *SAREC (Servicio Ambulante Rural de Extensión Cultural) y sus principales actividades*. Quito: 1951. Various pagination.

*462. SALAZAR, SEGUNDO MIGUEL. "SAREC y la educación fundamental para adultos," *Educación*, Quito, Nueva Epoca, 123 (April, 1952), 112-119.

463. *Servicio Ecuatoriano de Voluntarios*. Quito: 1973. No pagination.
Outlines the work of the youth volunteer service in literacy and co-operative education. Also describes the training programs for student brigades. Focuses efforts in four regions: Azuay-Cañar, Chimborazo-Bolívar, Guayas, and Pichincha.

464. VELOZ, RUBÉN. "Las escuelas radiofónicas en el Ecuador," *Arco*, 26 (October, 1962), 634-635.
Describes the Escuelas Radiofónicas Populares of Chimborazo, founded by the local bishop of the Catholic church and patterned after Radio Sutatenza in Colombia. Discusses organization and programming (running the gamut from religious instruction to literacy and health education).

AGRICULTURAL TRAINING

*465. FOOD AND AGRICULTURAL ORGANIZATION. *Ecuador: Actividades de extensión agrícola dentro del programa de la Misión Andina; informe al gobierno*, by V. L. Bolanos. EPTA Report, 1279. N.p.: 1960. 28 pp.

*466. FOOD AND AGRICULTURAL ORGANIZATION. *Ecuador: Agricultural Extension and Education; Report to the Government*, by N. T. Theodorou. EPTA Report, 14. N.p.: 1952. 51 pp.

*467. FOOD AND AGRICULTURAL ORGANIZATION. *Ecuador: El servicio nacional de extensión agropecuaria; informe al gobierno*, by J. Galecio Gómez. Document UNDP/TA 2970. N.p.: 1971. 21 pp.

*468. FOOD AND AGRICULTURAL ORGANIZATION. *Ecuador: Extensión*

agrícola y desarrollo rural; informe al gobierno, by R. Briceno.
Document UNDP/TA 2901. N.p.: 1970-1971. 28 pp.

469. INTER-AMERICAN COMMITTEE FOR AGRICULTURAL DEVELOPMENT.
*Study of Agricultural Education, Investigation and Extension,
1965: Ecuador.* Washington: Pan American Union, 1967. 155 pp.
Chapter 4 covers the organization of agricultural extension services
throughout the country, on local and national levels. Many organizations are involved in extension work and services have not been
coordinated to prevent overlap. Report intensively covers the organization and programs of the Servicio Nacional de Extensión Agrícola
(SCIA).

*470. YOUNGSTROM, C. O. *Report on Agricultural Extension in Ecuador,
July 12-August 19, 1965.* Quito: U.S. Agency for International
Development, 1965. 16 pp.

BASIC EDUCATION/LITERACY

*471. ALBERTUS, URSULA. "The Role of Libraries in the Functional
Literacy Programme," *Bulletin for Libraries,* 24:4 (July/August,
1970), 201-204.
UNESCO's adult functional literacy pilot project. (From: *Handbook
of Latin American Studies,* 33 [1971], 273)

472. ALBORNOZ, MIGUEL. "Alphabet in the Andes," *Inter-American,*
4:3 (March, 1945), 14-16.
Describes the literacy work of the Unión Nacional de Periodistas.

473. "Campaña de Alfabetización," Instituto Interamericano del Niño,
Noticiario, (October, 1945), 103.
Brief description of the literacy work of the Unión Nacional de
Periodistas in Ecuador.

*474. ECUADOR. MINISTERIO DE EDUCACIÓN PÚBLICA. *Alfabetización y
educación de adultos.* Quito: 1966. 54 pp.

475. HURTADO, OSVALDO. *Dos mundos superpuestos: Ensayo de diag-
nóstico de la realidad ecuatoriana.* 3rd. ed. Quito: Instituto
Ecuatoriano para el Desarrollo Social, 1973. 120 pp.
In the third part of this study of Ecuadorean society, which deals with
education, a section is devoted to fundamental education and briefly
describes several literacy efforts, including the Plan Nacional de

Alfabetización de Adultos (1964-1973), the Proyecto Piloto de Alfabetización de Adultos in Cuenca, Milagro, and Pesillo, radio schools, and several (anonymous) groups employing the Freire *conscientización* method.

476. LINKE, LILO. "Illiteracy in Ecuador: Meeting the Challenge," *Times Educational Supplement*, 1638 (September 21, 1946), 448; 1639 (September 28, 1946), 460.

Two-part article describing the work of Frank Laubach and the Liga de Enseñanza de Analfabetos (LEA) in Guayaquil and of the Unión Nacional de Periodistas in Quito and the Andean region.

477. MURGUEYTIO, REINALDO. "El arte Disney en la educación de los adultos," *Revista Ecuatoriana de Educación*, 2:7/8 (July/December, 1949), 97-105.

Discusses the project of the Unión Nacional de Periodistas in Ecuador's literacy campaign.

*478. *Plan Nacional de Alfabetización y Educación de Adultos*. Quito: Casa de la Cultura Ecuatoriana, 1964. 59 pp.

*479. UNIÓN NACIONAL DE PERIODISTAS DEL ECUADOR. *La campaña de alfabetización de adultos en el Ecuador, a cargo de la Unión Nacional de Periodistas; síntesis de enero de 1944 a junio de 1949*. Quito: 1949. 8 pp.

*480. UNIÓN NACIONAL DE PERIODISTAS DEL ECUADOR. *Cartilla del Dr. F. Laubach adaptada por la U.N.P.* Quito: Impr. Gran Colombia, 1949. 24 pp.

*481. UNIÓN NACIONAL DE PERIODISTAS DEL ECUADOR. *Incorporación de las masas populares a la cultura y al progreso; 15 años de labores*. [Quito: 1958.] 86 pp.

*482. UNIÓN NACIONAL DE PERIODISTAS DEL ECUADOR. *La UNP en la educación popular ecuatoriana*. [Quito: Editorial "La Unión," 1954.] 79 pp.

483. UZCÁTEGUI, EMILIO. *Compulsory Education in Ecuador*. Studies on Compulsory Education, 7. Paris: United Nations Educational, Scientific, and Cultural Organization, 1951. 60 pp.

Chapter 5 on the campaign against illiteracy talks about various programs to combat illiteracy, including the Mobile Rural Cultural Extension Service (SAREC), the army, the Unión Nacional de Periodistas, and the Liga de Enseñanza de Alfabetización (LEA). Other chapters following discuss the problems of and the obstacles to overcoming illiteracy on a national scope.

COOPERATIVE EDUCATION

484. *Agricultural Enterprise Promotion Program, P.P.E.A.* Guayaquil, Ecuador: [1974?]. 13 pp.

> Describes the program initially organized in 1971 which is designed to promote modernization of small farmers in the coastal region by promoting the formation of cooperatives. PPEA occasionally conducts courses on the principles and functions of cooperativism, but most of the cooperative education work is in the hands of the Federación Nacional de Cooperativas Arroceras (FENACOOPAR), which was established for that purpose by the Agency for International Development in the late 1960s.

HEALTH, HYGIENE, AND NUTRITION INSTRUCTION

*485. FOOD AND AGRICULTURAL ORGANIZATION. *Ecuador: Actividades de economía doméstica en el programa de desarrollo de comunidades de la Misión Andina y otros programas oficiales; informe al gobierno,* by V. G. Ortiz. CEP Report, 34. N.p.: 1966. 34 pp.

486. FOOD AND AGRICULTURAL ORGANIZATION. *Informe al gobierno del Ecuador sobre nutrición.* EPTA Report, 705. Rome: 1957. 12 pp.

> One of the activities of the FAO nutrition expert was to give a series of discussions over Radio Católica's educational program directed toward women in the home.

487. TORAL VITERI, MIGUEL. *Breve ensayo de educación sanitaria.* Quito: Casa de la Cultura Ecuatoriana, 1955. 236 pp.

> Talks about the need to develop methods of health education outside of, as well as in, the school. Suggests the creation of community centers, dissemination by means of radio, television, and lecture, particularly in rural areas where school programs are largely inadequate or nonexistent. Gives occasional examples of efforts in Ecuador on radio school programs or through extension services.

PROFESSIONAL/PARAPROFESSIONAL TRAINING

488. ALVAREZ A., JOSÉ. "Preparación de auxiliares de enfermería para

puestos de salud rural," *Anuario Indigenista,* 28 (December, 1968), 133-140.

Training program of the Andean Mission for rural health workers on the subprofessional level. Program involves training in basic hygiene, maternal and infant care, and rural sanitation problems.

VOCATIONAL SKILL TRAINING

489. INSTITUTO ECUATORIANO DE ANTROPOLOGÍA Y GEOGRAFÍA. "La Misión Andina en el Ecuador," *América Indígena,* 20:1 (January, 1960), 35-51.

Describes work of two training facilities available to indigenous people: the *taller de artes manuales* in the Casa de la Cultura Ecuatoriana in Quito and the Centro Textil in Otavalo under the direction of the Instituto Ecuatoriano de Antropología y Geografía (IEAG), which provides instruction in textile techniques. Offers a critique of these efforts.

MISCELLANEOUS

490. ALVARADO, RAFAEL. "Educación fundamental y sus proyecciones en el Ecuador," *Revista Ecuatoriana de Educación,* 7:31 (May/June, 1954), 122-129.

Discusses various fundamental education programs in Ecuador, such as the Misiones Sociales, Servicio Ambulante Rural de Extensión Cultural (SAREC), and the Campaña de Alfabetización.

491. BURBANO MARTÍNEZ, HECTOR. *La educación y el desarrollo económico y social del Ecuador.* Quito: Casa de la Cultura Ecuatoriana, 1966. 189 pp.

Chapter 7 deals with the national plan for adult and literacy education, stating objectives and describing the organization. Chapter 8 discusses educational efforts, both formal and nonformal, of the Andean Mission program, their inadequacies and achievements.

*492. ECUADOR. MINISTERIO DE EDUCACIÓN PÚBLICA. DEPARTAMENTO DE EDUCACIÓN DE ADULTOS. *Plan nacional de educación extraescolar 1973-1977.* Quito: [1973?]. 75 pp.

493. FUENTES ROLDÁN, ALFREDO. "Programas indigenistas ecuatorianos, 1954-1958," *América Indígena,* 19:4 (October, 1959), 275-304.

Taking the country by geographic sections (coast, Amazon region, Andes), the author discusses projects of various organizations (international, governmental, private, religious) directed toward improving the situation of the native population. Examples cited include: religious missionary work which has included instruction in health and sanitation, agricultural and vocational training, and literacy training; literacy work of the Unión Nacional de Periodistas; Centro de Artes Manuales in Otavalo; Misión Andina (which receives the most attention).

494. HURTADO, OSVALDO, and JOACHIM HERUDEK. *La organización popular en el Ecuador*. Quito: Instituto Ecuatoriano para el Desarrollo Social, 1974. 136 pp.

Provides one of the most comprehensive historical discussions of programs within a single country, including an analysis of their significance and effectiveness on a national level and for those involved in them. Concentrates on the 4-F clubs which originated in 1946, the Amas de Casa program which was initiated by Point Four in 1958, *barrio* organizations (which usually act as pressure groups to secure better community facilities), and activities of cooperatives.

495. "National Plan for Out-of-School Education in Ecuador," *Adult Education Information Notes*, 5 (January/February, 1974), 11.

Announces the new plan recently completed by the Department of Adult Education of the Ministry of Education. The plan is geared to the age groups between 15 and 35 years of age.

496. TRAIL, JoANN S. "Peace Corps Volunteers Learn New Techniques," *Journal of Home Economics*, 58:6 (June, 1966), 462.

Touches on Peace Corps work with 4-F clubs and the Amas de Casa (home demonstration) groups.

497. UNIÓN NACIONAL DE PERIODISTAS DEL ECUADOR. *Alfabetización y educación de adultos*. Quito: 1951. 32 pp.

Describes the literacy work of the Unión Nacional de Periodistas from 1944-1951 and the adult education activities of the Instituto Ecuatoriano de Investigaciones para Educación de Adultos.

498. WILSON, JACQUES M. P. *The Development of Education in Ecuador*. Hispanic-American Studies, 24. Miami: University of Miami Press, 1970. 169 pp.

Chapter 8 on adult education and acculturation of the natives briefly mentions several nonformal programs: the literacy program of the Unión Nacional de Periodistas; adult basic education pilot program in San Antonio de Pichincha (1954-1956); army literacy programs; Andean Mission program in the provinces of Chimborazo and Tungurahua; literacy and basic education program of the military *junta* begun in 1963-1964.

CONCEPTUALIZATION

499. BUITRÓN, ANÍBAL. "Vida y pasión del campesino ecuatoriano," *América Indígena*, 8:2 (April, 1948), 113-130.

    After discussing the range of social and economic problems afflicting the indigenous population, the author suggests possible steps toward solving them, such as the establishment of centers in rural towns to provide instruction in improved agricultural methods, hygiene, literacy, and technical advice and training for small businesses.

500. CISNEROS CISNEROS, CÉSAR. "Plan integral de rehabilitación campesina," Universidad Central del Ecuador, *Anales*, 87:342 (March 18, 1958), 193-219.

    Proposes three demonstration projects to raise the standard of living in rural areas by establishing: (1) textile demonstration centers, which would include apprenticeship training; (2) health units, to instruct in hygiene and nutrition; (3) agricultural missions; (4) small business missions, to offer technical advice and training.

501. TOBAR, JULIO. "Un plan de acción del magisterio para contribuir a la reivindicación del indio ecuatoriano," *Revista Ecuatoriana de Educación*, 6:22 (July/August, 1952), 70-77.

    Proposes a plan to expand educational facilities and programs beyond schools and school age.

El Salvador

MULTIFACETED PROGRAMS

502. "El Salvador's Laboratory for Better Living," in United Nations, Department of Public Information, *Basis for Better Living.* New York: 1954, pp. 13-14.

Account of the resettlement–community development program in Sitio del Niño. Activities include nutrition and health education and vocational training.

503. HALLETT, ROBERT M. *Food for El Salvador.* Building a Better Hemisphere Series, 27. Washington: Technical Cooperation Administration, Inter-American Regional Office, Institute of Inter-American Affairs, 1953. No pagination.

Superficial description of various aspects of the U.S. Point Four Program—mainly agricultural extension activities and vocational training centers.

AGRICULTURAL TRAINING

*504. DI FRANCO, JOSEPH, and ANTONIO M. ARCE. *Estudio del servicio de extensión de El Salvador.* Turrialba, Costa Rica: Instituto Interamericano de Ciencias Agrícolas, 1960. 35 pp.

*505. DI FRANCO, JOSEPH, and ANTONIO M. ARCE. *Preliminary Report on Study of Extension Service of El Salvador.* Turrialba, Costa Rica: Instituto Interamericano de Ciencias Agrícolas, 1960. No pagination.

506. HARVEY, W. E. " 'County agent' in El Salvador," *Foreign Agriculture,* 17:1 (January, 1953), 16-18.

Describes the work of a typical extension agent in the program administered by the Centro Nacional de Agronomía. Most of the work revolves around demonstration projects, general meetings, farm visits, and the distribution of publications.

507. HILDEBRAND, NORBERT. *Of Tractors and Tortillas.* Building a Better

Hemisphere Series, 20. Washington: Technical Cooperation Administration, Inter-American Regional Office, Institute of Inter-American Affairs, 1952. No pagination.

Describes the Point Four Program's agricultural extension station at Santa Tecla where work ranges from irrigation control to learning to drive a tractor.

LABOR UNION EDUCATION

508. GUILLÉN, CARLOS. "Labor Learns the Way," *Americas,* 5:11 (November, 1953), 30-31.

Describes educational efforts of the Labor Institute which consist of meetings and training sessions of representatives of labor unions and various government officials on such topics as industrial hygiene and accident prevention. Also mentions internal educational services of the unions themselves.

MISCELLANEOUS

509. EL SALVADOR. MINISTERIO DE EDUCACIÓN. *Situación demográfica, social, económica y educativa de El Salvador: Informe presentado a la Conferencia sobre Educación y Desarrollo Económico y Social en América Latina.* San Salvador: 1963. 131 pp.

Section devoted to adult education efforts in the literacy program, *brigadas culturales,* and cultural extension programs.

*510. EL SALVADOR. MINISTERIO DE EDUCACIÓN. DEPARTAMENTO DE EDUCACIÓN FUNDAMENTAL. *Bases para la organización y funcionamiento de nuevas instituciones de educación de adultos en El Salvador.* San Salvador: 1965. Various pagination.

511. *'Institutos de trabajo' en El Salvador.* Serie sobre Educación Social del Trabajador, 12. Washington: División de Trabajo y Asuntos Sociales, Unión Panamericana, 1955. 38 pp.

Prologue briefly mentions other aspects of nonformal education directed toward the worker, such as literacy centers in communities and in industrial and commercial establishments, the work of the Sección de Educación Obrera in the Ministerio de Trabajo y Previsión Social, and efforts in unions and cooperatives (in particular the Sindicato General de Matarifes in Matadero Municipal). The remainder of the publication is devoted to a description of the *institutos de labor* whose aims are to open discussion of workers' problems between workers and government specialists through meetings in which specific topics are addressed.

512. VELA, JOSÉ MANUEL. "Como se combate el analfabetismo de adultos en El Salvador," Instituto Interamericano del Niño, *Boletín*, 34:2: 133 (June, 1960), 181-186.

Includes descriptions of the literacy program of the Departamento de Alfabetización y Educación de Adultos of the Ministerio de Cultura Popular and of the organization and achievements (since 1958) of the *brigadas culturales*.

513. WAGGONER, GEORGE R., and BARBARA ASHTON WAGGONER. *Education in Central America*. Lawrence: University of Kansas Press, 1971. 180 pp.

Chapter 3 on El Salvador mentions the literacy campaign and the more than 1200 literacy centers (1966-1967 figures). Also briefly notes programs for community development, centers for training workers, and radio programs for literacy and community development.

Guatemala

MULTIFACETED PROGRAMS

514. "La acción educativa en el medio rural," *Educación,* Washington, 3:9 (January/March, 1958), 39-41.

    Describes the campaign of the Dirección General de Desarrollo Socio-educativo Rural begun in 1955. The program has school and community activities in areas of economics (agriculture, stock raising, and small businesses), health, home, recreation, and general culture.

515. "Alumnas del 'Centroamérica' van en misión cultural a San Andrés Itzapa," *Indice,* 1:4 (November/December, 1946), 29-35.

    Educational activities of normal school students visiting a cultural mission for a few days. They offered instruction in hygiene, agricultural techniques, and home improvement.

516. HILDEBRAND, JOHN R. "Guatemalan Rural Development Program: An Economist's Recommendations," *Inter-American Economic Affairs,* 17:1 (Summer, 1963), 59-71.

    Critique of a program, one of whose areas of activity is supervised credit, which the author feels should have the most emphasis. Suggests that cooperation and coordination between the extension and credit agents must be developed and maintained.

517. "Una importante misión cultural," *Revista del Maestro,* 2:5 (April/June, 1947), 97.

    Cultural mission work of normal school students in San Andrés Itzapa in hygiene, civics, and agricultural extension.

518. JICKLING, DAVID L. "Development in Rural Guatemala: The Country's Development Needs and Measures Being Taken to Meet Them," *Local Government Throughout the World,* 5:3 (June/August, 1966), 43-46.

    The agency for Indian integration (Servicio de Fomento de la Economía Indígena—SFEI) utilizes agricultural extension agents and training schools for the development of small craft industries to implement its program.

519. "Primera escuela de alfabetización," *Revista de Educación,* Guatemala, 13:1 (March, 1945), 51.

> Experimental literacy school in Quiché where horticulture will also be taught.

520. "El Programa Nacional de Desarrollo de la Comunidad y la atención al sector indígena en Guatemala," *América Indígena,* 32:2 (April/June, 1972), 419-421.

> Briefly describes the objectives and proposed projects of the Programa Nacional de Desarrollo de la Comunidad. One area of projected activity is to be broadly educational: health instruction and artisan (craft) training.

521. UNITED NATIONS. TECHNICAL ASSISTANCE ADMINISTRATION. *The Indian Economic Development Service of Guatemala.* Document ST/TAO/K/Guatemala/2. New York: 1960. 46 pp.

> Booklet describing the concepts, background, organization, and activities of the Servicio de Fomento de la Economía Indígena (SFEI). Among the latter are the program of supervised credit (agricultural extension), technical instruction in a variety of subjects to improve living conditions, skill training in special training centers, and literacy work.

AGRICULTURAL TRAINING

*522. FOOD AND AGRICULTURAL ORGANIZATION. *Guatemala; las actividades de extensión agrícola dentro de los planes nacionales de desarrollo rural,* by S. Pacheco. Document UNDP/TA 2522. N.p.: 1968. 12 pp.

BASIC EDUCATION/LITERACY

523. CHAVARRÍA FLORES, MANUEL. *Analfabetismo en Guatemala: Informe de seis años.* Guatemala: Comité Nacional de Alfabetización, 1952. 115 pp.

> Discusses the problem of illiteracy in Guatemala and various projects undertaken to alleviate the situation: the campaign in the capital; the campaign for indigenous literacy; the second regional campaign; the creation of a mobile library system.

524. CHURCH, CLARENCE. "The Summer Institute of Linguistics in Guatemala: 1959," *Boletín Indigenista,* 20:2 (June, 1960), 132-135.
General description of the literacy work of the Summer Institute of Linguistics.

525. GRAHAM, ALVA W. "Hope for Literacy in Guatemala," *Social Education,* 28:1 (January, 1964), 21-23, 28.
Literacy program developed by the Guatemalan army with American aid. Also describes the pilot literacy program in Jutiapa.

526. "Guatemala Attacks Illiteracy," Pan American Union, *Bulletin,* 74:7 (July, 1945), 422-423.
Describes the literacy campaign begun during the Arévalo regime. Each person who can read and write is required to teach one other person.

*527. MEYER, WALTER LANFORD. "Guatemala's Fight Against Illiteracy," *Pan American,* (May, 1948), 42-45.

528. WENDELL, MARGARITA. "En torno a un programa de alfabetización bilingüe: Un año en el proyecto de Tactic," *Guatemala Indígena,* 2:3 (July/September, 1962), 129-140.
Describes the literacy work of the Summer Institute of Linguistics in the Plan de Mejoramiento Integral de Tactic.

VOCATIONAL SKILL TRAINING

529. BEHRMAN, DANIEL. "The Mayans Modernize," *Courier,* 7:12 (May, 1955), 16-17.
UNESCO technical assistance program to modernize weaving techniques. Of particular interest is the spinning and weaving school in San Pedro Sacatepéquez directed toward future professional weavers who will go into business for themselves.

*530. GUATEMALA. MINISTERIO DE TRABAJO Y PREVISIÓN SOCIAL. INSTITUTO DE CAPACITACIÓN Y PRODUCTIVIDAD (INTECAP). *El qué y el porqué de INTECAP.* Guatemala: 1973. No pagination.

531. NASH, MANNING. *Machine Age Maya: The Industrialization of a Guatemalan Community.* American Anthropological Association, Memoir, 87. [Menasha, Wisconsin]: 1958. 118 pp.
Briefly describes the on-the-job training system used in the textile factory in Cantel.

MISCELLANEOUS

532. "Adult Education," *International Bureau of Education Bulletin*, 21:85 (4th Quarter, 1947), 156-157.
    Notes the stages of the literacy campaign in 1946 (including work of the army) and the introduction of traveling missions to rural areas.

533. BENJAMIN, GEORGIA K. "Community Goes to School in Guatemala," *Educational Outlook*, 26:3 (March, 1952), 91-101.
    Nuclear school at Esquintla offers special courses for adults, primarily at night, in literacy, basic education, health education, home improvement, and skill training. Also describes the mobile cultural mission program—most active from 1946-1950—in areas of health, agriculture, and home economics and which utilizes movies and demonstrations to instruct people; the literacy campaign; and the night classes for workers in Guatemala City.

534. CARDONA, RAFAEL. *El hombre, la tierra y el alfabeto en Guatemala: Una estructura pedagógica pentagonal echa sus raíces en el humus de la tierra*. Guatemala: 1957. 50 pp.
    Talks about the work of the Dirección General de Asuntos Agrarios and the Crédito Agrícola Supervisado (credit with technical advice). Also discusses the Sistema Socio-Educativo Rural whereby new concepts in rural development and education are being initiated.

535. CONFERENCE ON EDUCATION AND ECONOMIC AND SOCIAL DEVELOPMENT IN LATIN AMERICA, SANTIAGO DE CHILE, 1962. *Situación demográfica, económica, social y educativa de Guatemala*. 3rd ed. Guatemala: Ministerio de Educación Pública, 1962. 251 pp.
    Includes a section on adult education (literacy training, popular education, cultural extension, vocational training). Discusses various institutions and agencies involved in adult education activities, such as the Dirección de Educación de Adultos, Dirección de Desarrollo Socio-educativo Rural, Universidad Popular, Dirección de Bellas Artes, the army, Summer Institute of Linguistics, and the Servicio Cooperativo Interamericano de Educación.

536. LEON PALACIOS, O. DE. "Rural Education in Guatemala," *National Elementary Principal*, 37:6 (April, 1958), 24-25.
    Briefly describes the organizations called the Direction for Social Rural Educative Development and the Farmer Nucleo School, part of the rural development program which administers activities in the areas of economy, health, home improvement, and general culture directed toward the community as a whole.

537. ORDÓÑEZ, MARÍA VICTORIA DE. "Educación de adultos en Guatemala." Unpublished thesis. Universidad de San Carlos de Guatemala, 1967. 79 numb. leaves.

Includes sections on the literacy campaigns (including efforts of the army) and on work done by such organizations as the Summer Institute of Linguistics, the Sínodo Evangélico de Guatemala, the Catholic chuch, and through the medium of television. A further section on special programs describes the work of organizations such as the Universidad Popular.

538. RUIZ FRANCO, ARCADIO. "Memoria de labores del Instituto Indigenista Nacional de Guatemala durante el tiempo comprendido de julio de 1966 a junio de 1970," *América Indígena,* 30:4 (October, 1970), 1097-1117.

Several pages under the heading *"trabajos prácticos"* are devoted to descriptions of programs and projects undertaken in communities throughout the country. Listed by community, these activities range from health programs to literacy training to agricultural improvement programs.

Guyana

MISCELLANEOUS

539. THOMASSON, F. H. "Training in the Sugar Industry in Guyana," in Joseph A. Lauwerys, and David O. Scanlon, eds., *World Year Book of Education, 1968: Education within Industry*. London: Evans Brothers, 1968, pp. 341-344.
    Discusses the management training and apprenticeship programs of the Brooker Sugar Estates company. The apprenticeship program provides training for fitters, machinists, electricians, agricultural mechanics, and sugar boilers.

Haiti

MULTIFACETED PROGRAMS

540. "Assistance from U.N.: Haiti Tackles Ignorance and Disease,"
    Times Educational Supplement, 1989 (June 12, 1953), 541.
    Résumé of United Nations Technical Assistance Program efforts in
    literacy and fundamental education.

541. BERNARD, JOSEPH C. "Las escuelas de orientación," *Educación,*
    Washington, 3:9 (January/March, 1958), 42-43.
    Briefly describes community development and literacy work of the
    Misiones Sociales, the community arm of the Escuelas de Orienta-
    ción in rural areas.

542. BURNS, BRENDA. "With the U.N. in Haiti," *United Nations News,*
    8:1· (January/March, 1953), 19-22.
    Describes the Marbial Valley fundamental education project. The
    literacy program is the primary task, but technical assistance teams
    work to improve agricultural and health conditions in the valley.

543. FERNÁNDEZ BALLESTEROS, ALBERTO. *Toulon: Una experiencia en
    Haití.* México: Beatriz de Silva, 1954. 485 pp.
    Personal account of the UNESCO fundamental education project in
    the Marbial Valley, written by the former director.

544. HART, DONN V. "UNESCO Goes to Work in Haiti," *School and
    Society,* 66:1707 (September 13, 1947), 205.
    Brief summary of the aims and project goals of the Marbial project.

545. LIND, LARDS. "Marbial Valley of Haiti," *Midland Schools,* 64:4
    (December, 1949), 16-17.
    Describes work in literacy, health, agricultural, and skill training of
    the UNESCO fundamental education project in the valley.

546. MARSHALL, KENDRIC N. "Fundamental Education Programme of
    UNESCO," *Harvard Educational Review,* 20:3 (Summer, 1950),
    139-148.
    Section 5 covers the UNESCO project in the Marbial Valley—back-
    ground information, description of the area, and activities undertaken.

*547. MENDE, TIBOR. "Marbial Valley Project," *Caribbean Quarterly,* 2:3 (July/September, 1951), 18-21.

548. "The Re-Birth of a Valley," *Courier,* 2:5 (June, 1949), Supplement. 4 pp.
> Outlines various aspects of the Marbial Valley project: literacy work; craft training; health education; agricultural training; visual education museum.

549. UNITED NATIONS EDUCATIONAL, SCIENTIFIC, AND CULTURAL ORGANIZATION. *The Haiti Pilot Project: Phase One 1947-1949.* Monographs on Fundamental Education, 4. Paris: 1951. 83 pp.
> Provides a detailed description of the early stages of the community development project whose programs run the gamut from literacy education to agricultural and craft training to health education. The bulk of the document is devoted to a description of the community and a survey of people's values and receptivity to new ideas from an anthropological-sociological viewpoint.

550. UNITED NATIONS EDUCATIONAL, SCIENTIFIC, AND CULTURAL ORGANIZATION. SECRETARIAT. *Fundamental Education: Pilot Project in Haiti.* Document 18 EX/9. Paris: 1949. 8 pp.
> Annex 1 describes the purposes and proposed activities (health and hygiene education, agricultural training, development of local crafts) for the Marbial Valley project.

551. WILSON, EDMUND. "Haiti: UNESCO at Marbial," *The Reporter,* 2:11 (May 23, 1950), 29-33.
> First hand account of UNESCO efforts in Haiti in literacy work, craft instruction, and agricultural training. Also discusses some of the problems encountered.

BASIC EDUCATION/LITERACY

552. "Art, Science, and Education," Pan American Union, *Bulletin,* 66:2 (February, 1932), 136-140.
> Briefly mentions formation of an organization called the League for Instructing Illiterate Laborers. Free literacy lessons would be available in the evening to any laborer wishing to attend.

553. BELLEGARDE, DANTÉS. "Mass Education in Latin America," *Institute of International Education News Bulletin,* 30:7 (April, 1955), 19-23, 67.
> Briefly comments on the literacy campaign.

554. DALE, GEORGE A. *Education in the Republic of Haiti.* U.S. Office of Education, Bulletin 1959, no. 20. Washington: Government Printing Office, 1959. 180 pp.

Chapter 7 deals with adult education, reviewing various efforts on the part of private and religious organizations and governmental agencies in literacy work. Also describes the organization of the adult education centers whose primary emphasis is on literacy training.

555. ROMERO, FERNANDO. *Vocational Education in Haiti.* Series N on Vocational Education, 11. Washington: Division of Education, Pan American Union, 1952. 187 pp.

Appendix 5 on workers' education comments briefly on the literacy campaign directed by the Section of Workers' Education of the Labor Office.

MISCELLANEOUS

556. DARTIQUE, MAURICE. "Haiti," in *Educational Yearbook, 1942.* New York: International Institute, Teachers College, Columbia University, 1942, pp. 221-246.

Section on adult education notes in particular the program of rural adult education administered by the Department of Agriculture through its Division of Rural Education and Division of Agricultural Extension. A wide variety of activities have been undertaken, mainly centering around agriculture, but also touching on hygiene and civic education. Urban areas are relatively poor in adult education programs, with only a few night schools to teach literacy in operation.

557. McCONNELL, H. ORMONDE. "Teaching Them to Read: Literacy Campaign in Haiti," *International Review of Missions,* 42:168 (October, 1953), 438-445.

Focuses on the government literacy campaign in Creole begun in May, 1940, but also covers various activities of the UNESCO pilot project in the Marbial Valley.

Honduras

MULTIFACETED PROGRAMS

558. ACCIÓN CULTURAL POPULAR HONDUREÑA. *The Agricultural Education Program (Programa de Promoción Agrícola) of Acción Cultural Popular Hondureña: An Experimental Program in Agricultural Extension for Small Farmers in Latin America; a Summary Description.* Tegucigalpa: 1973. 48 pp.

> Report covering the background, objectives, operational structure, and financing of the agricultural extension program directed by ACPH. Also provides an overview of ACPH work in other types of endeavors (radio schools, vocational training, paraprofessional training) throughout the country.

559. LYLE, JACK. "The Radio Schools of Honduras," in *New Educational Media in Action: Case Studies for Planners.* Paris: International Institute for Educational Planning, United Nations Educational, Scientific, and Cultural Organization, 1967. Vol. 3, pp. 95-110.

> Description of the program sponsored by Acción Cultural Popular Hondureña (ACPH) and inspired by Radio Sutatenza in Colombia which attempts to bring literacy and basic education to the rural population. Heavily influenced by the Catholic church.

*560. WHITE, ROBERT A. *An Evaluation of the Radio Schools and the Radio School Movement in Honduras (Summary Report).* St. Louis: Department of Sociology and Anthropology, St. Louis University, 1972. 146 pp.

AGRICULTURAL TRAINING

*561. DI FRANCO, JOSEPH, and ROY A. CLIFFORD. *Analytical Study of the Extension Service of Honduras: Status Report 1962.* Turrialba, Costa Rica: Instituto Interamericano de Ciencias Agrícolas, 1962. 17 pp.

*562. DI FRANCO, JOSEPH, et al. *Estudio analítico del servicio de extensión de Honduras*. Turrialba, Costa Rica: Instituto Interamericano de Ciencias Agrícolas, 1961. 69 pp.

563. GINGERICH, GARLAND E. "Working as an Agricultural Missionary," *Agricultural Education Magazine,* 41:3 (September, 1968), 64-65. Personal account of experiences as an agricultural extension agent with a project administered by Agricultural Missions, Inc. of New York. Also comments on the special training program in agricultural techniques for community leaders in San Pedro Sula.

*564. VALLE, ARMANDO J. *Nuevo enfoque de extensión agrícola en Honduras*. Tegucigalpa: Servicio Técnico Interamericano de Cooperación Agrícola, 1963. 16 pp.

BASIC EDUCATION/LITERACY

565. AGUILAR PAZ, JESÚS, and RAFAEL BARDALES B. "El alfabetismo en Honduras," *Revista del Archivo y Biblioteca Nacionales,* Tegucigalpa, 28:7/8 (January/February, 1950), 368-374. Part of a series of articles on illiteracy in Honduras, this article is devoted to a history of literacy campaigns beginning with the Manuel Bonilla administration. Most of the article covers the campaign of Carías Andino which began in 1942.

*566. HONDURAS. MINISTERIO DE EDUCACIÓN PÚBLICA. CONSEJO NACIONAL DE ALFABETIZACIÓN. *Memoria de la campaña nacional de alfabetización 1950-1951*. Tegucigalpa: 1951. 26 pp.

567. "Literacy Campaign in Honduras," Pan American Union, *Bulletin,* 80:5 (May, 1946), 289. Describes the organization and administration of the literacy campaign begun in 1945.

Jamaica

MULTIFACETED PROGRAMS

568. ANDERSON, ANN. "Peace Corps Helps Give New Life to Old Arts,"
Art Education, 18:8 (November, 1965), 22-23.
Peace Corps work with the newly formed Crafts Development Agency
designed to develop the handicrafts industry. They offer instruction
in designing and updating techniques, establishing cooperatives, and
developing efficient production and marketing techniques. One hun-
dred craft centers have been established as part of the program.

569. GILL, C. H. S. "Setting up Training Schemes in a Jamaican Mining
Company," in Joseph A. Lauwerys, and David O. Scanlon, eds.,
World Year Book of Education, 1968: Education within Industry.
London: Evans Brothers, 1968, pp. 345-351.
Management and workers' training programs offered by Alcan Jamaica
Ltd. The company maintains a trades training center and offers courses
in basic supervision to managerial staff.

570. MARIER, ROGER. *Social Welfare Work in Jamaica: A Study of the
Jamaica Social Welfare Commission.* Monographs on Fundamental
Education, 7. Paris: United Nations Educational, Scientific, and
Cultural Organization, 1953. 166 pp.
Detailed and lengthy tract on the work of the Commission since its
inception in 1937. Activities have included: educational film service;
community center program (adult education, craft classes, agricultural
instruction, health education); campaigns on nutrition and agriculture;
literacy work.

AGRICULTURAL TRAINING

571. WAKEFIELD, A. J. "Memorandum of Agricultural Development in
Jamaica," Jamaica Agricultural Society, *Journal,* 47:6/8 (June/
August, 1943), 155-217.
Section 19 on agricultural education includes information about the
4-H clubs, the apprentice-settlement program, and the educational

118

film program. Section 25 pertains to the Jamaica Agricultural Society, which has as part of its responsibilities the development of agricultural extension.

BASIC EDUCATION/LITERACY

572. JAMAICA. MINISTRY OF YOUTH AND COMMUNITY DEVELOPMENT. SOCIAL DEVELOPMENT COMMISSION. "Literacy Through Radio and Television in Jamaica," *Educational Television International,* 4:1 (March, 1970), 50-54.
     Describes the literacy program with particular emphasis on the period since the introduction of television and radio on an experimental basis in 1966. Program content is discussed and an evaluation of the program is offered.

573. KIRKALDY, JOHN. "Major Campaign Aims to Stamp Out Illiteracy," *Times Educational Supplement,* 2989 (September 1, 1972), 12.
     New literacy campaign conducted on a voluntary basis.

VOCATIONAL SKILL TRAINING

574. HUGILL, J. A. C. "Jamaica's Shortage of Mechanics and Artisans," *West India Committee Circular,* 72:1316 (August, 1957), 221-222.
     Describes the apprenticeship training program (Central School at Monymusk) organized and funded by private enterprise.

575. INTERNATIONAL LABOUR OFICE, GENEVA. *Report to the Government of Jamaica on the Development of Vocational Training.* Document ILO/TAP/Jamaica/R3. Geneva: 1962. 24 pp.
     Brief mention of night school training for adult workers, and a somewhat longer discourse on the apprenticeship and "adult accelerated training" programs. Difficult to ascertain in some cases whether the training facility is part of the formal school system or not.

Mexico

MULTIFACETED PROGRAMS

576. AGUILERA DORANTES, MARIO. "El proyecto piloto mexicano de la educación básica," *El Maestro Mexicano,* 4 (February, 1949), 9-10.

    General description of the UNESCO pilot basic education project in Nayarit.

577. AGUILERA DORANTES, MARIO. "Three Villages on the March: The Nayarit Project," *Fundamental Education,* 3:3/4 (October, 1951), 116-123.

    Detailed firsthand account of the community development activities in the towns of Amapa, Pantano Grande, and Campo de Limones in Nayarit. Mobile cultural missions are sent to the towns. Efforts include literacy classes, teaching of domestic skills, health education, vocational training, basic education courses, and agricultural instruction.

578. AGUILERA DORANTES, MARIO, and ISIDRO CASTILLO. *Santiago Ixcuintla: Un ensayo de educación básica.* México: Ediciones Oasis, 1970. 319 pp.

    Lengthy account of the Ensayo Piloto de Educación Básica in Nayarit written by two men personally involved. Describes in detail the activities and projects undertaken during Aguilera's term there (around 1950). Most detailed personal report available. Very positive.

*579. ALLEN, D. "Cultural Missions Bringing Light to Mexican Masses," *Hispania,* 27 (February, 1944), 69-70.

580. ANZOLA GÓMEZ, GABRIEL. *Cómo llegar hasta los campesinos por medio de la educación: Resultados de una experiencia en el CREFAL.* Biblioteca de Autores Contemporáneos, 4. Bogotá: Ministerio de Educación Nacional, 1962. 398 pp.

    Detailed study of and personal reflections on the educational work done at the Centro Regional de Educación Fundamental para la América Latina (CREFAL) during the period of the author's residence there.

581. AVILA GARIBAY, JOSÉ. "Misiones culturales motorizadas," *Educación*, México, 2. época, 2 (September, 1959), 127-130.
Brief history and outline of the functions of the mobile Cultural Missions.

582. BAILEY, BERNARDINE. "Mexico: Laboratory of the Future," *United Nations World*, 6:12 (December, 1952), 47-50.
Description of the fundamental education work at CREFAL's Pátzcuaro center and in the surrounding countryside.

583. BARRIGA VÁZQUEZ, BENJAMÍN. "The Rural Cultural Missions of Mexico," *Social Sciences in Mexico and South and Central America*, 1:2 (Fall, 1947), 30-38.
Describes the principles, goals, organization, and activities of the rural Cultural Mission program after reorganization in 1942. Projects in particular villages also described.

584. "Basic Education in Mexico: The Nayarit Project," *Times Educational Supplement*, 1924 (March 14, 1952), 220.
Includes background information and a general description of the area. Discusses aims of the project and mentions some activities (literacy work, skill instruction, health instruction, agricultural education).

585. BONILLA Y SEGURA, GUILLERMO. "Cultural Missions in Mexico," *Fundamental Education*, 1:1 (January, 1949), 16-23.
Recounts the history of the Cultural Mission program dating back to 1924 and its revival in 1943. Comments on aims and methods, organization and administration of the contemporary program in some detail.

*586. BONILLA Y SEGURA, GUILLERMO. "As missões culturais no México," *Revista Brasileira de Estudos Pedagógicos*, (January/April, 1950), 51-58.

587. BONILLA Y SEGURA, GUILLERMO. *Report on the Cultural Missions of Mexico*. U.S. Office of Education, Bulletin 1945, no. 11. Washington: Government Printing Office, 1945. 61 pp.
Written by the director of the program, the report covers activities of 1942-1943. Part 1 describes the objectives, organization, and finances, with sections devoted to rural, workers', and urban missions. Part 2 recounts the specific operation of the missions and tasks to be accomplished. Part 3 discusses achievements and future plans.

588. BUITRÓN, ANÍBAL. "El desarrollo de la comunidad en la teoría y en la práctica," *América Indígena*, 21:2 (April, 1961), 141-150.
Advances some theoretical discussion of elements deemed necessary

by some for successful implementation of community development programs. Proceeds with a discussion of the success of CREFAL and descriptions of some of its projects. Success was realized in spite of not meeting all essential requirements previously noted.

589. CASTRO, ANGÉLICA. "El Instituto de Alfabetización para Indígenas Monolingües," *Boletín Indigenista,* 11:1 (March, 1951), 66-75.
Work in the Tarascan zone of Michoacán and with the Otomí in Hidalgo. Describes problems encountered and offers a fairly detailed report of activities, including comments on the annual training course offered to teachers and others involved in the literacy campaign and on the success of the campaign itself.

590. CASTRO DE LA FUENTE, ANGÉLICA, and EZEQUIEL GUERRERO AMAYA. "Promotores agropecuarios y de salubridad," *Anuario Indigenista,* 28 (December, 1968), 111-114.
Briefly describes the program of *promotorías culturales bilingües* which began in 1964 as a means of disseminating information to indigenous people in subjects of agriculture and general health. Offers suggestions for improvement of the program.

*591. CENTRO REGIONAL DE EDUCACIÓN FUNDAMENTAL PARA LA AMÉRICA LATINA. *Acción del CREFAL en América Latina; informe: 2° semestre de 1971.* Pátzcuaro: 1972. 53 pp.

592. CENTRO REGIONAL DE EDUCACIÓN FUNDAMENTAL PARA LA AMÉRICA LATINA. *El CREFAL.* Pátzcuaro: 1966. 40 pp.
More detailed description of the organization of CREFAL, its programs of study, and activities of students in the field.

593. CENTRO REGIONAL DE EDUCACIÓN FUNDAMENTAL PARA LA AMÉRICA LATINA. *CREFAL: Its Nature and Purpose.* Pátzcuaro: 1959. 14 pp.
A description of courses for those being trained as fundamental education specialists and a résumé of activities undertaken in local communities are included.

*594. CENTRO REGIONAL DE EDUCACIÓN FUNDAMENTAL PARA LA AMÉRICA LATINA. *Cuadro del plan de trabajo para la zona de influencia del CREFAL.* Pátzcuaro: 1955. 27 pp.

595. CENTRO REGIONAL DE EDUCACIÓN FUNDAMENTAL PARA LA AMÉRICA LATINA. *Ellos lo hicieron: Narración de una experiencia en el campo de la salud pública dentro de un programa de desarrollo de la comunidad.* Pátzcuaro: 1964. 74 pp.
Describes CREFAL's supervised credit program on the island of

Pacanda for developing the chicken industry, as well as the simultaneous program of health education.

596. CENTRO REGIONAL DE EDUCACIÓN FUNDAMENTAL PARA LA AMÉRICA LATINA. *Etapa de actividades*. Pátzcuaro: 1953. 28 pp.
Reviews the activities of CREFAL in the areas of home-nutrition education, health education, agricultural extension, and basic education. Describes various projects in the Pátzcuaro area.

597. CENTRO REGIONAL DE EDUCACIÓN FUNDAMENTAL PARA LA AMÉRICA LATINA. *Informe de actividades*. Pátzcuaro: 1959-1960. 4 vols.
Formal report of CREFAL activities on a semi-annual basis. Reports both on courses given within the Center and on programs carried out in the nearby communities.

598. CENTRO REGIONAL DE EDUCACIÓN FUNDAMENTAL PARA LA AMÉRICA LATINA. "El trabajo de educación en el CREFAL," *Educación*, Washington, 1:3 (July/September, 1956), 21-25.
Describes CREFAL's fundamental education work in the environs of Pátzcuaro, such as leadership training, literacy programs, and supervised credit.

599. CHACÓN NARDI, RAFAELA. "Educación de la comunidad en México," Cuba, Comisión Nacional de la UNESCO, *Boletín*, 5:5 (May, 1956), 21-22; 5:6 (June, 1956), 9-11.
Describes the Comunidades de Promoción Indígena project initiated in 1953, incorporating technical training through an apprenticeship program, health education, agricultural instruction, and literacy training. New communities were established as demonstration areas. Objectives of the project are discussed.

600. CHAPIN, BARBARA. "CREFAL Means New Horizons," *New York State Education*, 42:7 (April, 1955), 474-476.
Describes training at CREFAL, types of field work done in the locality, and methods employed.

601. COBOS, BERNARDO. "Labour Education in Mexico," *Labour Education*, 18 (April, 1970), 21-24.
Historical account, written in somewhat glowing terms, of the educational activities of the Confederación de Trabajadores Mexicanos (CTM). The CTM has organized a number of educational seminars for its members which concentrate on specific aspects of the labor movement, and it has actively participated in literacy campaigns and vocational training programs, such as the Adiestramiento Rápido de la Mano-de-Obra (ARMO).

602. "Community Development and Fundamental Education," *Technical Assistance Newsletter,* 48 (December, 1958), 1-12.

Includes a brief description of CREFAL and its activities in Pátzcuaro.

603. COOK, KATHERINE M. *La casa del pueblo: Un relato acerca de las escuelas nuevas de acción de México.* Translated by Rafael Ramírez. México: 1936. 157 pp.

Chapter 2 describes in some detail the organization of the Cultural Missions in the early phase of their existence.

604. COUTIÑO RUIZ, ORALIA. "Humanización de la reforma agraria: Proyección del Centro de Bienestar Social como centro de extensión rural." Unpublished thesis. Universidad Nacional Autónoma de México, 1963. 136 numb. leaves.

Chapter 10 describes the educational activities (e.g., literacy courses, history and geography courses) of the Casas de la Asegurada, part of the Instituto Mexicano de Seguro Social. Work was later carried on by the Centros de Seguridad Social para el Bienestar Familiar and expanded to include courses in nutrition, health, home improvement, and civic education. Chapter 11 discusses the importance of the Centros de Seguridad Social para el Bienestar Familiar as rural extension centers.

605. "Cultural Missions," *International Bureau of Education Bulletin,* 20:81 (4th Quarter, 1946), 162.

Reports on the revival of the Cultural Mission program, of which there are three types: rural, workers', and urban.

606. DÉLMEZ, ALBERT JUÁRES. "The History of the Cultural Missions in Mexican Education." Unpublished Ph.D. dissertation, University of Missouri, 1949. 308 numb. leaves.

Role and achievements of the Cultural Missions in the broad scope of post-revolutionary education.

607. ELSON, BENJAMIN F. "Summer Institute of Linguistics in Mexico, 1958-1959," *Boletín Indigenista,* 20:1 (March, 1960), 44-51.

Two-year report of the activities of the Institute, including literacy and community development work.

608. EVANS, LUTHER H. "Some Activities of UNESCO in the Caribbean," in A. Curtis Wilgus, ed., *The Caribbean: Contemporary Education.* Caribbean Conference Series, 10. Gainesville: University of Florida Press, 1960, pp. 233-241.

Short section on CREFAL, focusing on current finances and the training program at the Center.

609. FABILA, ALFONSO. *La misión cultural de Amanalco, escuela sin muros (ensayo sobre educación fundamental mexicana)*. México: Editorial Bolívar, 1948. 126 pp.

> Bulk of this work is devoted to a community study, but the introduction provides some information on the goals and objectives of the Cultural Missions. Appendixes 2 and 3 offer some idea of the activities undertaken at Amanalco by the Cultural Mission and expenditures made on them.

610. FIGUEROA ORTIZ, JOSÉ. "The Rural Community Development Programme in Mexico," *International Journal of Adult and Youth Education*, 14:2 (1962), 77-81.

> Relates the development of rural social welfare centers administered by the Department of Public Health and Welfare which act as principal community development agents. They are involved in activities ranging from community improvement projects to health education campaigns. Also mentions the special training courses of the Department for "social organizers" and local leaders known as "community organizers."

611. FISHER, GLEN H. *Desarrollo de la comunidad local de Nayarit (México)*. Organización y Desarrollo de las Comunidades Locales, 18. Document ST/SOA/Ser.O/18; ST/TAA/Ser.D/18. New York: United Nations, 1954. 62 pp.

> Covering the period 1949-1952, this study goes into great detail about the pilot fundamental education program in Nayarit, whose basic goal was to integrate all local community development projects, from the Cultural Missions to public health projects, under one administration. Following a general socio-politico-geographical description of the Valle de Santiago, various aspects of the program are discussed. Educational efforts included agricultural extension, literacy programs, health and nutrition programs, home economics extension, and skill training. The school became a community center where much of the activity was focused. A detailed description of the administration is provided and the author talks candidly about problems encountered and in what areas the project suffered and did not live up to expectations. Many of the basic problems are attributed to lack of qualified and dedicated personnel and lack of adequate federal support.

612. FISHER, GLEN. "Directed Culture Change in Nayarit, Mexico: Analysis of a Pilot Project in Basic Education," in Munro S. Edmonson, et al, eds., *Synoptic Studies of Mexican Culture*. Tulane University, Middle American Research Institute, Publication 17. New

Orleans: Middle American Research Institute, Tulane University, 1957, pp. 67-173.

Comprehensive study of the pilot basic education project in Nayarit. First sections of the work give background information, leading to a full description of the project in part 3, including origins of the project, methodology, organization, and activities in areas of agriculture, health, and domestic life. Part 5 offers an analysis of the overall program and specific components.

613. FOSTER, GEORGE M. *Tzintzuntzan: Mexican Peasant in a Changing World.* Boston: Little, Brown, 1967. 372 pp.

Describes the work of CREFAL in Tzintzuntzan, which was not considered to be successful.

614. FUENTE, JULIO DE LA. "El centro coordinador Tzeltal-Tzotzil," *América Indígena*, 13:1 (January, 1953), 55-64.

Activities in agricultural extension, literacy training, and health education at the Chiapas Centro Coordinador of the Instituto Nacional Indigenista, as well as descriptive background information on the geographical region.

615. FUENTE, JULIO DE LA. "Development of Indian Communities in Mexico," in Egbert de Vries, ed., *Social Research and Rural Life in Central America, Mexico and the Caribbean Region: Proceedings of a Seminar Organized by UNESCO in Cooperation with the United Nations Economic Commission for Latin America, Mexico City, 17-27 October 1962.* Paris: United Nations Educational, Scientific, and Cultural Organization, 1966, pp. 167-177.

Good description of the scope and activities of the Centros Coordinadores of the Instituto Nacional Indigenista, with particular reference to the center in Tzeltal-Tzotzil region of Chiapas. Work is in the areas of health education (for which a puppet theater was developed), agricultural extension, training for small business operation, and vocational training.

*616. FUENZALIDA, J. B. "Las misiones culturales en México," *Revista de Educación*, Santiago, 3:15 (June, 1943), 50-52.

617. FULTON, DAVID C. "A New Nayarit," *Americas*, 2:10 (October, 1950), 32-34.

Activities of American Friends Service Committee volunteers at the UNESCO pilot fundamental education program in Nayarit. Work included instruction in health, farming techniques, and care of children, in addition to practical tasks of improving the community.

618. GILLEN, JOHN. "Latin America," in Phillips Ruopp, ed., *Approaches*

to *Community Development: A Symposium Introductory to Prob-
lems and Methods of Village Welfare in Underdeveloped Areas.*
The Hague: W. Van Hoeve, 1953, pp. 331-344.
Includes a very general report on the UNESCO pilot project in Nayarit.

619. GLUCKSTADT, ILSE. "The Indian in Mexican Life," *Institute of International Education News Bulletin,* 31:1 (October, 1955), 20-24.
Sparse account of the Instituto Nacional Indigenista (INI) program of
community development in Chiapas. Local men are offered one-month
training courses at the Centro Coordinador Tzeltal-Tzotzil, where a
demonstration farm is also maintained.

620. GONZÁLEZ SALAZAR, GLORIA. *La educación obrera a través de las
organizaciones de trabajadores: Aspectos generales en México.*
México: 1959. 95 pp.
Chapter 2 is devoted to workers' education in Mexico. Part 4 of the
chapter describes educational activities and programs of various
unions, ranging from literacy training to vocational skill training.

621. HATCH, D. SPENCER. "Rural Reconstruction in Mexico," *Agriculture in the Americas,* 4:3 (March, 1944), 51-53, 57.
YMCA-sponsored community development program near Tepoztlán.
Principal activities revolve around the farm demonstration project at
the Camohmila Center. Other efforts include health education and
craft training.

622. HATCH, D. SPENCER. "Rural Reconstruction in Mexico: Self-Help
Method for All-Round Rural Development," *Applied Anthropology,* 2:4 (July/September, 1943), 17-21.
Community development project sponsored by the YMCA. See entry
621.

623. HATCH, D. SPENCER. *Toward Freedom from Want: From India to
Mexico.* Bombay: Oxford University Press, 1949. 303 pp.
Final chapter devoted to a personal recollection of the establishment
of the rural demonstration center at Camohmila sponsored by the
YMCA. Activities included agricultural instruction, training classes
in weaving and other cottage industries, literacy work, and basic
education.

624. HUGHES, LLOYD H. *CREFAL: Formador de líderes de educación
fundamental.* Translated by Lucas Ortiz Benítez and Bernabé León
de la Barra. Pátzcuaro: Centro Regional de Educación Fundamental
para la América Latina, 1958. 52 pp.
Provides a general description of the CREFAL program at Pátzcuaro,
including background information, descriptive data of the Pátzcuaro
area, and discussion of methodology. Primary areas of concern are:

health and sanitation; agriculture; home life; literacy; recreation; cooperatives; schooling.

625. HUGHES, LLOYD H. "CREFAL: Training Centre for Community Development for Latin America," *International Review of Education,* 9:2 (1963/1964), 226-235.

History, organization, and program of study for the training of community development specialists at the Center. Also offers a brief critique and evaluation of the Center's work.

*626. HUGHES, LLOYD H. *Mexican Cultural Mission Programme.* Monographs on Fundamental Education, 3. Paris: United Nations Educational, Scientific, and Cultural Organization, 1950. 77 pp.

627. INTERNATIONAL LABOUR OFFICE. *Conditions of Life and Work of Indigenous Population of Latin American Countries.* Fourth Conference of American States Members of the International Labor Organization, Montevideo, 1949, Report 2. Geneva: 1949. 142 pp.

Chapter 6 on the social policy of governments includes a description of Mexico's Brigadas de Promoción Indígena—mobile units staffed by specialists to travel the country and teach people agricultural and vocational skills, basic health and nutrition information, and so forth.

*628. KNIGHT, MABEL. "UNESCO Experiment in Patzcuaro," *Mexican-American Review,* 19:11 (November, 1951), 8-10, 38.

*629. LAGUERRE VELEZ, ENRIQUE A. "The International Project at Patzcuaro," *International House Quarterly,* 16:3 (Summer, 1952), 158-162.

630. LAMBERTO MORENO, J. "Mexico's Cultural Missions," *Fundamental Education,* 1:4 (October, 1949), 3-8.

Deals primarily with methods used by the mission staff in the field. Also offers further clarification of the administration of the program.

631. LANE, LAYLE. "Climbing Jacob's Ladder: The Cultural Missions in Mexico," *American Teacher Magazine,* 48:3 (February, 1964), 11-12.

Report of a visit to Cultural Missions near Mexico City. Provides description of objectives and general organization of the missions.

632. LENZ, FRANK B. "Rural Rebuilding in Mexico," *Inter-American,* 4:4 (April, 1945), 28-29.

Community development program sponsored by Mexico City's YMCA. Work included agricultural instruction and demonstration, health education program, and skill training to introduce new industry.

633. "Life in Patzcuaro," *Times Educational Supplement,* 2247 (June 13, 1958), 989.
Brief article outlining specialist training program at Pátzcuaro.

634. LÓPEZ RICOY, LUIS. "¿Es posible incorporar al campesino mexicano a la cultura nacional a trayés de la reforma agraria?" Unpublished thesis, Universidad Nacional Autónoma de México, 1962. 118 numb. leaves.
Includes a discussion of the Cultural Missions, their organization and activities in the section on rural education.

635. MACK, MARY D. "That All May Learn," U.S. Department of State, Division of Publications, *The Record,* 7:5 (September/October, 1951), 1-6.
Description of the early days of CREFAL operations in Pátzcuaro. Stresses the kinds of activities undertaken. Some financial figures included.

*636. MAITLAND, JOHN. "Experiment in Nayarit," *Mexican-American Review,* 18:2 (February, 1950), 16-21.

637. McEVOY, J. P. "A Neighbor in a Mexican Valley," *Survey Graphic,* 34:6 (June, 1945), 290-291, 301, 304.
Reflections on a visit to the rural demonstration-training center sponsored by the YMCA in Camohmila, near Tepoztlán.

*638. MEXICO. DIRECCIÓN GENERAL DE ALFABETIZACIÓN Y EDUCACIÓN EXTRAESCOLAR. *Misiones culturales.* México: 1961. No pagination.

*639. MEXICO. DIRECCIÓN GENERAL DE ALFABETIZACIÓN Y EDUCACIÓN EXTRAESCOLAR. *Nuevas misiones culturales motorizadas.* Folletos, 2. México: 1959. 12 pp.

640. MEXICO. DIRECCIÓN GENERAL DE ASUNTOS INDÍGENAS. *Seis años de labor: 1952-1958.* México: 1958. 131 pp.
Discusses a wide variety of projects undertaken by the division of indigenous affairs, such as agricultural instruction and demonstration projects, health education, vocational training, literacy work, and domestic arts.

641. MEXICO. INSTITUTO MEXICANO DEL SEGURO SOCIAL. *Centros de seguridad social para el bienestar familiar.* México: 1960. 24 pp.
Discusses the educational activities of the Centros: health and nutrition courses, home improvement courses, and civic instruction.

642. MEXICO. SECRETARÍA DE EDUCACIÓN. *Plan de trabajo del ensayo*

'*piloto*' *mexicano de la educación básica.* Santiago Ixcuintla: 1949. 55 pp.

Pilot project in Nayarit of integral community education in the fields of health, agriculture, home improvement, and literacy. Among institutions participating are: Misiones Culturales Rurales; Misión Cultural Motorizada; Servicio Extensivo de Educación Agrícola.

643. MEXICO. SECRETARÍA DE EDUCACIÓN PÚBLICA. *Acción educativa del gobierno federal.* México: 1956-1959/1960. 4 vols.

Provides annual statistical information on the literacy campaign and the Cultural Missions.

644. MEXICO. SECRETARÍA DE EDUCACIÓN PÚBLICA. *El ensayo piloto mexicano de educación básica de Santiago Ixcuintla, Estado de Nayarit, Mex.* México: 1952. 77 pp.

Outline and details of the background, objectives, organization, methods, activities, and financing of the Nayarit basic education project. Also includes an account of the work of the Cultural Missions in the area which are part of the program.

645. MEXICO. SECRETARÍA DE EDUCACIÓN PÚBLICA. *Las misiones culturales, 1932-1933.* México: 1933. 357 pp.

Beginning with a brief history, this document provides a detailed description of the activities of the Cultural Missions around the country.

646. MICHAELS, LEILA. "A Report on the Latin American Regional Fundamental Education Centre, CREFAL." Unpublished thesis, University of California, Los Angeles, 1956. 158 numb. leaves.

Begins with a definition of fundamental education, followed by a description of the Pátzcuaro region, the Center and its training curriculum, projects in selected communities in the area grouped by type (general culture, health and home, economy, and recreation), and an evaluation of the overall program.

647. "Las misiones culturales," *Educación Nacional,* 1:1 (February, 1944), 64-66.

General statement of the objectives of the program and goals that each individual should strive to attain.

648. "Nayarit Basic Education Project," *International Bureau of Education Bulletin,* 26:105 (4th Quarter, 1952), 158.

Brief comment on the Nayarit project, naming some accomplishments in literacy and skill training.

649. NORMAN, JAMES. "Teamwork Against Poverty," *Mexican Life,* 30:9 (September, 1954), 11-14, 58-63.
      Detailed report of CREFAL's activities in Pátzcuaro: health and agricultural education; literacy training; vocational skill training. Also describes the organization of the program.

650. OGDEN, HORACE G. " 'CREFAL' Trains Teachers for Community Leadership," in U.S. Office of Education. *1957 Yearbook on Education Around the World: Education for Better Living; the Role of the School in Community Improvement.* Bulletin 1956, no. 9. Washington: 1957, pp. 143-154.
      Discusses the training program at CREFAL and the field work done in the areas of literacy, agriculture, and health.

651. ORGANIZATION OF AMERICAN STATES. INTER-AMERICAN CULTURAL COUNCIL. COMMITTEE FOR CULTURAL ACTION. *Study on Coordinated Services for Indian Communities.* Document CAC-E-12. Washington: Department of Cultural Affairs, Pan American Union, 1954. 8 pp.
      Outline of the objectives and purposes of the Coordinated Services for Indian Communities, a fundamental education-community development program to assimilate the indigenous population into national life.

652. PUGA, MARIO. "Una obra de reivindicación: La integración del indio a la nacionalidad," *Humanismo,* 2:7/8 (January/February, 1953), 49-53.
      Discusses the underlying philosophy of the work of the Instituto Nacional Indigenista and its Centros de Coordinación. Focuses in particular on the work in literacy training, teaching practical agricultural techniques, and health education of the Centro in Chiapas.

653. "Radio Programs for 1929," Pan American Union, *Bulletin,* 63:7 (July, 1929), 739.
      Describes educational extension by radio. Programs directed primarily to workers in the city and rural laborers.

654. RADVANYI, LASZLO. "Measurement of the Effectiveness of Basic Education," *International Journal of Opinion and Attitude Research,* 5:3 (Fall, 1951), 347-366.
      Offers some analysis, based on a questionnaire technique over a five-year period, of the effectiveness of UNESCO's pilot fundamental education program in Nayarit.

655. REDFIELD, ROBERT. *A Village that Chose Progress: Chan Kom Revisited.* University of Chicago Publications in Anthropology; Social Anthropological Series. Chicago: University of Chicago Press, 1957. 187 pp.
   Analysis of the effects of changes wrought on a Mexican village which was exposed to community education projects, such as the Cultural Mission. Chapter 3 reveals on a first-hand level the educational experiences of a Cultural Mission in a small village during the mid-'40s. It describes the skills taught and the knowledge imparted and the changes which resulted from these efforts. Chapter 7 further describes some of the experiences of the Cultural Mission.

656. "The Right to Education Means the Right to Better Living," *Courier,* 5:11 (November, 1952), 4-5.
   Describes the activities of CREFAL such as training in agricultural techniques, nutrition, sewing, and hygiene.

657. SÁNCHEZ, GEORGE I. "Education in Mexico," in Arthur Henry Moehlman, and Joseph S. Roucek, eds., *Comparative Education.* Dryden Professional Books in Education. New York: Dryden Press, 1952, pp. 85-108.
   Includes a brief section describing the Cultural Mission program.

658. SAYRE, MRS. RAYMOND. "Building Bridges of Understanding," American Association of School Administrators, *Official Report,* (1954), 98-109.
   Includes a short personal account of CREFAL's activities.

659. SCHOLES, WALTER V. "Mexico: Illiteracy and Land Reforms," *Current History,* New Series, 22:127 (March, 1952), 130-133.
   Article in part offers a sketchy outline of the development of the Cultural Mission program.

660. SHEATS, PAUL HENRY. *Report on UNESCO's Regional Training and Production Center for Fundamental Education (CREFAL) at Patzcuaro, Mexico.* Los Angeles: 1952. 10 pp.

661. SMITH, HENRY LESTER. "Education in Mexico," Indiana University, School of Education, *Bulletin,* 18:4 (July, 1942), 1-95.
   Includes a general description of the early Cultural Mission program in the chapter on teacher training.

662. SODI M., DEMETRIO. "Actividades del Instituto Indigenista Interamericano, 1960-1962," *Boletín Bibliográfico de Antropología Americana,* 23/25:1 (1960/1962), 210-215.
   Brief entry on the Centro Piloto de la Sierra de Puebla, a joint project

of CREFAL, the Organization of American States, and the Mexican government, similar to the CREFAL program in Pátzcuaro. Local work in the areas of health and agricultural education mentioned.

663. STENTON, JEAN E. "Experiment in Education," *Canadian Geographical Journal,* 50:5 (May, 1955), 190-193.
Describes the CREFAL fundamental education project in Pátzcuaro.

664. UNITED NATIONS EDUCATIONAL, SCIENTIFIC, AND CULTURAL ORGANIZATION. *Learn and Live: A Way Out of Ignorance for 1,200,000,000 People.* Paris: 1951. 32 pp.
Describes the organization, functions, and activities of CREFAL in fundamental education.

665. UNITED NATIONS EDUCATIONAL, SCIENTIFIC, AND CULTURAL ORGANIZATION. *New Horizons at Tzentzenhuaro: One Year of Work at a Fundamental Education Centre for Latin America.* Paris: 1953. 33 pp.
Illustrated narrative of CREFAL's first year of work with the people of Tzentzenhuaro. Describes the training program and activities carried out in the community.

666. UNITED NATIONS EDUCATIONAL, SCIENTIFIC, AND CULTURAL ORGANIZATION. *Regional Fundamental Education Centre for Latin America.* Document UNESCO/ED/96. Paris: 1951. 6 pp.
General account of the aims and program of CREFAL. Also provides lists of activities which CREFAL is to undertake in the areas of economics, health and hygiene, home improvement, and civil and social education.

667. UNITED NATIONS EDUCATIONAL, SCIENTIFIC, AND CULTURAL ORGANIZATION. *Youth and Fundamental Education.* Monographs on Fundamental Education, 9. Paris: 1954. 86 pp.
One section describes the American Friends Service Committee work with the pilot project in fundamental education in Nayarit. Committee participated in health and nutrition education, skill training, and agricultural instruction.

*668. UNITED NATIONS EDUCATIONAL, SCIENTIFIC, AND CULTURAL ORGANIZATION. CONFERENCIA PLENARIA. DELEGACIÓN MEXICANA. *Plan de trabajo del ensayo 'piloto' mexicano de la educación básica: Santiago Ixcuintla, Nayarit.* México: Tip. Plus Ultra, 1949. 55 pp.

669. UNITED NATIONS EDUCATIONAL, SCIENTIFIC, AND CULTURAL ORGANIZATION. SECRETARIAT. *Progress Report on the Regional*

Centre for Fundamental Education in Latin America at Patzcuaro, Michoacan, Mexico. Document 28 EX/4. Paris: 1951. 4 pp.
Provides financial information and general remarks on the success of CREFAL programs.

670. "UNESCO's Fundamental Education Center in Patzcuaro, Mexico," *American Teacher Magazine,* 36:3 (December, 1951), 16-18.
Brief look at CREFAL activities in Pátzcuaro.

671. VALENZUELA KUNCKEL DE SÁNCHEZ, MARÍA. "Trabajo social que se desarrolla en algunas dependencias de la Secretaría de Educación Pública." Unpublished thesis, Universidad Nacional Autónoma de México, 1950. 69 numb. leaves.
Chapters 2 and 3 discuss the work of the Cultural Missions.

672. "Voluntary Manual Labour in Mexico," *Times Educational Supplement,* 2040 (June 4, 1954), 555.
Personal reminiscences of time spent as an American Friends Service Committee volunteer in Las Iguanas, Nayarit, working with the basic education project. Women taught health and sewing. Offers some critique of the program.

673. WALLS, FOREST WESLEY. "The Activities of Selected United Nations Specialized Agencies with Particular Reference to Field Projects in Mexico." Unpublished Ph.D. dissertation, University of Washington, 1958. 361 numb. leaves.
Chapter on UNESCO activities gives a fairly detailed report on that body's fundamental education training center, CREFAL, at Pátzcuaro, from its inception to date.

674. WISE, SIDNEY. "Sunday School Under the Trees," *Times Educational Supplement,* 2710 (April 28, 1967), 1408-1409.
Describes Mexico City's School of Popular Learning, a private venture with free classes offered in a wide range of subjects (hair styling, radio operating, electronics, language, for example).

*675. WOOLSEY, W. "CREFAL: UNESCO's School for Community Development Leadership in Latin America," *Hispania,* 46 (March, 1963), 115-118.

676. WOOLSEY, WALLACE. "Cultural Mission No. 53, San Pablo Huixtepec, Oaxaca," *Modern Language Journal,* 48:1 (January, 1964), 35-39.
General description of the Cultural Missions, followed by a report of a visit to a Cultural Mission near Oaxaca.

AGRICULTURAL TRAINING

677. ANTUÑA, SANTIAGO E. *Hacia una vida mejor: Apuntes sobre una experiencia realizada con el crédito agrícola supervisado.* Pátzcuaro: Centro Regional de Educación Fundamental para la América Latina, 1957. 31 pp.

Describes the credit–agricultural extension program in Pátzcuaro for raising chickens.

678. BRUNER, RICHARD. "The Puebla Project," *Rockefeller Foundation Quarterly,* 3 (1969), 20-39.

Project funded by the Rockefeller Foundation whose immediate aim is to increase corn crop yields and which is working through an intense program of agricultural extension agents training local farmers in new methods. Project began in early 1967 and is administered by the International Maize and Wheat Improvement Center (CIMMYT) in Mexico City.

*679. CENTRO INTERNACIONAL DE MEJORAMIENTO DE MAIZ Y TRIGO (CIMMYT). *The Puebla Project 1967-69: Progress Report of a Program to Rapidly Increase Corn Yields on Small Holdings.* Mexico: 1969. 120 pp.

680. CENTRO REGIONAL DE EDUCACIÓN FUNDAMENTAL PARA LA AMÉRICA LATINA. *Importancia del crédito agrícola supervisado y del cooperativismo en el proceso de desarrollo de comunidades rurales; experiencia de la comunidad—La Pacanda.* Pátzcuaro: 1965. 78 pp.

Describes the supervised credit program to develop the chicken industry which began in 1956 under the joint sponsorship of CREFAL and the Banco Nacional de Comercio Exterior in the island community of La Pacanda. Includes a community study and an analysis of the effects of the project.

681. FOOD AND AGRICULTURAL ORGANIZATION. *Activities of FAO under the Expanded Technical Assistance Program 1950-1952.* Rome: 1952. 76 pp.

Describes, in part, the agricultural extension work being done by the FAO at CREFAL.

*682. FOOD AND AGRICULTURAL ORGANIZATION. RURAL INSTITUTIONS DIVISION. *Mexico: Integrated Agricultural Programme for Education, Research and Extension Work, Chapingo; Report on Project*

Results, Conclusions and Recommendations; Terminal Report. Document UNDP/SF MEX/6. N.p.: 1970. 54 pp.

*683. FORD FOUNDATION. *Progress of the Agricultural Extension Project of the Secretariat of Agriculture and Livestock and the Ford Foundation: Mexico, 1968.* Mexico: 1968. 21 pp.

*684. JIMÉNEZ SÁNCHEZ, LEOBARDO. "The Puebla Project: A Regional Program for Rapidly Increasing Corn Yields among 50,000 Small Holders," in Delbert T. Myren, ed., *Strategies for Increasing Agricultural Production on Small Holdings: International Conference Proceedings, Puebla, Mexico, August, 1970.* Mexico: International Maize and Wheat Improvement Center, 1971, pp. 11-17.

*685. MEXICO (STATE). DIRECCIÓN DE AGRICULTURA Y GANADERÍA. *La extensión agrícola en el estado de México; sus tendencias y sus realizaciones.* Toluca: 1957. 74 pp.

686. OGDEN, H. G. *Hacia una vida mejor: El crédito agrícola supervisado abre nuevas esperanzas.* Pátzcuaro: Centro Regional de Educación Fundamental para la América Latina, 1957. No pagination.
    Program of credit–agricultural extension for those interested in raising chickens. Includes instruction in construction, feeding, and care of the chickens.

687. SIMMONS, JOHN L. "A Corporation for Peasant Farmers?" *International Development Review,* 13:2 (1971/1972), 19-21.
    Experimental program financed by the Agency for International Development (AID) and administered by the International Marketing Institute of Cambridge, Massachusetts which proposes a multiservice corporation to sell farm supplies and provide credit and technical advice to farmers.

688. SMITH, WILLIAM C. "Hens that Laid Golden Eggs," *International Development Review,* 3:3 (October, 1961), 2-5.
    Concerned with one of CREFAL's technical aid projects, the introduction of small-scale commercial chicken farming. The project involves the extension of credit and technical advice. Analyzes the process of acceptance of the project by the villagers in the Pátzcuaro area.

689. STANLEY, RUTH HOFFMAN. "Mexican Pueblo in Transition," *Journal of Geography,* 49:7 (October, 1950), 269-278.
    Describes the supervised credit program of the Banco Nacional de Crédito Ejidal as it operates in San Pablo Atlazalpan in the state of Mexico. An agricultural engineer is placed in charge of the local program.

BASIC EDUCATION/LITERACY

690. BAEZ CAMARGO, G. "Mexico Attacks Illiteracy: Mexico to Make War on Illiteracy," *Christian Century*, 61:39 (September 27, 1944), 1093, 1116-1117.
    Describes the Camacho literacy campaign begun in 1944, which was inspired by the Laubach method of "each one, teach one."

691. BARRERA VÁSQUEZ, ALFREDO. "Cómo resuelve México el problema de la alfabetización de sus indígenas monolingües," *Yikal Maya Than*, 7:79 (March 28, 1946), 66-69.
    Literacy campaign begun in 1944 and the methods of instruction employed.

692. BARRERA VÁSQUEZ, ALFREDO. "La UNESCO y la educación bilingüe de los amerindios," *Boletín Indigenista*, 12:2 (June, 1952), 86-105.
    Summary of papers given at a meeting of experts in Paris, 15 November-5 December 1951. Describes several literacy programs beginning in the late 1930s with the Tarasco Project and continuing with the work of the Consejo de Lenguas Indígenas (CLI) and its Instituto de Alfabetización en Lenguas Indígenas and the Summer Institute of Linguistics in the early 1940s.

693. "Buddy System," *Industrial Arts and Vocational Education*, 35:2 (February, 1946), 63.
    Brief report on Avila Camacho's literacy campaign begun in 1944.

694. "Campaign Against Illiteracy," *International Bureau of Education Bulletin*, 19:76 (3rd Quarter, 1945), 92.
    Brief note on the organization of the literacy campaign.

695. "La campaña alfabetizante en el estado de Campeche," *Hemisferio*, 4:15 (January, 1945), 72.
    Work of Lic. Eduardo L. Lavalle Urbina, governor of Campeche, in the literacy campaign, including the creation of the Departamento Cultural and the development of local libraries.

696. "La campaña pro-educación popular en México," *Educación y Cultura*, 1:4 (April 1, 1940), 204-207.
    Article focuses on part of the campaign initiated in 1937 that directed toward the eradication of illiteracy.

697. CASTILLO, IGNACIO M. DEL. "La alfabetización en lenguas indígenas:

El Proyecto Tarasco,'' *América Indígena,* 5:2 (April, 1945), 139-
151.

> Author describes his own work in the literacy program carried out in
> Michoacán during 1939 and 1940. Offers an analysis of the approaches
> taken and some background information.

698. CENTRO DE ESTUDIOS NACIONALES, MÉXICO. *La nueva cruzada en el
campo de la alfabetización.* Colección de Testimonios, Documentos, Acuerdos, Decretos y Leyes Importantes para la Historia
de un Régimen, 4. México: 1965. 239 pp.

> Collection of reprinted newspaper articles testifying to the extent of
> the literacy campaign throughout the country in 1965.

699. '' 'Each One-Teach One' Campaign,'' *International Bureau of Education Bulletin,* 20:80 (3rd Quarter, 1946), 111.

> Brief commentary on the literacy campaign launched in 1944.

*700. FERNÁNDEZ SERNA, GABINO. "Plan piloto Petatlán de alfabetiza-
ción," *Revista de Economía,* 31:5 (May, 1968), 158-160.

701. GARDNER, CLINTON HARVEY. "Mexico's Campaign Against Illiteracy," *Social Education,* 13:6 (October, 1949), 277-278.

> Organization, problems, and achievements of the literacy campaign
> launched in 1944.

702. GEORGI, A. A. "Education in Mexico," *Education,* Boston, 68:7
(March, 1948), 402-406.

> Includes section on Avila Camacho's literacy campaign. Reports on
> the progress of the campaign to 1947.

*703. GRAY, W. S. "Mexico's Campaign to Reduce Illiteracy," *Elementary
School Journal,* 47 (May, 1947), 480.

704. "Guides and Leaders for the Villagers of Latin America," *Courier,*
11:3 (March, 1958), 24.

> Brief discussion of CREFAL's literacy work in Pátzcuaro and sur-
> rounding areas.

705. KASDON, LAWRENCE M., and NORA S. KASDON. "Television: Vehicle
for Literacy Training in Mexico," *Adult Leadership,* 16:3 (September, 1967), 91-92, 124.

> Detailed description of the experiment begun in 1965 in Mexico City
> on closed circuit television and expanded to commercial television
> and radio in 1966. Provides information on course content and first-
> hand observations of the authors. Courses are televised in Mexico
> City, Guadalajara, and Monterrey.

706. KNIGHT, MABEL F. "Educator of the Masses," *Christian Science Monitor Magazine Section,* (September 14, 1946), 7.
Jaime Torres Bodet's role in the literacy campaign as the Minister of Education.

707. "Literacy Campaign," *International Bureau of Education Bulletin,* 21:84 (3rd Quarter, 1947), 114.
Progress report on the second anniversary of the literacy campaign.

708. LOWRY, DENNIS T. "Radio, TV and Literacy in Mexico," *Journal of Broadcasting,* 14 (Spring, 1970), 239-244.
Describes the national radio-television literacy program called "Alfabetización" which began in 1965. Administered by the Secretaría de Educación Pública, it involves approximately 130 radio stations and 12 television stations. Offers a critique of the program.

709. MEXICO. DIRECCIÓN GENERAL DE ALFABETIZACIÓN Y EDUCACIÓN EXTRAESCOLAR. *Salas populares móviles de lectura.* Folletos, 27. México: 1961. 16 pp.
Describes the traveling libraries (part of the Cultural Mission program) which not only provide reading materials but also offer direction in reading in order to broaden the scope of the reader. Project is directed toward the recently literate.

*710. MEXICO. SECRETARÍA DE EDUCACIÓN PÚBLICA. *Campaña nacional contra el analfabetismo; cartilla 1944-1946.* México: 1944. 110 pp.

*711. MEXICO. SECRETARÍA DE EDUCACIÓN PÚBLICA. DIRECCIÓN GENERAL DE ALFABETIZACIÓN Y EDUCACIÓN EXTRAESCOLAR. *Bases de organización para la campaña de alfabetización en los estados y territorios.* Serie Planes, Programas y Orientaciones Técnicas, 1. México: 1956. 15 pp.

*712. MEXICO. SECRETARÍA DE EDUCACIÓN PÚBLICA. DIRECCIÓN GENERAL DE ALFABETIZACIÓN Y EDUCACIÓN EXTRAESCOLAR. *Programas de alfabetización.* Serie Planes, Programas y Orientaciones Técnicas, 2. México: 1956. 17 pp.

713. "Mexico Fights Illiteracy," *Progressive Education,* 23:3 (January, 1946), 102-103.
Description of the "second phase" of Avila Camacho's literacy campaign, the distribution of primers.

714. "Mexico's Literacy Campaign," Pan American Union, *Bulletin,* 80:4 (April, 1946), 234-235.
Progress report on the literacy campaign for 1945.

715. "Mexico's Literacy Campaign," *Modern Mexico,* 17:7 (December, 1944), 3, 32.
   General report of the campaign, mentioning the work of the Indian Institute in preparing material to be used in the campaign.

716. NOEL, JOHN VAYASOUR. "Illiteracy Campaign Well Under Way," *Mexican News Digest,* 1:9 (1945), 12-13, 48.
   Discusses the year-long National Campaign Against Illiteracy decreed in 1944. Primarily focuses on the educational philosophy of Torres Bodet who, as Secretary of Public Education, directed the effort.

717. PACHECO CRUZ, SANTIAGO. *Campaña alfabetizante i la educación indígena en el territorio de Quintana Roo; Bosquejo de la labor.* Chetumal, Quintana Roo: 1956. 61 pp.
   Describes the literary campaign in Quintana Roo.

718. PERAZA MEDINA, FRANCISCO. "La lucha contra el analfabetismo," *Futuro,* 105 (October/November, 1945), 46-47, 59.
   Work of the Campaña Nacional contra el Analfabetismo. The plan originated with each literate person teaching an illiterate but was later expanded to include courses taught by certified instructors.

719. "Progress Toward the Liquidation of Illiteracy in Mexico," *School and Society,* 62:1610 (November 3, 1945), 288.
   Brief progress report on the literacy campaign and projections of future activities.

720. "Results of the Mexican Campaign Against Illiteracy," *International Labour Review,* 55:1/2 (January/February, 1947), 114-115.
   Provides statistics on the literacy campaign from 1944-1946. Also offers some analysis of the results and information regarding the organization of the campaign.

721. "Schools for Illiterates in the Army," Pan American Union, *Bulletin,* 63:2 (February, 1929), 205.
   Brief note on the literacy program in the Mexican army.

722. SCULLY, MICHAEL. "Mexico Gets Down to A-B-C's," *Readers Digest,* 47:283 (November, 1945), 87-90.
   Describes preparation of primers and organization of Avila Camacho's literacy campaign of the 1940s directed by Torres Bodet.

723. "Some Mexican Educational Activities," Pan American Union, *Bulletin,* 82:8 (August, 1948), 475.
   Progress report on the literacy campaign begun in 1944.

*724. SUMMER INSTITUTE OF LINGUISTICS. *Veinticinco años del Instituto Lingüístico de Verano en México, 1935-1960.* México: 1960-1961. 59 pp.

725. VANDERBILT, AMY. "Mexico's ABC's," *Collier's,* 118:24 (December 14, 1946), 86-87, 129, 131.
Tells of the national literacy campaign begun under Avila Camacho and organized by Jaime Torres Bodet. Mentions the use of educational film strips lit by lanterns in the rural campaign. The campaign utilized the Laubach method of "each one, teach one."

726. VANE, ERIK. "Required Reading," *Inter-American,* 4:8 (August, 1945), 12-14, 36-37.
Relates many personal experiences, problems which have arisen, and success achieved in Avila Camacho's literacy campaign based on the Laubach system.

727. "War on Ignorance," *Inter-American,* 3:10 (October, 1944), 5-6.
Further description of the goals and organization of Avila Camacho's literacy campaign.

728. YÁÑEZ, AGUSTÍN. "Balance de la campaña alfabetizadora," *El Libro y el Pueblo,* 6:10 (November, 1965), 8-11.
Reports on the achievements of the literacy campaign begun in 1944. Describes the organization of literacy work in rural areas.

729. ZUBRYN, EMIL. "Mexican Literacy Campaign," *Times Educational Supplement,* 2758 (March 29, 1968), 1087.
Describes radio and television efforts of the Ministry of Education literacy campaign. Pilot project covers the states of Hidalgo, Mexico, Morelos, Puebla, Oaxaca, Tlaxcala, and Veracruz, and the Federal District.

HEALTH, HYGIENE, AND NUTRITION INSTRUCTION

*730. FOOD AND AGRICULTURAL ORGANIZATION. *Report on Home Economics Education at CREFAL and Home Economics Extension Services in Mexico,* by P. H. Dino. Document TA/69/1. N.p.: 1969. 17 pp.

731. "Health Education for Workers in Mexico," Pan American Union, *Bulletin,* 78:6 (June, 1944), 353-354.
New program of health education developed jointly by the Depart-

ment of Public Health and the Department of Labor to take place both in labor centers and in homes.

*732. PINTO, LUIS EMILIO. *La educación sanitaria en un programa piloto de educación fundamental; dos años de experiencia en el Centro Regional de Educación Fundamental para la América Latina.* Pátzcuaro: Centro Regional de Educación Fundamental para la América Latina, 1953. 22 pp.

PROFESSIONAL/PARAPROFESSIONAL TRAINING

733. CORTÉS E., VALENTE. *Programa integral de capacitación en la empresa.* Instituto Tecnológico y de Estudios Superiores de Monterrey; Departamento de Relaciones Industriales; Serie: Monográficos, Cuadernos, 25. Monterrey: 1968. 60 pp.
General discussion of techniques and methods employed and planning of management training courses. Some associations which conduct courses and seminars in Mexico are listed in chapter 5.

*734. MEXICO (STATE). DIRECCIÓN DE AGRICULTURA Y GANADERÍA. *Primer curso de capacitación para orientadores del hogar rural.* Toluca: 1955. 88 pp.

735. MOLINA CÓRDOVA, ARMANDO. "The Struggle Against Illiteracy in Latin America: Concerted Action Against Ignorance in Mexico," *The Student,* Leiden, Netherlands, 8:5 (May, 1964), 6-8.
Report of the Adult Education Training Seminar organized by the Confederación Nacional de Estudiantes de México and the Coordinating Secretariat of National Unions of Students (COSEC) in February, 1964, which laid the foundation for student work in literacy and adult education campaigns in Mexico.

736. REYES SALCIDO, EDGARDO. "A Mexican Experiment in Industrial Education," in *Year Book of Education 1968: Education within Industry.* London: Evans Brothers, 1968, pp. 352-358.
Unique program of worker training sponsored by Fibras Químicas, S.A. in Monterrey. Selected workers are trained for supervisory positions both in the factory at Monterrey and in the cooperating firm in the Netherlands. Program content described and an evaluation of the program is tendered.

VOCATIONAL SKILL TRAINING

737. ALBA, VICTOR. "Mexico: A Country Report," *ILO Panorama,* 16 (January/February, 1966), 16-25.

Vocational training at Industrial Training Centers (CECATI) established under the guidance of the International Labor Organization. Specific courses at the Industrial Productivity Center in Santa Clara near Mexico City described which served as a model for CECATI. In 1965 the program became officially known as the National Vocational Training Service for Industry (Adiestramiento Rápido de la Mano-de-Obra—ARMO).

738. VEZZANI, A. A. "Technical Cooperation," *Industrial Arts and Vocational Education,* 47:4 (April, 1958), 113-119.

Reports on an apprenticeship program (Centro de Adiestramiento de Operadores—CAO) sponsored by the U.S. Technical Assistance Program and administered by Mexico's Ministry of Communications and Public Operations to train operators and mechanics for highway construction and farm equipment.

MISCELLANEOUS

739. BURBANO MARTÍNEZ, HECTOR. *Amerindia: La neuralgia del Nuevo Mundo; génesis y realidades de sus principales problemas económico-sociales.* Pátzcuaro: Centro Regional de Educación Fundamental para la América Latina, 1956. 108 pp.

Chapter 11 offers a critique of the Cultural Mission and pilot fundamental education programs of the Mexican government.

740. CANO, CELERINO. "Panorama de la educación rural," *Educación,* Washington, 3:9 (January/March, 1958), 44-48.

Antecedents to and descriptions of the Cultural Mission program and the Centros de Capacitación (the rural training and literacy centers).

741. CASTILLO LEDÓN, AMALIA. "The Struggle for Literacy and Rural Education in Mexico," in A. Curtis Wilgus, ed., *The Caribbean: Contemporary Education.* Caribbean Conference Series, 10. Gainesville: University of Florida Press, 1960, pp. 242-256.

Includes reports of the Cultural Mission program (with personal anecdotes from an early Mission staff member describing her work) and literacy campaigns, beginning with the campaign of 1944.

742. CORONA M., ENRIQUE. *Al servicio de la escuela popular.* 2d. ed. Biblioteca Pedagógica de Perfeccionamiento Profesional, 14. México: Instituto Federal de Capacitación del Magisterio, 1963. 181 pp.
Chapter 6, entitled "La Educación Extraescolar," contains a lengthy discussion of literacy programs dating back to 1922 and the broad cultural objectives of these programs. Also includes a shorter section on the Cultural Missions.

743. FARÍAS, LUIS M. "La radiodifusión y su aspecto educativo," *Humanitas,* 5 (1964), 593-606.
Calls for the expansion of radio school systems as the best means of disseminating information to all people and of solidifying the revolution. Notes that such schools already exist in Chihuahua, Hidalgo, Oaxaca, and Chiapas. Experimental radio literacy programs have been carried out in the states of Hidalgo, Mexico, and Oaxaca.

744. FUENTE, JULIO DE LA. *Educación, antropología y desarrollo de la comunidad.* Colección de Antropología Social. México: Instituto Nacional Indigenista, 1964. 315 pp.
Collection of essays by the author spanning a period of some twenty years. Speaks from the point of view of an anthropologist, calling for study and understanding of indigenous cultures before implementing programs designed to improve them. Analyzes the successes and failures of several programs directed toward the indigenous population, such as the Cultural Missions, literacy campaigns, programs of the Instituto Nacional Indigenista (e.g., Centros Coordinadores), and the work at CREFAL.

745. GILL, CLARK C. *Education in a Changing Mexico.* Washington: Institute of International Studies, U.S. Office of Education, 1969. 127 pp.
Chapter 8 on literacy and fundamental education covers "nonformal education (*educación extraescolar*)," including literacy training, Cultural Missions, Indian education programs, and agricultural education. Summary sections discuss the literacy campaign initiated in 1944, organization of the Cultural Missions, the training course offered by the Casa del Estudiante Indígena, programs of the Dirección General de Asuntos Indígenas and the Instituto Nacional Indigenista, and agricultural training offered at the Centros de Enseñanza Agropecuaria Fundamental and the Centros de Capacitación para el Trabajo Rural and by the Brigadas de Promoción de Agricultura y Agropecuaria. Very informative report.

746. GONZÁLEZ SALAZAR, GLORIA. *Problemas de la mano de obra en México: Subempleo, requisitos educativos y flexibilidad ocupacional.* México: Instituto de Investigaciones Económicas, Universidad Nacional Autónoma de México, 1971. 222 pp.

Chapter 3, section 2, talks about the short-term vocational training programs available in Mexico, such as the Sistema Nacional de Centros de Capacitación para el Trabajo Industrial y Rural, the Plan Nacional de Adiestramiento Rápido de la Mano-de-Obra (ARMO), and the Instituto Mexicano del Seguro Social. The section is divided into urban and rural programs. In the rural sector important programs are the Centros de Capacitación para el Trabajo Rural, the Brigadas de Promoción Agropecuaria, the Dirección General para el Desarrollo de la Comunidad Rural, and agricultural extension programs.

747. GUZMAN CRUZ, VICENTA. *La trabajadora social colaboradora de las misiones culturales y brigadas indígenas, en la organización y desarollo de las comunidades rurales e indígenas.* México: Escuela de Trabajo Social 'Vasco del Quiroga.' 1965. 50 pp.

Sections devoted to discussion of the origin, organization, and functions of the Brigadas Indígenas and the Cultural Missions. Also talks about work with a Brigada Indígena in Puebla.

748. HOLMES, LULA THOMAS. "Educating Mexican Masses," *Headline Series,* 94 (July/August, 1952), 55-62.

Includes sections on the work of the Cultural Missions, Avila Camacho's campaign against illiteracy begun in 1944, and UNESCO fundamental education projects in Pátzcuaro and Nayarit.

749. LANGROD, WITOLD, ed. *El campo de México: Organismos de desarrollo de la comunidad.* México: Universidad Iberoamérica, 1969. 321 pp.

All major community development projects and their activities are discussed, one by one, from the Cultural Mission program to various student projects. The types of programs discussed run the gamut from literacy training to agricultural extension.

750. LIRA LÓPEZ, SALVADOR, RAMÓN FERNÁNDEZ Y FERNÁNDEZ, and QUINTÍN OLAZCOAYA. *La pobreza rural en México.* México: 1945. 122 pp.

Chapter 2 gives some idea of the educational activities of the rural social service (health and nutrition instruction) and Cultural Missions (by viewing the components of a Mission).

751. MEXICO. DIRECCIÓN GENERAL DE ALFABETIZACIÓN Y EDUCACIÓN

EXTRAESCOLAR. *Informe de labores y nuevos lineamientos, 1944-1955.* México: 1956. 90 pp.

Describes in detail the literacy campaign from 1944 to 1954 and the work of the Cultural Missions, providing financial information for both programs.

*752. MEXICO. INSTITUTO NACIONAL DE LA JUVENTUD MEXICANA. *Centros de capacitación industrial y agrícola.* Ciclo Presidente López Mateos, 57. México: 1963. 54 pp.

753. MEXICO. SECRETARÍA DE EDUCACIÓN PÚBLICA. *Informe para la Tercera Reunión Interamericana de Ministros de Educación.* México: 1963. Various pagination.

Part 1, section 4, gives a detailed discussion of nonformal educational programs in Mexico: literacy campaigns; Centros de Educación Extra-Escolar; Misiones Culturales; Centros de Capacitación Indígena; Brigadas de Mejoramiento Indígena; work of the Instituto Nacional Indigenista; Centros de Enseñanza Agropecuaria Fundamental; Brigadas Móviles de Promoción Agropecuaria; agricultural clubs; Centros Nacionales de Capacitación (apprenticeship program); radio and television programs; Instituto Nacional de la Juventud Mexicana programs.

754. MEXICO. SECRETARÍA DE EDUCACIÓN PÚBLICA. CONSEJO NACIONAL TÉCNICO DE LA EDUCACIÓN. *Educación en el trabajo: Programas de adiestramiento para el trabajo agrícola e industrial.* México: 1963. 230 pp.

Includes a short discourse on the events leading to the creation of the rural and urban, industrial and agricultural training centers—Centros de Capacitación. Provides a program by program description of the training and courses offered in various technical fields.

755. MEXICO. SECRETARÍA DE RECURSOS HIDRÁULICOS. COMISIÓN DEL PAPALOAPÁN. *El Papaloapán, obra del presidente Alemán.* México: 1949. 108 pp.

Contains information about the literacy program, Cultural Missions, and the Brigada Cultural de Asuntos Indígenas in the Papaloapán area.

756. MORIN, RENEE. "Mexican Adults Crave Education," *Food for Thought,* 8:1 (October, 1947), 5-7.

Reports on the literacy campaign, the *"comedores familiares"* program which offers women courses in sewing, hygiene, and nutrition, and adult education programs in rural areas.

757. MYERS, CHARLES NASH. *Education and National Development in Mexico.* Research Report Series, 106. Princeton, New Jersey:

Industrial Relations Section, Department of Economics, Princeton University, 1965. 147 pp.

Chapter 4 provides a general discussion of the goals and organization of the Cultural Mission program during the 1920s and 1930s. Chapter 5, in the section on skilled workers, briefly mentions several avenues for skill training available: the armed forces, which train men in basic mechanical skills; apprenticeship programs required by the government; the program of vocational training sponsored by the Industrial Productivity Center; a new group of worker training schools offering short-term courses.

758. "Recent Educational Measures in Mexico," *International Labour Review*, 50:6 (December, 1944), 763-768.

Describes in some detail the provisions of the literacy campaign. Comments on the national organizational preparation for literacy work. The section on indigenous education notes the establishment of vocational training centers and the work of the Cultural Mission in Jalisco.

759. REYES ROSALES, JOSÉ JERÓNIMO. *Conocimiento y educación de los adultos*. Biblioteca del Maestro Veracruzano. Xalapa: I.F.C.M., 1959. 52 pp.

Includes a description of the literacy campaigns and the Cultural Mission program in the context of adult education. Makes specific proposals for an adult education campaign through the formation of Juntas de Mejoramiento Moral, Cívico y Material and outlines the types of instruction which should be given, concentrating primarily on health and hygiene.

760. SMITH, MARINOBEL. "Mexico's Stepped-Up Education Campaign," *Mexican-American Review*, 33:1 (January, 1965), 19-22.

Discusses, in part, the Misiones Culturales Motorizadas, originally created by Jaime Torres Bodet; each Mission stays a minimum of one year in a community. Also mentions the literacy program initiated by Avila Camacho in 1944 and the on-going work in literacy of the Salas Populares de Lectura.

761. TANNENBAUM, FRANK. *Mexico: The Struggle for Peace and Bread*. New York: Knopf, 1950. 293 pp.

Chapter 10 (on education) notes the literacy campaign begun during the Obregón administration and discusses in some detail the early Cultural Mission program of the same era.

762. THOMPSON, ADIA. "Where Organized Workers Go to College," *Progressive Education*, 25:3 (January, 1948), 24-25.

Describes the Universidad Obrera founded by Vicente Lombardo

Toledano: courses offered at night; open to adult workers; free of tuition; no degrees or grades. Courses run from the practical to the philosophical. The University is also active in the literacy campaign, for which it has created workers' centers.

763. UNITED NATIONS. OFFICE OF PUBLIC INFORMATION. *Acción de las Naciones Unidas en México, 1963.* New York: 1963. 91 pp.
Details U.N.-sponsored activities, including ILO efforts in establishing the vocational training center in Santa Clara, FAO work with the Banco de México in organizing supervised credit programs, and includes a special section on CREFAL.

764. VARELA RECÉNDEZ, SALVADOR. "Aspectos de la educación fundamental en México," Instituto Interamericano del Niño, *Boletín*, 34:2 (June, 1960), 187-196.
Article divided into three sections: the first deals with the functions and activities of the Cultural Missions; the second covers the literacy campaign begun in 1944; the third, and most lengthy, discusses CREFAL, its organization and activities.

765. WATSON, GOODWIN. *Education and Social Welfare in Mexico, 1939.* New York: Council for Pan American Democracy, 1940. 47 pp.
Mentions literacy and skill training efforts of the army and the small contribution of government radio stations to education.

766. WHETTEN, NATHAN L. *Rural Mexico.* Chicago: University of Chicago Press, 1948. 671 pp.
The section on illiteracy in chapter 17 describes the organization of the literacy campaign initiated by Avila Camacho and directed by Jaime Torres Bodet. Chapter 18 is devoted to the rural Cultural Missions, with a detailed account of the organization and activities of one mission in San Pablo in the state of Tlaxcala. This chapter also provides a description of the agricultural demonstration work of the Camohmila Center near Tepoztlán under the sponsorship of the YMCA.

767. ZETTERBERG, HANS L. *Museums and Adult Education.* London: Evelyn, Adams and Mackay, 1968. 89 pp.
Appendix C on adult education in Mexican museums mentions some activities of various museums in Mexico City, notably the museum tours arranged by the Instituto Nacional de Antropología e Historia (INAH) in conjunction with the Centro de Bienestar Social program and the Museo Nacional de Higiene programs for factory workers from trade union organizations.

CONCEPTUALIZATION

768. GONZÁLEZ DÍAZ LOMBARDO, FRANCISCO. "Instituto de Bienestar y Seguridad Social Campesino," Instituto Técnico Administrativo del Trabajo, *Revista,* 17 (May/August, 1962), 5-41.

Elaborate proposal (complete with organization chart) for the creation of the Instituto de Bienestar y Seguridad Social Campesino. Among the projected services would be both formal and nonformal educational programs, the latter including a type of agricultural extension described in the section on agricultural development services.

769. MANRIQUE DE LARA, JUANA. "La biblioteca pública y la educación de los adultos," Mexico, Biblioteca Nacional, *Boletín,* 2a. época, 1:2 (April/June, 1950), 16-27.

Calls for public libraries to take an active role in adult education. Should take on responsibility for providing information by offering specialized courses and literacy training or by having material available on request. Libraries should also serve as information centers where people can find out where other courses might be offered.

770. MEXICO. SECRETARÍA DE EDUCACIÓN PÚBLICA. *Educación en el trabajo: Programas de adiestramiento para el trabajo agrícola e industrial.* México: Consejo Nacional Técnico de la Educación, 1963. 230 pp.

Recognizing the lack of training facilities in the formal school system, this document proposes a system of vocational and agricultural training and an apprenticeship program for youth and adults to supplement it. Bulk of the report is devoted to descriptions of proposed courses for the various areas of training.

771. VICENS, JUAN. "El frente cultural," *Futuro,* 59 (January, 1941), 25-26.

Advocates the creation of workers' (union) libraries as important cultural and educational centers.

Nicaragua

MULTIFACETED PROGRAMS

772. MIÑANO GARCÍA, MAX H. "The Rio Coco Pilot Project in Fundamental Education, Nicaragua," *Fundamental and Adult Education,*
9:2 (April, 1957), 78-85.
Work of a UNESCO-sponsored project in such areas as health education, vocational skill training, civic education, and home improvement instruction. Describes the organization, working methods, intensive training courses for rural teachers, and achievements of the program to date.

*773. NICARAGUA. MINISTERIO DE EDUCACIÓN PÚBLICA. *Nicaragua en el
CREFAL.* Managua: 1955. 23 pp.
Describes the fundamental education project in Rio Coco. (From:
"Fundamental Education: Some Recent Publications," *Education
Abstracts,* 8:7 [September, 1956], 16)

*774. NICARAGUA. MINISTERIO DE EDUCACIÓN PÚBLICA. *Proyecto piloto,
educación fundamental: Informe de las actividades desarrolladas
en el área del proyecto piloto durante el período comprendido
entre el uno de marzo al 31 de julio de 1960.* Managua: 1960.
42 pp.

775. SCHICK, RENE. "Informe sobre el estado de la educación fundamental y de la alfabetización de adultos en Nicaragua," Instituto
Interamericano del Niño, *Boletín,* 35:2 (June, 1961), 85-106.
Report of the Rio Coco fundamental education project. Activities
include health education, literacy training, and agricultural training.

776. WEAVER, ANTHONY JOHN. "An Experience of Educational Theater
in Community Development in Nicaragua," *Community Development Journal,* 5:1 (January, 1970), 44-46.
Describes the work of the British Volunteer Programme in educational
theater in Santa Teresa in a program of community development
through rural educational theater sponsored by the Centro de Investigación y Acción Social (CIAS) of the Universidad Centroamericana
in Managua. Theater techniques are based on those of Alfredo Mendoza Gutiérrez at CREFAL in Mexico.

AGRICULTURAL TRAINING

*777. FOOD AND AGRICULTURAL ORGANIZATION. *Nicaragua: El servicio de extensión agrícola y desarrollo rural; informe al gobierno*, by R. Briceno. Document ESR-UNDP/TA 3115. N.p.: 1972. 21 pp.

BASIC EDUCATION/LITERACY

778. "Nicaragua Fights Illiteracy," Pan American Union, *Bulletin*, 80:5 (May, 1946), 290-291.
Briefly describes the organization of the literacy program begun in 1945.

PROFESSIONAL/PARAPROFESSIONAL TRAINING

779. PIJOAN, MICHEL. "The Miskito Indians: Some Remarks Concerning Their Health and the Lay Health Program," *América Indígena*, 4:4 (October, 1944), 255-263.
Brief description of the training program in health care for selected Miskito Indians at Bilwas-Karma.

Panama

MULTIFACETED PROGRAMS

780. HOOPER, OFELIA. "Rural Panama: Its Needs and Prospects," *Rural Sociology,* 8:3 (September, 1943), 247-253.

    Talks about the Department of Agriculture's rural extension program directed toward improving both the home (through health and nutrition information) and agricultural techniques. The author describes her own extension work from her days of teaching in rural areas.

AGRICULTURAL TRAINING

781. MCKAY, ALBERTO. "Un programa de nutrición del Ministerio de Salud en zonas indígenas de Panamá," *América Indígena,* 32:1 (January/March, 1972), 153-158.

    Describes the project which introduced to Cuna Indian communities new agricultural products and techniques designed to augment the traditional diet with basic nutrients that had been lacking.

HEALTH, HYGIENE, AND NUTRITION INSTRUCTION

*782. PANAMA. MINISTERIO DE TRABAJO, PREVISIÓN SOCIAL Y SALUD PÚBLICA. DEPARTAMENTO DE SALUD PÚBLICA. SECCIÓN DE BIOESTADÍSTICA Y EDUCACIÓN SANITARIA. *'Salud y Bienestar,'* *el radiograma sanitario panameño.* Ciencia y Sanidad: Publicaciones Especiales. Panamá: 1947. 80 pp.

VOCATIONAL SKILL TRAINING

783. PANAMA. SERVICIO COOPERATIVO INTERAMERICANO DE EDUCACIÓN. *A Vocational Occupation Survey: A Study of the Needs of Industry*

for Skilled and Semi-Skilled Workers with Proposals for the Development of the Vocational Education Program in the City of Panama. Publicaciones Serie A, 1. Panamá: 1949. 120 pp.

Fairly lengthy study of the existing vocational education requirements and programs. While supervised by the Ministry of Education, not all programs are part of the formal educational system. Specific information about schools and programs is sketchy, however. Study recommends evening extension courses for workers.

MISCELLANEOUS

784. PAN AMERICAN UNION. DEPARTMENT OF CULTURAL AFFAIRS. DIVISION OF EDUCATION. *Vocational Education in Panama.* Vocational Education, Series N, 16. Washington: 1952. 158 pp.

Chapter 5, dealing with extension programs, mentions several efforts in the area: vocational extension offered by the Escuela de Artes y Oficios for industrial workers, the Escuela Profesional for office workers, and the Colegio Félix Olivares for farmers; agricultural and home economics extension work of the Instituto Nacional de Agricultura in Divisa.

785. "Los trabajos de extensión agrícola y de economía doméstica," *Revista de Agricultura y Comercio,* 6:61 (September, 1946), 20-26.

Describes the work of agricultural and home extension agents in Panama.

Paraguay

MULTIFACETED PROGRAMS

786. FOGEL, GERARDO. "Programa integrado urbano-rural de desarrollo de la comunidad en Encarnación: Itapúa, Paraguay," *Revista Paraguaya de Sociología*, 6:14 (March, 1969), 5-69.

    Primary emphasis of the program is on literacy training. Mentions the literacy centers in Encarnación and Coronel Bogado and the adult education program of the Centro Regional de Educación. Special courses for women are offered in home economics and hair styling.

787. "Las mujeres del campo aprenden algo nuevo," *En Guardia*, 4:12 (July, 1945), 21-23.

    Describes the Centros de Trabajos Domésticos begun in 1944 which offer training in sewing, cooking, nutrition, and child care.

788. "Paraguay's Community Work Center," *Practical Home Economics*, 23:9 (November, 1945), 544, 572, 574.

    Activities of the Centro de Trabajos Domésticos in Capiata, a domestic skill training center established by a North American and a Paraguayan woman in 1944 to offer free instruction to anyone interested in domestic arts, hygiene, child care, nutrition, and literacy.

*789. "STICA Conducts an Agricultural Development Program in Paraguay," U. S. Institute of Inter-American Affairs, Food Supply Division, *Monthly Report*, (July, 1946), 3-11.

VOCATIONAL SKILL TRAINING

790. MAHLMAN, HAROLD E. *Point IV Vocational Education in Paraguay*. Building a Better Hemisphere Series, 25. Washington: Technical Cooperation Administration, Inter-American Regional Office, Institute of Inter-American Affairs, 1953. No pagination.

    Creation (in 1948) and organization of the vocational training school in Asunción sponsored by factory owners for the training of selected employees.

MISCELLANEOUS

791. INTERNATIONAL LABOUR OFFICE. *Informe al gobierno del Paraguay sobre una misión preliminar en el campo del desarrollo rural, con referencia particular a la capacitación campesina y a la organización cooperativa.* Programa de Desarrollo de las Naciones Unidas, Sector Cooperación Técnica; Document ILO/TAP/Paraguay/R.7. Geneva: 1967. 49 pp.

     Brief description of training programs offered both at the professional level and to the peasant population by the Programa de Alimentación y Educación Nutricional (PAEN), the Instituto de Bienestar Rural (IBR), and the Servicio Técnico Interamericano de Cooperación Agrícola (STICA). Also provides a detailed proposal for the formation of the Centro de Capacitación Campesina.

Peru

MULTIFACETED PROGRAMS

792. APARICIO VEGA, GUILLERMO. *Educación fundamental.* Cusco: Editorial Garcilaso, 1955. 259 pp.
   Provides a definition and philosophy of fundamental education and uses the work of the Peruvian *núcleos escolares* as examples of fundamental education–community development projects. The final section of the book is devoted to a description of the *núcleo* system in Peru, the program's history and philosophy. Describes the various activities of each of the specialists assigned to a central *núcleo.*

793. ASTETE MARAVI, LEOPOLDO. "Sello peruanista de los núcleos escolares campesinos," *Nueva Educación*, 9:11:57 (March, 1953), 6-13.
   Account of the development of the *núcleos escolares campesinos*, their basic philosophy, and a brief note of nonformal educational activities.

794. BAUM, JOHN A. *Estudio sobre la educación rural en el Perú: Los núcleos escolares campesinos.* 2d. ed. México: Centro Regional de Ayuda Técnica, Agencia para el Desarrollo Internacional, 1967. 150 pp.
   Describes the history and administration of the *núcleos escolares campesinos* program and devotes individual chapters to detailed discussion of the *núcleos* at Quiquijana and Huarocondo, near Cuzco.

795. BEBBINGTON, PETER C. "The Summer Institute of Linguistics: Rehabilitation Work among 30 Forest Indian Tribes of Peru," *Peruvian Times*, 22:1100 (January 12, 1962), 10-13.
   Good description of the organization and operation of the Summer Institute of Linguistics with emphasis on linguistic work and some comment on health education and agricultural instruction undertaken. Focuses on work with the Piros Indians.

796. BRISTER, WILLIAM C. "Adventure in Cooperation," *Pan American*, 10:1 (April, 1949), 21-24.
   Describes the agricultural and home extension work of the Servicio Cooperativo Interamericano de Producción de Alimentos (SCIPA). Also provides general financial information.

156

797. BURKE, MALCOLM K. " 'SCIPA' in Peru," *Peruvian Times,* 10: 485/486 (April 7/14, 1950), 11-12; 10:487 (April 21, 1950), 18, 20; 10:488 (April 28, 1950), 13-14; 10:489/490 (May 5/12, 1950), 18; 10:491 (May 19, 1950), 13-14; 10:492 (May 26, 1950), 17-18; 10:493 (June 2, 1950), 12-13; 10:497 (June 30, 1950), 7-8; 10: 500/501 (July 21/28, 1950), 14, 16; 10:505 (August 25, 1950), 17-18; 10:507 (September 8, 1950), 12-14; 10:508 (September 15, 1950), 21-22; 10:509 (September 22, 1950), 8, 10; 10:510/511 (September 29/October 6, 1950), 17-18; 10:512 (October 13, 1950), 16; 10:513 (October 20, 1950), 7; 10:514 (October 27, 1950), 15; 10:517 (November 17, 1950), 9-10; 10:519/520 (December 1/8, 1950), 25-26; 10:521 (December 15, 1950), 11, 13; 10:522 (December 22, 1950), 11.

Series of articles describing the work of the Servicio Cooperativo Interamericano de Producción de Alimentos (SCIPA). Very anecdotal and filled with locality descriptions. Places covered include the Iquitos center, Tacna-Moquegua centers, Ica's machinery pools, Cañete, Lima, Huarás and Casma Valleys, Trujillo and Chiclayo, Pacasmayo, Tumbes, Piura, Arequipa, Cuzco, Ayacucho, Huancavelica, Huancayo-Tarma, Huánuco, Cajamarca, and Ancash.

798. CHUECA SOTOMAYOR, CARLOS. "Vicos: Comunidad individualista," *Fanal,* 17:64 (1962), 2-11.

Describes the Peru-Cornell Project in general terms (includes illustrations), with sections devoted to the health and agriculture programs, including the program of supervised agricultural credit.

*799. DAVIGNON, CHARLES A. "A History of the Radio Schools of Peru (at Puno) from 1961 to 1969 and Their Contribution to Present and Future Education in Peru." Unpublished Ph.D. dissertation, Catholic University of America, 1973. 197 numb. leaves.

800. "Developments of the Peru-Cornell Project (1952)," *Boletín Indigenista,* 13:1 (March, 1953), 54-71.

Report includes sections on the historical background, development of the project, initial efforts (primarily in areas of agriculture and health), and research undertaken.

801. DOBYNS, HENRY F., CARLOS MONGE M., and MARIO C. VÁSQUEZ. "A Contagious Experiment: The Vicos Idea Has Spread Throughout Peru," *Peruvian Times,* 22:1146 (November 30, 1962), 15-17.

Discusses the influence of the Vicos project on the surrounding area of the Callejón de Huaylas, as well as on other areas of the country. The authors feel that the Andean Indian Program, the National Plan for

Integration of the Aboriginal Population, and other new programs
have used the successes of Vicos as their models.

*802. DOBYNS, HENRY F., CARLOS MONGE M., and MARIO C. VÁSQUEZ.
"Desarrollo comunal y regional: Experimento conjunto del proyecto 'Peru-Cornell'," *Perú Indígena*, 9:20/21 (January/June,
1961), 133-139.

*803. DOBYNS, HENRY F., PAUL L. DOUGHTY, and HAROLD D. CASSWELL,
eds. *Peasants, Power and Applied Social Change: Vicos as a
Model.* Beverly Hills, California: Sage Publications, 1971. 237 pp.

804. GIBSON, RAYMOND C. *Rural Schools of Peru: Peruvian-North American Cooperative Program in Rural Education.* Studies in Comparative Education, 5. Washington: Division of International Education, U. S. Office of Education, 1955. 23 pp.
Fairly superficial look at the organization of the system of *núcleos
escolares campesinos.* Includes a case study of the Quiquijana school,
an evaluation of and recommendations for the project, and a map showing the locations of the central schools within the system.

805. GILLETTE, ARTHUR. "When 'School' Becomes a Non-Word," *Times
Educational Supplement,* 3100 (October 25, 1974), 14.
Describes formal and nonformal aspects of the new educational system
called the Núcleo Educativo Comunal (NEC). In addition to regular
schooling for children, NECs offer, for example, literacy courses and
cottage industry training to the out-of-school population.

806. GODALL, HAROLD L. "La obra del Instituto Lingüístico de Verano,"
Perú Indígena, 6:14/15 (July, 1957), 175-190.
Reports on the activities of the Summer Institute of Linguistics from
May, 1956 to May, 1957, with emphasis on linguistic-literacy work,
but also including sections on the training course for tribal leaders and
special agricultural training. Ends with projected work for 1957.

*807. HOLMBERG, ALLAN R. "Changing Community Attitudes and Values
in Peru: A Case Study in Guided Change," in Richard N. Adams,
ed., *Social Change in Latin America Today.* New York: Harper,
1960, pp. 63-107.

808. HOLMBERG, ALLAN R. "Folk Hero, Dr. Carlos Monge M., " *Peru-
vian Times,* 22:1146 (November 30, 1962), 15.
General article providing some background information about the
Peru-Cornell Project in Vicos.

809. HOLMBERG, ALLAN R. "Informe sobre el desarrollo del proyecto

Perú-Cornell,'' *Perú Indígena,* 3:7/8 (December, 1952), 237-248; 5:12 (December, 1953), 153-159.

Annual reports of activities undertaken at Vicos.

810. HOLMBERG, ALLAN R., and MARIO C. VÁSQUEZ. ''Un proyecto de antropología aplicada en el Perú,'' Lima, Museo Nacional, *Revista,* 19/20 (1950/1951), 311-320.

Outline of the goals, financing, and plan of action for the Peru-Cornell Project in Vicos.

*811. HOLMBERG, ALLAN R., et al. ''The Transformation of the Political, Legal and Social Systems of Suppressed Peasant Societies: The Vicos Case,'' *American Behavioral Scientist,* 8:7 (March, 1965), 3-33.

812. HUXLEY, MATTHEW, and CORNELL CAPA. *Farewell to Eden.* New York: Harper and Row, 1964. 244 pp.

Discusses, in part, the work of the Summer Institute of Linguistics with the Amahuaca tribe in a jungle outpost called Puesto Veradero and the impact on the tribe of new ideas and techniques. Also talks about work with other tribes in the Peruvian jungle.

813. ''Informe del proyecto Perú-Cornell: 1955,'' *Boletín Indigenista,* 16:2/3 (August, 1956), 202-215.

Section on agriculture and the economy describes programs of instruction and introduction of new methods and technology in agriculture, as well as vocational training available. Ends with projections for 1956.

814. ''Informe sobre el desarrollo del proyecto Perú-Cornell: 1954,'' *Boletín Indigenista,* 15:3 (September, 1955), 274-285.

Comments on specific projects undertaken at Vicos during the year—health education, literacy program, skill training, and agricultural instruction. Article concludes with projections for 1955.

815. ''Intensification of Education among the Indians of Peru,'' Pan American Union, *Bulletin,* 73:11 (November, 1939), 671-672.

Brief description of the new mobile cultural brigades—units designed to take information on ways of improving living conditions to rural areas.

816. ''The Interamerican Cooperative and Food Production Service in Peru,'' *Peruvian Times,* 8:387 (May 21, 1948), 9-10.

Describes the program designed to increase food production through a system of rural extension agents who provide the technical know-how. The program was initiated in 1943, is staffed jointly by Peruvians and

Americans, and is administered by the Institute of Inter-American
Affairs (IIAA). Projects and activities are described, including the
dissemination of nutritional information by the home economics extension section of the program. Includes a list of people involved in the
program.

817. LEAR, JOHN. "The Vicos Project," *Peruvian Times,* 22:1146 (November 30, 1962), 13-14.
General interest article offering some background information about
the project.

818. LLOSA LARRABURE, JAIME. " *'Cooperación Popular'*: A New Approach to Community Development in Peru," *International Labour
Review,* 94:3 (September, 1966), 221-236.
Organization of the new community development program whose
local centers will hold classes in handicraft and vocational training
and training for local leaders, as well as administer specific improvement projects. Student volunteers, both Peruvian and foreign, parti-
pated in the program during the summer months of 1964 and 1965,
teaching agricultural skills and providing health information. Lists
accomplishments.

819. LYLE, JACK. "La Telescuela Popular Americana of Arequipa, Peru,"
in International Institute for Educational Planning, *New Educational Media in Action: Case Studies for Planners.* Paris: United
Nations Educational, Scientific, and Cultural Organization, 1967.
Vol. 2, pp. 77-98.
Description of the educational television station initiated by local
teachers in 1962 to reach the community at large. In 1965 there were
five series being broadcast: (1) kindergarten and transition level instruction for children not enrolled in regular school; (2) primary
education instruction for working adolescents; (3) literacy and fundamental education for adults; (4) community development; (5) broadcasts directed toward housewives for cultural enrichment. TEPA is
heavily influenced by the Catholic church.

820. MENDOZA R., SAMUEL. "Instituto Lingüístico de Verano: Aglutin-
ante nacional," *Revista Militar del Perú,* 62:694 (September/
October, 1966), 87-106.
Relates twenty years of Summer Institute of Linguistics work in the
jungles of Peru, describing literacy training and other educational
activities, particularly in the areas of home improvement and sanita-
tion-nutrition practices.

821. MONGE MEDRANO, CARLOS, and MARIO C. VÁSQUEZ. "Antropo-

logía y medicina," *Perú Indígena*, 6:14/15 (July, 1957), 19-33.
Talks about the changes introduced into Vicos and the success of the
projects. A number of specific projects are mentioned, such as supervised credit and health and nutrition education, with emphasis on the
latter.

822. MONGRUT MUÑOZ, OCTAVIO. "Un plan nacional para el desarrollo
e integración de la población indígena," *Fanal*, 22:81 (1967), 2-9.
Describes the aims and intentions of the new national plan for the
integration of the indigenous population: to be a multilevel, community development program in seven Andean zones.

823. MONTALVO, ABNER SELIM. *Sociocultural Change and Differentiation
in a Rural Peruvian Community: An Analysis in Health Culture.*
Dissertation Series, 5. Ithaca, New York: Latin American Studies
Program, Cornell University, 1967. 184 pp.
Describes the Peru-Cornell Project in general terms, then focuses on
the health education program.

824. MONTALVO, ABNER. "Vicos: experimento antropológico," *Fanal*,
13:51 (1957), 2-7.
Written in general terms, this article provides a résumé of background
information and a picture of Vicos before, during, and after the Peru-
Cornell Project, as well as describing objectives of the program.

825. NÚÑEZ DEL PRADO C., OSCAR. *Un ensayo de integración de la
población campesina: El caso del Kuyo Chico (Cuzco).* Serie:
Estudios del Valle del Urubamba, 2. Lima: Instituto de Estudios
Peruanos, 1970. 156 pp.
Detailed account of the community development program in Kuyo
Chico, which is part of the Plan Nacional de Integración de la Pobla-
ción Aborigen, written by one of the designers of the program. Mod-
eled on the Vicos project, it concentrates on introducing new agri-
cultural methods, nutrition and health instruction, and literacy training.
Difficult to read because of the lack of an index and table of contents.

826. NÚÑEZ DEL PRADO C., OSCAR. "El proyecto de antropología aplicada
del Cuzco," *Revista Universitaria*, 49:119 (2nd Quarter, 1960),
195-224.
Describes the Kuyo Chico project in the Department of Cuzco which is
modeled on both the Peru-Cornell Project in Vicos and the Puno-
Tambopata project of the Andean Mission program. This article provides a detailed account of the program begun in 1955, and its activities, including literacy work, artisan training, agricultural instruction,
and health and nutrition education.

827. O'HARA, HAZEL. "Science and the Indians," *Natural History*, 62:6 (June, 1953), 268-275, 282-283.
Personal account of a visit to Vicos by the author and her impressions of the people and projects.

*828. PALACIOS R., JULIÁN. "Brigadas de culturización indígena," *Educar*, 2a. época, 3:6 (December, 1940), 121-124.

*829. PATCH, RICHARD WILBUR. "Vicos and the Peace Corps: A Failure in Intercultural Communications," American Universities Field Staff, Report Service, *West Coast South America Series*, 11:2 (1964), 8 pp.

830. PERU. PLAN NACIONAL DE INTEGRACIÓN DE LA POBLACIÓN ABORIGEN. *Actividades julio 1964-junio 1965: Tercer informe*. Lima: Ministerio de Trabajo y Asuntos Indígenas, 1965. 132 pp.
Annual report of activities undertaken, area by area.

831. PERU. PLAN NACIONAL DE INTEGRACIÓN DE LA POBLACIÓN ABORIGEN. *Informe: Planteamiento del problema indígena; realizaciones enero 1962-junio 1963*. Lima: Ministerio de Trabajo y Asuntos Indígenas, 1963. 144 pp.
Detailed annual report of activities in each area.

832. PERU. PLAN NACIONAL DE INTEGRACIÓN DE LA POBLACIÓN ABORIGEN. *Proyecto de desarrollo e integración de la población indígena*. Lima: n. d. Various pagination.
Presents detailed plan for the nationally directed community development programs in the rural areas of the Mantaro Valley, Meseta de Bombón, Puno, Sicuani, Andahuaylas, Cangallo, and the Callejón de Huaylas. Activities include agricultural extension, supervised credit, vocational and artisan training, and the training of rural teachers, community leaders, and student volunteers.

833. "La respuesta del gobierno peruano," *Convergence*, 5:1 (1972), 61-65.
Describes the aims of the government for adult education for the period 1971-1975. Educación Básica Laboral (EBL) is directed to those without regular educational opportunities and to those who desire an accelerated learning situation designed to fit individual needs. Other adult education programs include cultural extension and the incorporation of educational opportunities in agrarian reform programs, industrial and fishing centers, and cooperatives.

834. ROMERO, FERNANDO. "New Design for an Old University: San

Cristóbal de Huamanga," *Americas,* 13:12 (December, 1961), 9-16.

Included in this report on the growth of the University in Ayacucho is a comment on the extension work in a project of applied social anthropology in the surrounding rural area.

835. ROSTEN, FRANK. "The Vicos Experiment," *Peruvian Times,* 18:917 (July 11, 1958), 6, 8-9.

Personal observations of the Vicos experiment. In this somewhat ethnocentric article, the author views the introjection of "progressive ideas" such as "establishing competitive spirit" as essential and, at least in part, successful. He also expresses firm ideas about the place Indians should assume, particularly with regard to those who are better educated (some Indians "assume more authority than is their due").

836. SANDELMANN, JOHN C. "Agricultural Extension Work Through the Servicio in Peru," in Howard M. Teaf, Jr., and Peter G. Franck, eds., *Hands Across Frontiers: Case Studies in Technical Cooperation.* Publications of the Netherlands Universities Foundation for International Cooperation. Ithaca, New York: Cornell University Press, 1955, pp. 217-263.

Provides background information about the Institute of Inter-American Affairs (IIAA) and the creation of the Servicio Cooperativo Interamericano de Producción de Alimientos (SCIPA) in 1943. Includes sections on financing and organization. Most of the article, however, is devoted to a description of the principle areas of SCIPA activity: surveying and engineering; services for farmers (including training in the use of machinery and maintenance of demonstration farms); agricultural extension service (which includes nutrition and home management programs); community organization and information (cooperative education, formation of Clubs Agrícolas Juveniles Perú—CAJP). Concludes with an evaluation of the organization and its effectiveness.

837. SCHNEIDER, ROBERT G. "Indian Tongues: A Report on the Summer Institute of Linguistics in Peru—March 1951," *Peruvian Times,* 11:540 (April 27, 1951), 9-10.

Describes all facets of the Institute's work—methods used, tribes with which it has worked, radio and aviation services, and the base at Yarinacocha.

838. SERVICIO COOPERATIVO INTERAMERICANO DE PRODUCCIÓN DE ALIMIENTOS. "Fundamento de nuestra campaña nacional en pro de

los Clubs Agrícolas Juveniles Perú," *Informaciones del SCIPA,*
19 (January, 1950), 28-30.

Describes the organization and programs of agricultural youth clubs,
locally directed by the SCIPA extension agent. Similar to 4-H clubs,
the programs include home and agricultural extension activities.

839. SERVICIO COOPERATIVO INTERAMERICANO DE SALUD PÚBLICA, PERU.
Informe sobre las actividades y programas. Lima: Ministerio de
Salud Pública y Asistencia Social, 1959. 73 pp.

Reports on professional and paraprofessional training programs and
social service work in community development programs.

840. SERVICIO COOPERATIVO INTERAMERICANO DE SALUD PÚBLICA, PERU.
Informe sobre las actividades y programas. Lima: Ministerio de
Salud Pública y Asistencia Social, 1960. 142 pp.

See entry 839.

841. SERVICIO COOPERATIVO PERUANO NORTEAMERICANO DE EDUCACIÓN.
Cartilla de los núcleos escolares rurales. Lima: 1956. No pagination.

Covers the educational tasks of the *núcleos* for the community at large:
literacy training, agricultural extension, vocational training, and the
program of educational films.

842. SMITH, LUCILLE, and MARJORIE BANKS. "Rehabilitation of the Andean Indian—a United Nations Project: Report on a Visit to the
Puno Region in the Highlands of Southern Peru," *Peruvian Times,*
19:984 (October 23, 1959), 6-11.

Report of a visit to the Puno base of the ILO-administered Andean
Mission program, followed by a short article on the program's organization. Comments on the artisan craft center at Vilque Chico, the
Tambopata colonization program, the Chucuito community workshop
where basic skills are taught, the fundamental education center at
Platería, the experimental-demonstration farms, and the Camicachi
community center.

843. SOINIT, ALBERT. "Another Light on the Amazon: A Further Report
on the Ticuna Indian Village of Cushillo Cocha," *Peruvian
Times,* 24:1207 (February 7, 1964), 6-10.

Close look at the results of Summer Institute of Linguistics work with
the Indians at Cushillo Cocha. Discusses the training given to tribal
leaders in medicine and health care and agricultural practices, as well
as literacy training for the community as a whole.

844. "Spanish by Radio in South America," *Times Educational Supplement,* 2606 (April 30, 1965), 1296.

Discusses the radio school and model farm programs of the Maryknoll order in Puno. Radio courses include literacy in Spanish, agricultural instruction, health education, and technical skill training.

845. ST. CLAIR, DAVID. "Yarinacocha," *Peruvian Times*, 18:912 (June 6, 1958), 6, 8, 10; 18:913 (June 13, 1958), 6, 8.
Provides background information about the Summer Institute of Linguistics and describes the activities in literacy work and the training course for native leaders (basic education, health and agricultural instruction).

846. STOWE, LELAND. "Miracle at Vicos," *Peruvian Times*, 23:1169 (May 10, 1963), 9-10.
Remarks drawn from a personal visit to Vicos. Briefly mentions agricultural and health work.

847. SUMMER INSTITUTE OF LINGUISTICS. *Dos lustros entre los selvícolas, 1945-1955*. Lima: G.P.S.A., 1956. 95 pp.
Relates the experiences and activities of the Summer Institute of Linguistics in the Peruvian jungle.

848. TANNER, LOUISE BRANTLEY. "The Forest Indians of Peru and the Work of the Summer Institute of Linguistics," *Peruvian Times*, 17:849 (March 29, 1957), 9-11; 17:850 (April 5, 1957), 11-12, 14; 17:851 (April 12, 1957), 7-8, 10.
Personal account of a five-year period in Peru as part of a Summer Institute of Linguistics team. Describes the literacy work, training course for tribal leaders, and agricultural instruction in the context of a commentary on experiences with various tribes.

*849. TELESCUELA POPULAR AMERICANA. *TEPA memoria: Año escolar 1968*. Arequipa, Perú: 1968. No pagination.

850. THE TIMES, LONDON. "The Radio School of the Maryknoll Fathers in Puno," *Peruvian Times*, 25:1273 (May 14, 1965), 6.
Programming includes literacy training, agricultural information, health courses, and technical skills, as well as a basic education course. The order also maintains a model farm for demonstration purposes and publishes booklets with practical information for distribution among the native population.

851. TINAGEROS GOIZUETA, NICANOR, et al. "Los núcleos escolares campesinos y la campaña de educación rural," *Nueva Educación*, 7:8:46 (December, 1951), 46-57.
Detailed report of the organization, administration, and activities of the system of *núcleos escolares campesinos*.

852. U.S. INSTITUTE OF INTER-AMERICAN AFFAIRS. *Nuclear Schools: A Report on the Programme of Rural Education*. Lima: Division of

Rural Education, Ministry of Public Education, and Servicio Cooperativo Peruano Norteamericano de Educación, 1949. 51 pp.
Brief section describing "social work" of the schools: educational activities extended to the community, usually in the area of agriculture or home improvement or hygiene.

853. VELASCO NÚÑEZ, MANUEL D., and CARLOS D'UGARD. "Instituto Indigenista Peruano: El programa Puno-Tambopata," *Industria Peruana*, 28:318 (November, 1958), 22-30.
Activities of the program are grouped in seven areas, including the following: vocational and artisan training; agricultural training; fundamental education (literacy, basic education, home improvement); and health education (training health workers and fundamental education in health and nutrition).

854. VENEZUELA. COMISIÓN INDIGENISTA. " 'Programa Puno-Tambopata'," *Boletín Indigenista Venezolano*, 6:1/4 (1958), 175-188.
Good résumé of the work of the Andean Mission in Peru. Offers fairly detailed reporting of various activities undertaken, such as agricultural instruction, artisan and vocational training, and health education.

855. "The Vicos Experiment: Rehabilitation of the Andean Indian," *Peruvian Times*, 20:1026 (August 12, 1960), 9-11.
More detail than most *Peruvian Times* articles on Vicos. Gives some concrete examples of agricultural and health instruction projects which are a continuing part of the program.

856. WALKER, FLORENCE G. "Rehabilitation of the Indian in Peru," *Peruvian Times*, 11:575 (December 28, 1951), 8.
Provides background information to the Peru-Cornell Project, such as the process of selection of the area and a description of the Vicos hacienda before the project began. Lists the economic, nutritional, sanitation, educational, and social-recreational aims of the experiment.

857. WALKER, FLORENCE. "Tingo María Agricultural Experiment Station," *Peruvian Times*, 11:525 (January 12, 1951), 7-8.
The principal objective of the experiment station established as a joint effort of the Peruvian Ministry of Agriculture and the U.S. Department of Agriculture in 1942 is to assist colonists in the area. Educational work is carried out by demonstration farms and extension agents. Activities of each department within the station are described in some detail, including work done in the community at large.

858. WARE, CAROLINE F. *Trabajos prácticos en organización y desarrollo de la comunidad.* Washington: Division of Labor and Social Affairs, Pan American Union, 1960. 97 pp.

Includes a detailed description of two short-term community development projects carried out in the *barriadas* of Lima by students of the Escuela de Servicio Social. Several educational activities were initiated, such as an educational film series, a program of health education, lectures on cooperatives and the care of domestic animals, and a course on home economics.

859. WISE, MARY RUTH. "Utilizing Languages of Minority Groups in a Bilingual Experiment in the Amazon Jungle of Peru," *Community Development Journal*, 4:3 (July, 1969), 117-122.

Describes the program initiated in 1952 and administered by the Summer Institute of Linguistics. The program is actually a combination of literacy work and paraprofessional training of tribal leaders.

860. WOOLLEY, GEORGE A. *Boomtown, South America: The Story of Tingo María.* Building a Better Hemisphere Series, 5. Washington: Technical Cooperation Administration, Inter-American Regional Office, Institute of Inter-American Affairs, 1952. 7 pp.

Focuses on the home and agricultural extension work of the agricultural experiment station in Tingo María.

861. ZALVIDEA R., EDMUNDO. "La labor del SCIPA," Facultad de Ciencias Económicas y Comerciales, *Revista*, 39 (July, 1948), 64-75.

General description of the major areas of activity for the Servicio Cooperativo Interamericano de Producción de Alimientos (SCIPA), including extension work and nutrition education.

AGRICULTURAL TRAINING

862. ARMSTRONG, O. K. *When Good Neighbors Get Together.* Washington: Technical Cooperation Administration, Inter-American Regional Office, Institute of Inter-American Affairs, n.d. 3 pp.

Describes the Point Four agricultural assistance programs in Peru directed by the Servicio Cooperativo Interamericano de Producción de Alimientos (SCIPA).

863. ALERS MONTALVO, MANUEL. "Social Systems Analysis of Super-

vised Agricultural Credit in an Andean Community," *Rural Sociology*, 25:1 (March, 1960), 51-64.

Analysis of the first year of operation (1953-1954) of a project in the community of Pucará in the Mantaro Valley. The project is administered by the Extension Service and the Peruvian Agricultural Development Bank. Offers background information, details of the operation, and a sociological analysis of the program.

864. BARACCO GANDOLFO, CARLOS. "La importancia de la extensión rural en la difusión de la técnica agrícola en el Perú," *Informaciones del SCIPA*, 9 (June, 1946), 11-12.

Discusses the activities of the Servicio de Extensión Rural Agrícola since its inception in 1943 and the future of the Service in its educational role.

865. "La cooperación práctica interamericana," *Grace Log*, 24:5 (September/October, 1949), 20-21.

Briefly describes the agricultural extension program sponsored by the Institute for Inter-American Affairs in Peru.

866. "Extension Service Flourishes in Peru," *Extension Service Review*, 17:3 (March, 1946), 42-43.

An optimistic account describing the background and activities of the Servicio de Extensión Agrícola Rural.

*867. FOOD AND AGRICULTURAL ORGANIZATION. *Perú; extensión agrícola—informe al gobierno*, by F. Rojas. Document UNDP/TA 2514. N.p.: 1968. 30 pp.

*868. FOOD AND AGRICULTURAL ORGANIZATION. *Perú; las actividades de extensión agrícola de los programas integrados de nutrición aplicada*, by F. Perlaza Saavedra. Document UNDP/TA 2348; TA/67/8. N.p.: 1967. 18 pp.

869. GUEVARA, LUIS ALFREDO. *Granjas comunales indígenas*. Lima: Empresa Periodística, 1945. 51 pp.

Describes the system of *granjas* initiated throughout the country in 1938 by the Dirección de Asuntos Indígenas to improve methods and production of rural products in indigenous settlements. Involves instruction of the *campesinos* by a type of extension agent.

*870. HIMES, JAMES R. "The Utilization of Research for Development: Two Case Studies in Rural Modernization and Agriculture in Peru." Unpublished Ph.D. dissertation, Princeton University, 1972. 364 numb. leaves.

Analysis of the effects of an agricultural project of the Peru-Cornell

Project in Vicos. (From: *Dissertation Abstracts International,* 33:3 [September, 1972], 873-A)

871. LOOMIS, CHARLES P. "Applied Anthropology in Latin America: Extension Work at Tingo Maria, Peru," *Applied Anthropology,* 3:1 (December, 1943), 18-34.
Describes the areas of concentration for extension agents and the organization of the experiment station and its work. Article is directed toward the future extension agent who might be considering working at Tingo, but nonetheless it gives an idea of the type of work involved.

872. MILLER, RAYMOND W. *Point 4 Builds Strength in the Americas.* Building a Better Hemisphere Series, 19. Washington: Technical Cooperation Administration, Inter-American Regional Office, Institute of Inter-American Affairs, 1952. 7 pp.
Activities of the cooperative agricultural program in Peru since 1943. Comments on the system of rural extension agents throughout the country.

*873. NICHOLS, ANDREW J. *Development of the Peruvian Extension Service.* Washington: Office of Foreign Agricultural Relations, U.S. Department of Agriculture, and Technical Cooperation Administration, Institute of Inter-American Affairs, 1952. No pagination.

874. PAN AMERICAN UNION. Comité Interamericano de Desarrollo Agrícola. *Estudio de educación, investigación y extensión agrícolas, 1967: Perú.* Washington: 1968. 376 pp.
Part 5 is devoted to a description and analysis of the agricultural extension services in the country: the División de Extensión Agrícola of the Servicio de Investigación y Promoción Agraria (SIPA); agricultural extension of other public agencies; and extension services of private organizations.

*875. SERVICIO COOPERATIVO INTERAMERICANO DE PRODUCCIÓN DE ALIMIENTOS. *5 años de actividad del plan de fomento del valle del Mantaro: 1955-1960.* Huancayo, Perú: 1960. 109 pp.

876. SHELLABY, ROBERT K. "SCIPA Means Food," *Americas,* 1:3 (May, 1949), 15-19, 39.
General article discussing SCIPA's activities in agricultural extension.

877. STEIN, WILLIAM W. "Nuevas semillas de papa para Vicos: cambio agrícola en los Andes," *América Indígena,* 31:1 (January, 1971), 50-83.
Report of agricultural innovations introduced by the Peru-Cornell Project at Vicos in 1952-1953.

*878. U.S. Institute of Inter-American Affairs. Food Supply Division. *Agricultural Progress in Peru: A Report of the IIAA-SCIPA Program, 1943-1949.* Washington: 1950. 35 pp.

BASIC EDUCATION/LITERACY

879. "Anniversary of League Against Illiteracy," Pan American Union, *Bulletin,* 64:10 (October, 1930), 1074-1075.
Relates efforts of a private organization founded in 1925 in Lima and Callao which is attempting to eradicate illiteracy.

880. Bazán, Juan Francisco. *La escuela y la comunidad.* 2d ed. Lima: 1964. 145 pp.
Brief section describes the organization of the literacy campaign begun in 1944 and renewed in 1957.

*881. "La campaña nacional de alfabetización," *Revista de Educación,* Lima, 2:1 (March/April, 1944), 121-124.

882. "Las escuelas nocturnas y vespertinas, desarrollarán una labor de alfabetización obligatoria: Necesidad de disposiciones complementarias; escuelas rotativas de tipo popular," *Nueva Educación,* 9:11: 58 (April, 1953), 61-62.
Outlines the new literacy program to be available to all in a system of night schools.

883. Grim, George. "Among the Indians of the Peruvian Amazon Country: The Work of the Summer Institute of Linguistics," *Peruvian Times,* 20:1042 (December 2, 1960), 6-9.
Describes the literacy work of the Institute and the environment in which they work.

*884. Peru. Dirección de Educación Común. *Plan y programa de tipo mínimo para la alfabetización del adolescente y el adulto.* Lima: 1944. 16 pp.

*885. Peru. Dirección de Educación Común. Campaña Nacional de Alfabetización. *Planes y programas de tipo mínimo para las secciones de alfabetización.* Lima: 1944. 16 pp.

886. Rivera Ramírez, Alejandro. "La batalla contra el analfabetismo

en el Perú: Un vasto plan educativo en marcha," *Fanal*, 16:60 (1961), 2-7.

After preliminary background information, the author describes the literacy plan in effect since 1956, which is administered on a national level, often with the collaboration of international and private organizations such as the Andean Mission program, Summer Institute of Linguistics, and the Servicio Cooperativo Peruano Norteamericano de Educación (SECPANE). Also briefly describes the work of the Unidades Móviles de Educación Fundamental.

887. SALAZAR ROMERO, CARLOS. *La realidad educacional del Perú.* Lima: Imp. Lux, 1945. 248 pp.

Chapter 14 deals with the literacy campaign initiated in 1944, giving some figures of enrollment and offering a critique of the program.

888. VÁZQUEZ, MARIO C. *Educación rural en el Callejón de Huaylas, el caso de Vicos: Un punto de vista antropológico.* Investigaciones Sociales; Serie: Monografías Andinas, 4. Lima: Editorial Estudios Andinos, 1965. 184 pp.

Chapter 10 devotes several pages to a description of the literacy training efforts of the Peru-Cornell Project in the evening schools established for that purpose.

*889. VILLANUEVA PINILLOS, ALFONSO. "La campaña de alfabetización," *Peruanidad*, 17 (March/June, 1944), 1131-1134.

HEALTH, HYGIENE, AND NUTRITION INSTRUCTION

890. BURKE, MALCOLM K. " 'SCISP' in Peru," *Peruvian Times*, 11:525 (January 12, 1951), 5; 11:526 (January 19, 1951), 13; 11:527 (January 26, 1951), 3; 11:528/529 (February 2/9, 1951), 7-8; 11:530 (February 16, 1951), 17-18; 11:531 (February 23, 1951), 5-6; 11:532 (March 2, 1951), 17-18.

Describes the educational work of the health center in Chimbote administered by the Servicio Cooperativo Interamericano de Salud Pública (SCISP), including educational films and demonstrations of preventive techniques. Also mentions work at the Tingo María center and at outposts on the Huallaga River.

891. "Program of the Servicio Cooperativo Inter-Americano de Salud

Pública for 1947," *Peruvian Times*, 7:341 (July 4, 1947), 7.
Comments on educational efforts which have been limited largely to
preparation and distribution of pamphlets on critical health problems.

PROFESSIONAL/PARAPROFESSIONAL TRAINING

892. "The Use of Social Promoters at the Puno Base of the Andean Indian
Programme," *International Labour Review*, 86:3 (September,
1962), 247-259.
Outline of training given to indigenous leaders and their role as "social
promoters" within their communities. Three basic types of instruction
are provided: (1) practical, "how-to" approaches to problems; (2) theoretical, meaning basic knowledge in areas of health and hygiene,
literacy, agriculture, and organizing local resources; (3) informational,
regarding public services available to communities and how to work
with them.

VOCATIONAL SKILL TRAINING

893. BARRY, MARION. "United Nations-Peruvian Training Center in
Huancayo," *Peruvian Times*, 24:1234 (August 14, 1964), 11.
Newly established training center offers a wide variety of short-term
skill training for potential instructors, some sent by their employers
in Lima (by means of a selection process by SENATI), others coming
from rural communities needing to develop new small-scale industry.
Courses range from agricultural mechanics to handicrafts to carpentry.

894. BEECK, RODOLFO. "A propósito de la educación técnica industrial,"
Nueva Educación, 18:30:154 (October, 1962), 6-8.
Brief description and analysis of the Servicio Nacional de Aprendizaje
y Trabajo Industrial (SENATI), one of the new approaches being taken
to train workers for an industrializing society. Also mentions vocational training offered to conscripts by the army.

*895. GARRISON, RAY L. *A Survey of the Servicio Nacional de Aprendizaje
y Trabajo, SENATI*. Lima: Technical Assistance Team, Teachers
College, Columbia University, 1968. 29 pp.

896. HARRISON, STEVE. "SENATI, National Apprenticeship and Industrial

Labor Service,'' *Peruvian Times*, 25:1299 (November 12, 1965), 4-5.

Describes the physical plant, financing, and international assistance for the new facility in Lima which will offer a broad range of industrial training courses. Also notes training being carried out in factories in Lima, Callao, Arequipa, and Chimbote.

897. INTERNATIONAL LABOR ORGANIZATION. *Perú: Servicio Nacional de Aprendizaje y Trabajo Industrial (SENATI); descripción y evaluación de los resultados logrados en los centros de capacitación de Chiclayo y Arequipa*. Informe Técnico, 1. Geneva: 1971. 42 pp.

Provides a general description of SENATI and its breakdown into northern and southern zones. Activities in each zone are discussed and the report ends with the conclusions and recommendations of the ILO mission. Appendixes provide some financial and personnel information.

898. ROMERO P., FERNANDO. "Hombres y desarrollo económico," *Fanal*, 19:71 (1964), 2-9.

Thoughtful and well written article on the goals and programs of SENATI.

MISCELLANEOUS

899. ARGUEDAS, JOSÉ MARÍA. "Mesa redonda y seminario de ciencias sociales," *Etnología y Arqueología*, 1:1 (May, 1960), 237-288.

Some discussion of the Vicos (Peru-Cornell) project and the Puno-Tambopata program of the Andean Mission from the point of view of applied social science. A critical account of their effectiveness.

900. BOURQUE, SUSAN CAROLYN. *Cholification and the Campesino: A Study of Three Peruvian Peasant Organizations in the Process of Societal Change*. Dissertation Series, 21. Ithaca, New York: Latin American Studies Program, Cornell University, 1971. 286 pp.

Describes in some detail three organizations whose activities are directed toward peasant education. The Instituto de Educación Rural (IER) is primarily concerned with vocational and agricultural training in centers for men and women throughout the country. The IER also provides training for rural community leaders for community development and administers agricultural extension services. The Asociación de Ligas Peruanas Agrarias de Campesinos de Avanzada (ALPACA) is an organization training for community development administered by Acción Popular and the International Development Corporation. Its courses cover such areas as sanitary education, cooperatives, and agricultural techniques. The Federación Nacional de Campesinos del Perú (FENCAP) is an APRA-sponsored peasant organization which, among many activities, administers short-term training courses in rural areas on such topics as cooperatives, agricultural techniques, and forming local organizations.

901. "Cornell Experiment in Indian Rehabilitation in the Callejón de Huaylas," *Peruvian Times,* 12:609/610 (August 22/29, 1952), 12.
    Background information, description of the hacienda prior to the project, and the goals of the project for the first year (1952-1953). Also discusses agricultural extension activities of SCIPA.

902. EBAUGH, CAMERON D. *Education in Peru.* U.S. Office of Education, Bulletin 1946, no. 3. Washington: Government Printing Office, 1946. 91 pp.
    Brief sections included on the organization of the national literacy campaign and the work of the Brigadas de Culturización.

903. FOOD AND AGRICULTURAL ORGANIZATION and INTERNATIONAL BANK FOR RECONSTRUCTION AND DEVELOPMENT. *The Agricultural Development of Peru: Part II, Detailed Report.* Washington: 1959. 407 pp.
    Chapter 10 on agricultural education, research, and extension offers a critique of the extension services of SCIPA and other organizations (e.g., Banco Agropecuario, Compañía Administradora del Guano, Sociedad Nacional Agraria). Chapter 13 on nutrition recommends a national program of health education through health workers, agricultural extension agents, home demonstration agents, and teachers.

904. FREEBURGER, ADELA R., and CHARLES C. HAUCH. *Education in Peru.* U.S. Office of Education, Bulletin 1964, no. 33; Studies in Comparative Education. Washington: Government Printing Office, 1964. 69 pp.
    Section on illiteracy and adult education programs gives a brief history of literacy programs and various adult education programs, such as the Centros y Talleres Artesanales, Planes de Colonización y Programas de la Población Aborigen, the University of San Cristóbal de Huamanga adult education program, and the Maryknoll radio school in Puno. Brief mention of SENATI in the section on educational centers and services.

905. GALVÁN, LUIS ENRIQUE. "Peru," in *Educational Yearbook, 1942.*

New York: International Institute, Teachers College, Columbia University, 1942, pp. 339-356.
Briefly notes the literacy programs and the work of the Brigadas de Culturización Indígena.

*906. JARA TÁMARA, ABRAHAM F. *Campaña de alfabetización y educación de adultos; informe de 1953-1954.* Lima: Servicio Cooperativo Peruano Norteamericano de Educación, 1965. 13 pp.

907. MONTALVO, EFRAÍN, and JORGE CASTRO HARRISON. "El plan nacional de educación rural," *Educación,* Washington, 3:9 (January/March, 1958), 56-62.
Good description of the rural education system developed in 1952 which includes the literacy program, mobile units, an adult education program, and the nuclear school system.

908. OSORIO, JOSÉ. "Las comunidades indígenas en el Perú y su adaptación al sistema cooperativo," *Informaciones Sociales,* 15:1 (January/March, 1960), 18-42.
Covers general aspects of the Peru-Cornell Project, the Puno-Tambopata project, the Plan Nacional de Integración de las Poblaciones Aborígenes, the Servicio de Extensión Agrícola, and the Programa de Crédito Agrícola Supervisado, all of which work in the areas of fundamental education, agricultural and vocational training, and health and nutrition education.

909. PALMER, DAVID SCOTT. "The U.S. Peace Corps in Peru," *Peruvian Times,* 23:1173 (June 14, 1963), 4-7.
Describes the wide range of Peace Corps activities in Peru—work in Puno and Cuzco with the Plan Nacional de Integración de la Población Aborigen, artisans teaching their skills in rural areas, vocational training in a reformatory in Arequipa, literacy work in Chimbote, home improvement instruction, community development work at Vicos, and vocational training with the Andean Mission program in the Puno area.

910. PAULSTON, ROLLAND G. "Education and Community Development in Peru: Problems at the Cultural Interface," in American Educational Research Association, *Paper and Symposia Abstracts, 1971 Annual Meeting.* Washington: 1971, p. 139.
Provides case studies of the *núcleos escolares,* the Crecer project, the Fe y Alegría movement, and the Peru-Cornell Project.

911. PAULSTON, ROLLAND G. "Maestros como agentes del cambio comunal: Cuatro programas peruanos," *América Indígena,* 30:4 (October, 1970), 929-944.
Examines the programs, problems, and achievements of four programs,

all of which have some nonformal aspects. Fe y Alegría, supported by the Catholic church and begun in 1965, concentrates on work in the *"barriadas urbanas"* of Lima and Arequipa. In addition to a regular school program, it offers vocational instruction and training in community development techniques. Crecer (Campaña para la Reforma Eficaz de las Comunidades Escolares de la República) provides a teacher training program for community development work. The author concludes that this program is largely unsuccessful because it is "interventionist," conceived and directed by a North American staff. Also included are descriptions of the work of the Summer Institute of Linguistics and the *núcleos escolares* system.

912. PAULSTON, ROLLAND G. "The 'Shadow School System' in Peru," in Cole S. Brembeck, and Timothy J. Thompson, eds., *New Strategies for Educational Development: The Cross-Cultural Search for Nonformal Alternatives*. Lexington, Massachusetts: Heath, 1973, pp. 185-194.

Provides a relatively current overview of a broad range of nonformal programs, such as the Servicio Nacional de Aprendizaje y Trabajo Industrial (SENATI), the national industrial training service; programs within the military services, including literacy and basic education, vocational skill training, and cultural assimilation; trade union leadership training at the Peruvian Labor Studies Centers in Lima and Arequipa. Also mentions in passing a wide diversity of other programs: farm extension and land reform courses offered by the Ministry of Agriculture; instruction in literacy, cooperative methods, and community development techniques by the Ministry of Labor and Communities; literacy and adult education programs of the Ministry of Education.

913. PAULSTON, ROLLAND G. *Society, Schools and Progress in Peru*. Oxford: Pergamon Press, 1971. 312 pp.

Chapter 7, entitled "Nonformal Education—the 'Shadow School System'," mentions specifically the programs of SENATI, the military, and the trade unions. See entry 912.

*914. PERU. MINISTERIO DE EDUCACIÓN PÚBLICA. DIRECCIÓN DE EDUCACIÓN PRIMARIA Y DEL ADULTO. *Plan nacional de alfabetización y educación de adultos*. Lima: 1963. 23 pp.

915. PERU. PRESIDENTE. *Mensaje presentado al congreso por el presidente constitucional de la República 1940*. Lima: 1940. 235 pp.

Ministerial reports comment on several nonformal educational programs. The Ministry of Education reports on the literacy campaign. The Ministerio de Fomento y Obras Públicas describes several agricultural extension–demonstration projects. The Ministerio de Salud

Pública, Trabajo y Previsión Social details the efforts of the Brigadas de Culturización Indígena (mostly literacy, but also home extension, health and nutrition education, and civic education).

916. "Programas de integración de las poblaciones aborígenes," *Perú Indígena*, 8:18/19 (January/June, 1959), 209-285.

Describes in detail four community development programs directed toward the indigenous population: the Proyecto de Antropología Aplicada in Cuzco, modeled on the Vicos program; the Junín program; the Peru-Cornell Project in Vicos, with a lengthy description of accomplishments both in the field and in publications; the Andean Mission program directed by the International Labor Organization in Puno-Tambopata. Very informative report.

917. ROMAÑA, JOSÉ M. DE. "La Iglesia en el desarrollo actual del Perú," *Fanal*, 20:73 (1965), 2-8.

Comments on the Escuelas Radiofónicas of the Maryknolls in Puno, literacy training in Lima and Cuzco, family education centers in Lima, and vocational training in Puno.

918. U.S. DEPARTMENT OF HEALTH, EDUCATION AND WELFARE. *Educación fundamental*. Lima: Servicio Cooperativo Peruano Norteamericano de Educación, 1959. No pagination.

Devoted principally to defining fundamental education and discussing the socioeconomic significance of illiteracy. It does include, however, a brief listing of organizations and programs active in the area of fundamental education, such as the Andean Mission program, the Peru-Cornell Project, and the Servicio Cooperativo Peruano Norteamericano de Educación (SECPANE).

919. VÁSQUEZ, EMILIO. "Trayectoría de la educación rural en el Perú," *Nueva Educación*, 4:4:19 (January/February, 1949), 13-20.

Describes several programs of nonformal education (the Brigadas de Culturización, *escuelas rurales experimentales*, and the *núcleo escolar* of Titicaca) and offers an analysis and critique of these efforts.

CONCEPTUALIZATION

920. BARRANTES, EMILIO. "Conceptos fundamentales sobre la educación del indio," *Nueva Educación*, 2:1:4 (July/August, 1946), 32-35.

Education must be thought of in the broadest of terms, not confined solely to schools, and educational planning must take this broad meaning into account.

921. CORNEHLS, JAMES V. "Forecasting Manpower and Education Requirements for Economic and Social Development in Peru," *Comparative Education Review,* 12:1 (February, 1968), 1-27.
Specifically states that educational planning is not restricted to the formal education system, but that it includes "special institutions and on-the-job training programs," such as SENATI, agricultural extension services, and the army. While dealing more with the problems of effective educational planning in Peru, there is a basic assumption that nonformal education is included in the larger educational frame of reference.

922. OPPER, C. G. "Cómo se lleva a cabo una campaña de educación fundamental," *Nueva Educación,* 7:7:39 (May, 1951), 26-29.
Talks about various types of fundamental education programs and how they can be effective in educating the population outside of school.

923. ROMERO, FERNANDO. *La industria peruana y sus obreros: Análisis de la necesidad económica de obreros calificados que se experimentará en el período 1955/65 y forma de satisfacerla.* Lima: Imprenta del Politécnico Nacional 'José Pardo', 1958. 74 pp.
Proposes a national apprenticeship service (chapter 4) based on the models in Brazil and Colombia. Industry must be willing to participate because the formal education system is incapable of producing sufficient numbers of qualified technicians. Chapter 5 deals with the advantages of such a system.

924. SACO, ALFREDO. *Programa agrario del aprismo.* Lima: Edición Populares, 1946. 63 pp.
Calls for the creation of mobile missions to reach the rural population and instruct them in modern agricultural techniques. Schools are not sufficient.

925. UNITED NATIONS. TECHNICAL ASSISTANCE ADMINISTRATION. *Report of an Exploratory Mission of the United Nations on the Economic and Social Development of the Department of Cuzco (Peru).* Document ST/TAA/K/Peru/1. New York: 1952. 18 pp.
Specifically recommends a supervised credit program as the only reasonable way of wedding education and adequate credit given the conditions of a rural area where educational facilities are either lacking or do not satisfy the needs of the rural agricultural population.

Puerto Rico

MULTIFACETED PROGRAMS

926. HOLSINGER, JUSTUS G. *Serving Rural Puerto Rico: A History of Eight Years of Service by the Mennonite Church.* Scottdale, Pennsylvania: Mennonite Publishing House, 1952. 231 pp.
  Describes the educational activities of the Mennonite Mission in La Plata since 1943. Included are the nurse-aide training course offered through the hospital; educational film series; public programs of instruction in the English language and literature; organization of 4-H clubs; sewing classes for women; nutrition education program; craft instruction; agricultural education program.

927. ISALES, CARMEN, and FRED G. WALE. "The Field Program of the Puerto Rican Division of Community Education," in Lyle W. Shannon, ed., *Underdeveloped Areas: A Book of Readings and Research.* New York: Harper, 1957, pp. 350-360.
  Personal account of the selection and training process and the work of rural community leaders in the program of community development.

928. PÉREZ YACOMOTTI, NÉLIDA. "Puerto Rico y educación de la comunidad," *Revista de Educación,* La Plata, 5:7/8 (July/August, 1960), 504-506.
  Brief account of the Community Education program, administered by the Department of Public Instruction, which trains rural organizers and provides educational material for use in community meetings.

*929. PUERTO RICO. CONGRESO. CÁMARA DE REPRESENTANTES. *Un programa de educación de la comunidad en Puerto Rico. Community Education Program in Puerto Rico.* New York: International Division, Radio Corporation of America, 1956. 24 pp.

*930. PUERTO RICO. DIVISIÓN DE EDUCACIÓN DE LA COMUNIDAD. *The Work of the Division of Community Education from the Time of the Passage of the Law May 14, 1949 to Present.* San Juan: 1951. 56 pp.

931. WALE, FRED G. "Community Education in Puerto Rico," in U.S. Office of Education, *Education for Better Living.* Bulletin 1956, no. 9. Washington: 1957, pp. 25-45.
  Describes the work of the Division of Community Education and gives

some examples of the kinds of activities undertaken by the program. This adult education–community development project offers instruction in vocational, agricultural, and domestic skills and health and nutrition education. It also includes a training program for rural leaders.

932. WARE, CAROLINE F. *Iniciativa de un pueblo: Ayuda mutua en Puerto Rico.* Serie sobre Organización de la Comunidad, 5. Washington: División de Trabajo y Asuntos Sociales, Unión Panamericana, 1953. No pagination.
Personal account of the activities of the Programa de Educación de la Comunidad of the Division of Community Education.

933. ZALDUONDO, CELESTINA. "A Family Planning Program Using Volunteers as Health Educators," *American Journal of Public Health and the Nation's Health,* 54:2 (February, 1964), 301-307.
Describes, in part, the educational program of the Family Planning Association which involves training of local volunteer leaders by area supervisors as well as dissemination of information regarding birth control and contraceptive devices.

AGRICULTURAL TRAINING

934. PUERTO RICO. COMMONWEALTH BOARD FOR VOCATIONAL EDUCATION. *Vocational Education in Puerto Rico.* San Juan: 1940. 64 pp.
Covers the programs for out-of-school farm workers in agricultural education—short-term extension courses, part-time and in the evening.

935. TONKIN, JOSEPH D. "Puerto Rico's Farm Radio Program," *Foreign Agriculture,* 13:1 (January, 1949), 19-20.
The cooperative Extension Service's daily broadcast, "Actualidad Agrícola," is directed toward the farm population with instruction in agricultural techniques.

936. VÁZQUEZ CALCERRADA, P. B. *The Study of a Planned Rural Community in Puerto Rico.* Agricultural Experiment Station, Rio Piedras, Bulletin, 109. Rio Piedras: Agricultural Experiment Station, University of Puerto Rico, 1953. 84 pp.
Describes the efforts of the Puerto Rico Reconstruction Administration

(PRRA) in a particular resettlement project at Castañer. One of the services provided is agricultural extension, whose primary activities center around the formation of cooperatives.

BASIC EDUCATION/LITERACY

937. "Puerto Rico Fights Illiteracy," *Caribbean,* 10:3 (October, 1956), 51-56; 10:5 (December, 1956), 142-145.
Lengthy discussion of the administration, content, and methodology of the literacy program begun in 1953.

*938. VILLARONGA, MARIANO. *El programa de alfabetización de Puerto Rico.* San Juan: Editorial del Departamento de Instrucción Pública, 1956. 17 pp.

COOPERATIVE EDUCATION

939. LUGO DE SENDRA, CLARA. "Co-operative Education in Puerto Rico," *Caribbean Commission,* 4:11 (June, 1951), 813-817.
Discusses, in part, the program of cooperative education created by the Land Authority in 1946 and administered by the Social Programs Administration of the Department of Agriculture and Commerce. The program is directed toward the rural peasant population for the purpose of developing cooperatives and offering instruction in basic cooperative philosophy and organization. One phase is a small industries program which trains peasants for organization into industrial cooperative associations. Also mentions the educational work of such existing cooperatives as the Tobacco Marketing Association (which gives special training to members and sponsors educational radio programs) and the Lafayette Cooperative Sugar Association.

CULTURAL EXTENSION

940. ATKINSON, CARROLL. "Radio as a Tool of Education in Puerto Rico,"

Modern Language Journal, 26:1 (January, 1942), 21-22.
The Escuela del Aire de Puerto Rico broadcasts programs of general cultural interest (music, literature, English language instruction) directed toward the rural population.

HEALTH, HYGIENE, AND NUTRITION INSTRUCTION

941. LUBE, CATALINA, and ANGELES CEBELLERO. "Puerto Rico Launches an Island-Wide Program of Health Education," *High School Journal,* 30:3 (May, 1947), 129-130.
Creation of community health centers administered by the Department of Health which arrange lectures and films on various health problems and sponsor a series of radio programs.

PROFESSIONAL/PARAPROFESSIONAL TRAINING

942. PUERTO RICO. DEPARTMENT OF EDUCATION. DIVISION OF COMMUNITY EDUCATION. *Community Education in Puerto Rico.* Occasional Papers in Education, 14. Paris: Education Clearing House, United Nations Educational, Scientific, and Cultural Organization, 1952. 25 pp.
Includes a good description of the Division's three-month training program for community organizers. Covers the period from July, 1949 to October, 1951.

VOCATIONAL SKILL TRAINING

943. OTERO, JORGE. "La educación y la industrialización de Puerto Rico," Hato Rey, Asociación de Maestros, *Revista,* 12:4 (August, 1953), 125, 129.
Describes the special vocational training courses for workers initiated by the División de Instrucción Vocacional outside of the regular vocational schools.

MISCELLANEOUS

944. BOURNE, DOROTHY DULLES, and JAMES R. BOURNE. *Thirty Years of Change in Puerto Rico: A Case Study of Ten Selected Rural Areas.* Praeger Special Studies in International Economics and Development. New York: Praeger, 1966. 411 pp.

Chapter 4 on government agency programs includes: (1) the Community Education program, designed to broaden basic cultural knowledge by means of radio, film, pamphlets, and lectures and to train selected community leaders in organizational techniques; (2) the Commission for Improvement of Isolated Communities' rural nutrition education program carried out by home economists and agronomists living in selected communities.

945. JIMÉNEZ MALARET, RENÉ. "Síntesis de los trabajos realizados en Puerto Rico por la División de Rehabilitación Rural de la PRRA," *Revista de Agricultura, Industria y Comercio de Puerto Rico,* 31:4 (December, 1939), 532-538; 32:2 (April/June, 1940), 207-215.

Activities of the Puerto Rican Reconstruction Administration and its rural rehabilitation program (agrarian reform). Efforts include literacy training and agricultural and home extension as part of rural reform.

946. KIDD, J. R. "Renaissance in Puerto Rico," *Food for Thought,* 19:4 (January, 1959), 156-160.

Briefly discusses a variety of programs in literacy training, agricultural extension, and community development.

947. RODRÍGUEZ BOU, ISMAEL. *Educación de adultos (orientaciones y técnicas).* Publicaciones Pedagógicas, Serie 2, 13. Rio Piedras: Consejo Superior de Enseñanza, Universidad de Puerto Rico, 1952. 365 pp.

Part 2 presents a thorough description of various adult education projects including: commercial and vocational instruction; agricultural extension service; workers' education courses of the Departamento de Trabajo; apprenticeship programs; health and sanitation instruction offered by the Oficina de Salud; cooperative education program of the Departamento de Agricultura y Comercio; home education program of the Administración del Hogar del Agricultor; Community Education program.

948. STEAD, WILLIAM H. *Fomento: The Economic Development of Puerto*

Rico. Planning Pamphlet, 103. Washington: National Planning
Association, 1958. 151 pp.

> Briefly mentions vocational and professional training programs organ-
> ized in various governmental departments in conjunction with the
> Economic Development Administration. As examples: an "accelerated
> program" of the Department of Education for training for new indus-
> tries in specially equipped centers or by in-plant training; the Admin-
> istration's Department of Industrial Services program to assist new
> manufacturing firms in training supervisory and managerial personnel.

CONCEPTUALIZATION

949. GONZÁLEZ DE DÁVILA, CECELIA. "A Proposal for Community Education in Selected Resettlements in Puerto Rico." Unpublished
thesis, New York University, 1955. 224 numb. leaves.

> Proposes a rural community education program to assist in resettlement
> areas. Included would be instruction in health, sanitation, nutrition,
> agricultural techniques, home improvement, and literacy through the
> use of film, radio, pamphlets, discussion, demonstration, study groups,
> and libraries. Report includes community studies for nine resettlement
> areas.

Trinidad and Tobago

HEALTH, HYGIENE, AND NUTRITION INSTRUCTION

950. MOOSAI MAHARJI, S. "Health Education in the West Indies," *Health Education Journal,* 8:1 (January, 1950), 31-35.

Health information is disseminated to the population by volunteer workers and health educators through special community classes, pamphlets, films, and mass meetings.

MISCELLANEOUS

951. RISKE, ROGER, and VAL D. RUST., "Nonformal Education and the Labor Force in Port of Spain, Trinidad," in Thomas J. La Belle, ed., *Educational Alternatives in Latin America: Social Change and Social Stratification.* Latin American Studies Series, 30. Los Angeles: Latin American Center, University of California, 1975, pp. 293-333.

Describes a number of nonformal training programs in the country. Corporate-sponsored training schemes include those of the Trinidad and Tobago Telephone Company and the Management and Productivity Center, both on the professional level. Also describes the government youth camp program which offers training in agricultural, livestock, crafts, and industrial skills and the government-sponsored Community Centers which concentrate on practical training in civics, practical teaching of home economics and budgeting, and some handicraft instruction. Briefer descriptions of Community Education Center programs of adult education and skill training, the Adult Education program, and the Population Council's family planning clinics are included.

Uruguay

MULTIFACETED PROGRAMS

952. BOLÍVAR LÓPEZ, LUIS. "Desarrollo de comunidades en Paguero," Consejo Nacional de Enseñanza Primaria y Normal, *Anales,* 29:7/ 12 (July/December, 1965), 26-35.
Community development program in Artigas in 1964 which was under the sponsorship of the Centro de Misiones Sociopedagógicas de Artigas. Activities include agricultural education, literacy training, and health education administered by a team of specialists.

953. ROLFO, FEDERICO. "El Movimiento de la Juventud Agraria en el Uruguay," Instituto Interamericano del Niño, *Boletín,* 41:163 (December, 1967), 486-490.
Reports on the educational activities begun in 1945 of the Movimiento (a private organization) through its Clubes Agrarios Juveniles. Concentrates on agricultural and domestic skill instruction and a program of supervised credit for farmers. Describes the organization and its financial and technical support.

BASIC EDUCATION/LITERACY

954. ABADIE SORIANO, ROBERTO. "La campaña de alfabetización en el Uruguay," Consejo Nacional de Enseñanza Primaria y Normal, *Anales,* 21:10/12 (October/December, 1958), 211-220.
Detailed description of the organization and administration of the literacy and fundamental education campaign begun in 1954. Mentions the UNESCO technical and financial contributions. Calls for the creation of literacy and fundamental education centers throughout the country.

955. ABADIE SORIANO, ROBERTO. "The Literacy Campaign in Uruguay," *Fundamental and Adult Education,* 10:1 (1958), 11-15.
Describes the plans for the literacy and fundamental education campaign which is to be carried out in special centers in villages and rural areas. Methods will include both book and audio-visual instruction.

956. Puig, José Pedro. "El teatro de Humberto Zarrilli en la educación de adultos," *Anales de Instrucción Primaria,* 13:3 (March, 1950), 123-126.

    Briefly describes the use of and reception to dramatic presentations in the evening adult schools in Montevideo.

957. Radio Escuela (Radio Program). *Radio Escuela: Radiotelefonía educativa en el Uruguay, 1931-1941.* Montevideo: Casa A. Barreiro y Ramos, 1941. 60 pp.

    Year-by-year outline of educational radio programming, ranging from literature to hygiene.

958. "Uruguay Makes Intensive Campaign Against Illiteracy," Pan American Union, *Bulletin,* 63:4 (April, 1929), 355-358.

    Brief description of the literacy campaign.

HEALTH, HYGIENE, AND NUTRITION INSTRUCTION

959. "Public Health and Social Welfare," Pan American Union, *Bulletin,* 66:3 (March, 1932), 222.

    Notes the active health education program of the Office of Health Education of the National Council of Hygiene, which utilizes radio broadcasts as the primary medium of instruction.

CONCEPTUALIZATION

960. Páez Formoso, Miguel A. *El drama campesino: El Partido Agrario en el Uruguay.* Montevideo: Prometeo, 1951. 111 pp.

    Sees the need for educational programs outside of school, especially in rural areas where schools are inadequate in quantity and quality. Also calls for broad health education and literacy campaigns.

Venezuela

MULTIFACETED PROGRAMS

961. BETHENCOURT R., OMAR J., and T. S. NICOLETTA SOLINAS. "Algunas consideraciones generales entre educación familiar y la salud pública," Universidad del Zulia, *Revista*, 4:18 (April/June, 1962), 203-215.

> Relates the activities of the Centros de Educación y Desarrollo de la Comunidad in Caracas which are under the direction of the Consejo Venezolano del Niño. Educational efforts include instruction in home economics, sewing, nutrition, and literacy.

962. "Better Ways of Country Living Shown by CBR," *Venezuela Up-to-Date*, 3:8 (July/August, 1952), 8-9, 15.

> General discussion of the organization and programs of the Consejo de Bienestar Rural (CBR). Supervised credit, home and agricultural extension, and community services are the primary areas of work.

963. BRADY, JERRY. "Old Barrios Make New Communities," *Overseas*, 2:6 (February, 1963), 4-9.

> Work of the American-based community development agency ACCION (affiliated with the Institute of International Education) whose efforts have been concentrated in urban areas of Venezuela. Activities include the organization of adult education and vocational training courses.

964. CHESTERFIELD, RAY A., and KENNETH R. RUDDLE. "Nondeliberate Education: Venezuelan Campesino Perceptions of Extension Agents and Their Message," in Thomas J. La Belle, ed., *Educational Alternatives in Latin America: Social Change and Social Stratification*. Latin American Studies Series, 30. Los Angeles: Latin American Center, University of California, 1975, pp. 149-168.

> Evaluates the effectiveness of extension agents and a home demonstrator in transmitting information in an extension program on the Isla de Guara by examining the process of interaction between agent and

campesino. Provides a brief history of extension education in the country from its inception in the 1930s.

965. "Notes on the Venezuelan Illiteracy Campaign for 1949-1950," *Foreign Education Digest,* 17:3 (January/March, 1953), 286-287.
Achievements of the centers of popular culture and mobile units in the literacy campaign. In addition to literacy training, the cultural centers provide apprenticeship and vocational skill training.

*966. ROMERO O., EDDIE J. "Desarrollo de la comunidad," *Boletín Indigenista Venezolano,* 12/15:1/4 (May, 1968), 59-67.
Describes the community development project in the Guajira. (From: Pan American Union. Columbus Memorial Library. *Index to Latin American Periodicals: Humanities and Social Sciences.* Vol. 8, 1968. Metuchen, New Jersey: Scarecrow Press, 1970, p. 97)

*967. ROMERO O., EDDIE J., and MANUEL DRUCKER. "Proyecto La Guajira, guía de trabajo," *Boletín Indigenista Venezolano,* 10:1/4 (1966), 81-130.

*968. VENEZUELA. COMISIÓN INDIGENISTA. "Proyecto del programa de educación fundamental por desarrollarse en la Guajira venezolana," *Boletín Indigenista Venezolano,* 6:1/4 (1958), 36-61.

969. VENEZUELA. CONSEJO DE BIENESTAR RURAL. *Consejo de Bienestar Rural, 25 años, 1948-1973.* Caracas: 1973. 64 pp.
Glowing account of the growth of CBR and its wide range of activities, including supervised credit programs, home demonstration, agricultural extension, professional training, demonstration farms, rural youth clubs, training program in agricultural mechanics, cooperative education, and mobile agricultural training units.

970. VENEZUELA. CONSEJO DE BIENESTAR RURAL. *Informe anual, 1951-1952.* Caracas: 1952. No pagination.
Describes extension activities (health, home improvement, farming techniques) and activities of the program of supervised credit, which also offers instruction and training in agricultural methods.

971. "Venezuela: A National Literacy Project," *UNESCO Chronicle,* 12:9 (September, 1966), 334-337.
Organization and achievements of the literacy program begun in 1958 and a discussion of the proposed expansion of the program, which seeks to combine literacy with vocational training. The program is to be administered jointly by several government departments. Pilot areas have been designated in the states of Bolívar, Portuguesa, and Lara.

AGRICULTURAL TRAINING

972. CAMP, JOHN R. *Agricultural Development in Venezuela: Report of the SCIPA, 1943-1946.* Washington: Food Supply Division, Institute of Inter-American Affairs, 1946. 93 pp.

    In the section of general observations several rural nonformal educational efforts are mentioned, including the Escuela Práctica de Agricultura in Maracay which was established in 1942 and is devoted to short-term practical courses for adults. Activities of the Servicio Cooperativo Interamericano de Producción de Alimentos (SCIPA) in the Chirgua, Montalbán, and Miranda areas are discussed, as well as efforts in other areas.

*973. CROY, OTTO C. *Análisis del progreso logrado en la extensión agrícola en Venezuela.* Caracas: Consejo de Bienestar Rural, 1959. No pagination.

*974. LEPAGE BARRETO, RAMÓN. *An Evaluation of Extension's Impact in Three Venezuelan Communities.* Turrialba, Costa Rica: Instituto Interamericano de Ciencias Agrícolas, 1963. 121 pp.

*975. MARTÍNEZ SALAS, ANTONIO, SONIA CASTILLO TRUJILLO, and MERCEDES FORNOZA DE RINCÓN. *Evaluación del servicio de extensión de Venezuela: Estructura.* Caracas: Dirección de Extensión, Ministerio de Agricultura y Cria, 1966. 180 pp.

976. VENEZUELA. INSTITUTO NACIONAL DE COOPERACIÓN EDUCATIVA. *Centro Nacional de Formación de Agricultores, San Carlos— Estado Cojedes.* Caracas: n.d. 12 pp.

    Describes the INCE apprenticeship-training center and programs in the field of agriculture.

BASIC EDUCATION/LITERACY

977. ADAM, FÉLIX. "La alfabetización en el medio rural," *Educación,* Caracas, 26:113 (December, 1964), 35-46.

    Includes analysis of the national literacy campaign begun in 1958, with reference to problems in rural areas. Article ends with a number of recommendations, among which is that future literacy programs should have priority in urban areas.

978. CARRUTHERS, BEN FREDERIC. "Venezuela Tries Intensive Literacy Experiment," *School and Society*, 67:1726 (January 24, 1948), 61-62.
Basic education and literacy program in the state of Aragua during the summer months of 1948.

979. "Development of Adult Education," *International Bureau of Education Bulletin*, 26:105 (4th Quarter, 1952), 164.
Comments on plans to expand the literacy campaign by providing more mobile units.

980. "En dos años han sido alfabetizadas más de noventa mil personas," *Farol*, 10:118 (March, 1949), 16-19.
Describes the work begun in 1944 by the Oficina Nacional de Alfabetización y Cultura Popular and the Patronato Nacional de Alfabetización. Campaigns utilize drama presentations.

981. LLOVERA LL., B. "El obrero en la escuela," *Revista de Educación Obrera*, 1:1 (March, 1940), 21-23.
Literacy campaign in government sponsored workers' schools.

982. MEDINA, JOSÉ RAMÓN. "Alfabetización y cultura popular," *Educación*, Caracas, 8/9:50/52 (August, 1947/January, 1948), 81-86.
Discusses problems encountered in the Campaña de Alfabetización y Cultura Popular, drawing from experiences of the campaign in Aragua. Deals in particular with incorporating the recently literate into the national culture.

983. MONTESINOS, ROBERTO. "Construir y educar," *Revista de Educación Obrera*, 1:2 (May, 1940), 13-14.
Describes the adult education classes (literacy and mathematics) in the workers' schools sponsored by the government.

984. "La nueva organización de la campaña nacional de alfabetización," *Educación*, Caracas, 10:59 (April/May, 1949), 76-78.
Discusses the reorganization and centralization of the literacy campaign. Also comments on the state of the campaign in Yaracuy and on the use of mobile library units in conjunction with the campaign.

*985. OFICINA DE EDUCACIÓN IBEROAMERICANA. *Informe sobre la alfabetización y educación popular de adultos en Venezuela*. Madrid: 1965. 17 pp.

986. THORNTON, BASIL. "Signals Across Venezuela," *Overseas*, 1:3 (November, 1961), 8-11.
Experiment in educational television in Caracas. Some programs are

directed toward young people and women, offering practical advice as well as attempting to instruct in national customs, folklore, and history. Viewing centers have been established in poorer areas of the city. The project is funded by the Creole Foundation.

987. VENEZUELA. EMBASSY. U.S. "War on Illiteracy Waged by Modern Organization," *Venezuela Up-to-Date,* 3:8 (July/August, 1952), 10-11.

> Describes the literacy and basic education program and its organization into five cooperating agencies—collective literacy centers, popular culture centers, mobile units, traveling libraries, and the Bureau of Literacy and Popular Culture.

988. VENEZUELA. INSTITUTO NACIONAL DE COOPERACIÓN EDUCATIVA. *Alfabetización y extensión cultural en las empresas.* Caracas: 1967. 16 pp.

> Program of literacy training and cultural extension courses in places of work (*empresas*) which are sponsored by INCE. Extension courses focus on language, mathematics, social studies, natural sciences, and drawing.

*989. VENEZUELA. MINISTERIO DE EDUCACIÓN NACIONAL. OFICINA DE ALFABETIZACIÓN Y CULTURA POPULAR. *Plan general de la campaña nacional de alfabetización y cultura popular durante el año 1949-1950.* Caracas: 1949. 65 pp.

*990. VENEZUELA. OFICINA DE ALFABETIZACIÓN Y CULTURA POPULAR DEL ESTADO DE ARAGUA. *Bases y organización de la campaña experimental de alfabetización y cultura popular en el estado de Aragua.* Caracas: 1947. 22 pp.

*991. VENEZUELA. OFICINA DE ALFABETIZACIÓN Y CULTURA POPULAR DEL ESTADO DE NUEVA ESPARTA. *Bases y organización de la campaña de alfabetización y cultura popular en el estado de Nueva Esparta.* Caracas: Editorial Bolívar, 1948. 22 pp.

*992. VENEZUELA. OFICINA DE ALFABETIZACIÓN Y CULTURA POPULAR DEL ESTADO YARACUY. *Bases y organización de la campaña intensiva de alfabetización y cultura popular en el estado de Yaracuy.* Caracas: Editorial Bolívar, 1958. 23 pp.

*993. VENEZUELA. OFICINA DE EDUCACIÓN DE ADULTOS. *Bases teóricas, organizativas y técnicas del plan quinquenal de alfabetización y cultura popular.* Caracas: 1957. 45 pp.

HEALTH, HYGIENE, AND NUTRITION INSTRUCTION

994. "Experiencias del servicio social sobre desarrollo de la comunidad en el sector de Catia," *Salud Pública*, 7:26 (1965), 53-65.
Describes the Unidad Sanitaria health education–community development work in the community of Catia.

995. LEWIS, MARY GUNNELL. "Home Demonstrators in Venezuela," *Journal of Home Economics*, 38:1 (January, 1946), 1-6.
Work of the Servicio Cooperativo Interamericano de Producción de Alimientos (SCIPA) and the Servicio de Demonstración del Hogar Campesino, focusing on the pilot program in the Montalbán Valley.

996. SAHAGÚN TORRES, J. "La experiencia sanitaria de Santa Teresa del Tuy," *Revista Venezolana de Sanidad y Asistencia Social*, 6:6 (December, 1941), 898-927.
Section describing the community health education work of the Unidad Sanitaria in Santa Teresa del Tuy.

PROFESSIONAL/PARAPROFESSIONAL TRAINING

997. "El Centro Interamericano de Educación Rural," *Educación*, Washington, 3:9 (January/March, 1958), 70-72.
Describes the professional training courses offered by the Institute, one of ten months duration and one of four months duration, for rural normal school teachers and directors and for administrators of rural educational services.

998. LLERANDI, FELIPE. "El Mácaro: El problema de la educación rural," *Farol*, 23:197 (November/December, 1961), 29-32.
Describes the work of the Centro de Capacitación Rural, a training center for rural teachers offering short-term courses in community development, agricultural education, home economics, and manual skills.

999. STEVENSON, GORDON K. "Improving Rural Education in Venezuela," Institute of International Education, *News Bulletin*, 36:2 (October, 1960), 20-24.
Activities of the Rural Teacher Training Center in Maracay (funded by

the Creole Foundation) which offers intensive, short-term courses for rural teachers to improve techniques and methods.

VOCATIONAL SKILL TRAINING

1000. DÍAZ, ANGEL. "Industrial Education in Venezuela," in Joseph A. Lauwerys, and David G. Scanlon, eds., *World Year Book of Education 1968: Education Within Industry.* London: Evans Brothers, 1968, pp. 226-234.

Good description of the aims and organization of the industrial training and apprenticeship programs of the Instituto Nacional de Cooperación Educativa (INCE), which are funded by contributions from employers, workers, and the federal government.

1001. "El Instituto Nacional de Cooperación Educativa (INCE)," *Política,* 8 (April, 1960), 103-104.

Briefly discusses the philosophy, goals, and financing of INCE.

1002. PADRÓN, HIRAM. "El Instituto Nacional de Cooperación Educativa," *Convergence,* 5:2 (1972), 60-63.

General discussion of INCE which was established in 1963 and which is financed by a federal tax levied on business and industry. Comments on the apprenticeship program, noncredit and correspondence classes, and training programs in the military.

1003. PALACIOS HERRERA, OSCAR, PEDRO B. PÉREZ SALINAS, and VICTOR HUGO MANZANILLA. "El INCE en el proceso de desarrollo económico del país," *Política,* 4:41/42 (August/September, 1965), 85-109.

Focuses on INCE's role in economic development. One section is devoted to a description of the goals, organization, finances, programs, and enrollment statistics of INCE, which is described as the *unidad de adiestramiento* for the country.

1004. SÁNCHEZ, GEORGE I. *The Development of Education in Venezuela.* U.S. Office of Education, Bulletin 1963, no. 7. Washington: 1963. 114 pp.

Chapter 7 deals briefly with INCE and its program of apprenticeship training.

1005. VENEZUELA. MINISTERIO DE EDUCACIÓN. "Vigoroso impulso a la educación artesanal, industrial y comercial,'' *Política*, 16 (June/ July, 1961), 58a-b.

One facet of the new educational plan to supply industry with skilled labor is a program of night training courses for workers offered at a variety of institutions. It is unclear, however, whether or not this is part of the formal school system.

1006. ''Vocational Training in South and Central America,'' *International Labour Review*, 55:6 (June, 1947), 570-575.

Includes a brief description of the new Practical School of Skilled Workers in the Cultivation of Coffee which offers a short-term practical training course in the growing and care of coffee. There are no prerequisites for the course and no degree or diploma is awarded upon its completion.

MISCELLANEOUS

1007. ADAM, FÉLIX, and PEDRO TOMÁS VÁSQUEZ. *La educación de adultos y los planes de desarrollo económico y social en Venezuela*. Ediciones ODEA. Caracas: Oficina de Educación de Adultos, 1965. 71 pp.

Includes sections on the literacy campaign and on INCE. The literacy program involves radio school efforts, *centros colectivos de alfabetización,* mobile units, *centros de extensión cultural, centros de cultura popular, centros de especialidades femeninas,* and agricultural training courses. An organization chart and enrollment figures are included. The section on INCE describes the organization, programming, and financing of the Institute. The concept of adult education is tied into national priorities.

1008. BAMBERGER, MICHAEL, and THOMAS A. BAUSCH. ''In Defense of Urban Community Development—the Venezuelan Case,'' *Review of Social Economy*, 26:2 (September, 1968), 130-144.

In expounding a justification for urban community development schemes, the authors mention several programs which have been implemented, though they offer no substantive information about any of the programs except INCE. Those mentioned include: INCE's vocational training program; ORDEC (the government community development agency); the Instituto Venezolano de Acción Comunitaria—IVAC (a private agency); Acción en Venezuela (also private).

1009. GOETZ, DELIA. *Education in Venezuela*. U.S. Office of Education, Bulletin 1948, no. 14. Washington: Government Printing Office, 1948. 104 pp.

> Chapter 6 on special education includes descriptions of the Practical Agriculture and Demonstration Center in Aragua (established in 1936) which serves in part as a training center for local farmers, the training of rural home demonstration agents, and the literacy campaign.

1010. INTERNATIONAL LABOR OFFICE. *Informe al gobierno de Venezuela sobre el proyecto para la integración de las poblaciones indígenas.* Programa de las Naciones Unidas para el Desarrollo, Sector Cooperación Técnica; Document ILO/TAP/Venezuela/R.9. Geneva: 1970. 31 pp.

> Focuses on a description of INCE efforts in the area of La Guajira, state of Zulia. Also discusses vocational and agricultural training programs of the Centro de Coordinación Indigenista in Yaguásiru, the Centro de Formación Agropecuaria in San Carlos, and the Centro de Aprendizaje Agrícola Don Bosco in Carrasquero (which has the financial support of Shell Oil of Venezuela). The Centro de Coordinación Indigenista also offers home improvement courses, such as sewing, cooking, and health, and training courses for professionals involved on all levels of community development programs. The efforts described above are all part of the larger joint Venezuela-Colombia development project in the area known as the Alta and Media Guajira.

1011. UNITED NATIONS. DEPARTMENT OF ECONOMIC AND SOCIAL AFFAIRS. COMMISSIONER FOR TECHNICAL ASSISTANCE. *Report of a Community Development Evaluation Mission to Venezuela*, by Caroline F. Ware, Rubén Darío Utria, and Antoni Wojcicki. Document TAO/VEN 15. New York: 1963. 88 pp.

> Evaluation report of the Programa Nacional de Desarrollo Comunal and other public and private agencies in the field of community development. Brief descriptions are provided for: (1) the Foundation for Community Development and Municipal Improvement, which maintains a training program; (2) the Ministry of Agriculture's housewives' clubs and rural youth clubs; (3) the National Agrarian Institute; (4) Ministry of Health and Welfare programs; (5) INCE; (6) the Instituto Venezolano de Acción Comunitaria (IVAC) and its training program for community leaders; (7) the Consejo de Bienestar Rural's supervised credit and farm machinery training programs; (8) Acción en Venezuela, or Organizadores de Acción Comunal, which provides a training program for organizers. The report also discusses the outlook for community development programs in Venezuela.

1012. VENEZUELA. PRESIDENTE. *Mensaje del presidente de la República ante el congreso nacional en sus sesiones ordinarias de 1960: Plan cuatrienal.* Caracas: Editorial del Arte, 1960. 70 pp.

Includes a short report on agricultural extension activities in the section on agriculture. The section on primary and teacher education comments on the literacy and adult education programs. The section on vocational education mentions the experimental Escuelas Artesanales de Producción for adults where crafts are taught and objects made can be removed and sold in the market place. This section also reports on INCE.

1013. WHARTON, CLIFTON R., JR. "CBR in Venezuela," *Inter-American Economic Affairs*, 4:3 (Winter, 1950), 3-15.

Reports on the technical assistance programs sponsored by the American International Association for Economic and Social Development, including the national nutrition information program, the training program in practical agriculture, and the rural development program of the Consejo de Bienestar Rural (CBR), the latter being the focus of the article. Regional offices of CBR are in the states of Táchira, Nueva Esparta, Carabobo, Lara, and Bolívar. Programs in each state are described, noting regional differences. Programs include technical guidance, supervised agricultural credit, skill training, home economics classes and extension, and agricultural extension.

CONCEPTUALIZATION

1014. BRUNO, JAMES E., and CORNELIS J. VAN ZEYL. "Educational Ideology in Venezuela: A Counterforce to Innovation," in Thomas J. La Belle, ed., *Educational Alternatives in Latin America: Social Change and Social Stratification*. Latin American Studies Series, 30. Los Angeles: Latin American Center, University of California, 1975, pp. 462-488.

This study, based on a survey of Venezuelan managers, concludes that nonformal modes of education are unlikely to meet with much success in Latin America because those who play key roles in the hiring process are firmly committed to the idea of formal education.

1015. McGINN, NOEL F., and RUSSELL G. DAVIS. *Build a Mill, Build a City, Build a School: Industrialization, Urbanization and Education in Ciudad Guayana, Venezuela*. Publication of the Joint Center for Urban Studies of the Massachusetts Institute of Technology and Harvard University. Cambridge, Massachusetts: MIT Press, 1969. 334 pp.

Proposes a number of different levels of nonformal education to supplement the formal school system—vocational training (to be co-ordinated with needs of local industry through INCE), basic education, apprenticeship programs. Offers advice about planning such programs based on known needs, values, and reactions of the citizens of the town.

1016. VENEZUELA. INSTITUTO TÉCNICO DE INMIGRACIÓN Y COLONIZACIÓN. *Memoria, 1940-1941: Parte expositiva*. Caracas: n.d. 2 vols. Calls for the creation of *"colonias escuelas"* to instruct *campesinos* in agricultural techniques. Seen as vital to the success of colonization programs.

Central America and the Caribbean

MULTIFACETED PROGRAMS

1017. VINTINNER, FREDERICK J. "A Mobile Rural Health Services Program in Central America and Panama," *American Journal of Public Health and the Nation's Health*, 58:5 (May, 1968), 907-914. Informative article describing the mobile rural health program funded by the U. S. Agency for International Development. In addition to medical aid, the program provides health and nutrition education and participates in community development activities (including instruction in basic agricultural and stock raising techniques). Offers an assessment of the three-year period since the program's inception in 1963 and outlines the achievements to date.

AGRICULTURAL TRAINING

1018. INTER-AMERICAN INSTITUTE OF AGRICULTURAL SCIENCES. *Estudio de educación, investigación y extensión agrícolas, 1966: Centroamérica.* Washington: Unión Panamericana, 1967. 369 pp. Part 3 describes the organization and activities of the agricultural extension services in the Central American countries of Costa Rica, El Salvador, Guatemala, Honduras, and Nicaragua.

*1019. ROSADO, HUMBERTO, and MARÍA JUSTINA LABOY. *Estudio de impacto de los servicios de extensión en el Istmo Centroamericano.* Publicación Miscelánea, 70. Guatemala: Instituto Interamericano de Ciencias Agrícolas, Zona Norte, 1970. 154 pp.

BASIC EDUCATION/LITERACY

1020. DOLFF, HELMUTH. "Educational Aid for Latin America," *Adult*

Leadership, 17:1 (May, 1968), 14, 35.
Work of the Costa Rica-based Instituto Centroamericano de Extensión de la Cultura (ICECU) which uses radio broadcasting as its primary medium for educational programs directed toward the adult population. The Institute works in cooperation with the German Volkshockschulen-Verband.

*1021. SUMMER INSTITUTE OF LINGUISTICS. *Instituto Lingüístico de Verano en Centro América, 1952-1962*. Guatemala: 1962. 15 pp.

HEALTH, HYGIENE, AND NUTRITION INSTRUCTION

1022. AVALA, V. O. "Home Economics Education in the Caribbean," *Caribbean Commission Monthly Information Bulletin*, 6:9 (April, 1953), 199-201.
Comments briefly on home extension work in the Caribbean in general and in particular on the program carried out by the University of Puerto Rico.

*1023. FOOD AND AGRICULTURAL ORGANIZATION. *Home Economic Education and Extension in the Caribbean*. Rome: 1952. 31 pp.

VOCATIONAL SKILL TRAINING

1024. ALCALA, V. O. "Apprenticeship and On-the-Job Training," *Caribbean Commission Monthly Information Bulletin*, 6:7 (February, 1953), 151-152, 154.
Describes the organization of apprenticeship programs in Trinidad and Tobago and Puerto Rico. Also comments on in-service training offered by several companies in Trinidad as a private initiative.

MISCELLANEOUS

1025. "Agricultural Education in Mexico and the Dominican Republic," Pan American Union, *Bulletin*, 81:2 (February, 1947), 110-111.
Describes the new program of agricultural education in Mexico

involving "practical and special" training in Practical Agricultural Schools and through extension. The Dominican Republic program specifically includes "demonstration teaching" as one of its four components which will be administered by the Department of Agriculture. Home economics courses directed toward farm women will be conducted both in schools and through short special training periods. Agricultural clubs for rural youth are to be established.

1026. CHACÓN NARDI, RAFAELA. *La alfabetización en México: Una experiencia educativa que pudiera utilizarse en Cuba.* México: Ediciones Lyceum, 1951. 160 pp.

Describes the literacy campaign, Cultural Mission program, and the Nayarit pilot project in basic education in Mexico. Based on observation of these programs, the author proposes a plan for literacy and fundamental education programs in Cuba.

1027. CHÁVEZ, IGNACIO. "La obra del bienestar social de la población rural de México," Mexico, Colegio Nacional, *Memoria*, 2:8 (1953), 21-32.

Briefly describes the fundamental education project in the Marbial Valley in Haiti and the CREFAL and Instituto Indigenista programs in Mexico.

1028. COMAS, JUAN. "Cultural Anthropology and Fundamental Education in Latin America," *International Social Science Bulletin*, 4:3 (1952), 451-461.

Good historical overview of fundamental education programs which focuses particular attention on the Cultural Mission program in Mexico and the Marbial Valley project in Haiti.

1029. HOWES, H. W. *Fundamental, Adult, Literacy and Community Education in the West Indies.* Educational Studies and Documents, 15. Paris: United Nations Educational, Scientific, and Cultural Organization, 1955. 79 pp.

Commences with definitions of fundamental, adult, literacy, and community education and goes on to describe programs in the various Caribbean countries. Included are the Jamaica Social Welfare Commission's literacy and nutrition education program; Puerto Rico's Division of Community Education's training program for selected rural community leaders and its literacy campaign; Mexico's Cultural Mission program; Cuba's cultural missions and literacy campaign; Haiti's literacy campaign, adult education centers, and the UNESCO pilot project in fundamental education at Marbial.

1030. KING, CLARENCE. *Working with People in Small Communities: Case*

Records of Community Development in Different Countries. New York: Harper, 1958. 130 pp.

A very superficial account. Chapter 4 notes the work of American Friends Service Committee volunteers in Ocampo, Mexico, in English language and craft training. Chapter 11 reports on the daily work of a field organizer for the Division of Community Education in Barrio Cuyón, Puerto Rico. Concentrates on the educational film series and evaluates the effectiveness of this medium to introduce new concepts.

1031. MEJÍA CASTRO, ARÍSTIDES. "Workers' Education in Central America," *Labour Education*, 9 (March, 1967), 7-9.

General discussion of organized educational efforts of trade unions in the region: Honduran trade union activities in literacy education; work of the Organización Regional Interamericana de Trabajadores (ORIT), Mexico; efforts on the part of the Instituto de Estudios Sindicales de Centro América (IESCA).

1032. PAULSTON, ROLLAND G. "Nonformal Educational Alternatives," in Cole S. Brembeck, and Timothy J. Thompson, eds., *New Strategies for Educational Development: The Cross-Cultural Search for Nonformal Alternatives.* Lexington, Massachusetts: Heath, 1973, pp. 65-82.

Focuses on national youth service organizations. The Jamaica Youth Corps (JYC) was created in 1956 and is a semi-autonomous governmental agency. Designed for the school dropout population, it has developed a program providing training in agricultural skills in rural camps, literacy and basic education, civic education, and on-the-job training. Depends a great deal on volunteer services and on aid from international corporations. In Cuba, the Centennial Youth Column, designed to reach the same population as the JYC, has three basic objectives: to provide basic education; to prepare agricultural workers; and to inculcate a socialist consciousness. Paulston offers an overview of both programs and an insight into some problems encountered.

1033. PEARSE, ANDREW C. "Vocational and Community Education in the Caribbean," in A. Curtis Wilgus, ed., *The Caribbean: Its Culture.* Publications of the School of Inter-American Studies, Series 1, 5. Gainesville: University of Florida Press, 1955, pp. 118-135.

Section on community education briefly explores some alternative programs: Puerto Rico's Division of Community Education; Haiti's Schools of Orientation and the Marbial Valley project; Jamaica Welfare Ltd.; Mexico's Cultural Missions and CREFAL.

1034. TECHNICAL MEETING ON AGRICULTURAL EXTENSION, TURRIALBA,

COSTA RICA. *Educational Approaches to Rural Welfare*. Washington: Food and Agricultural Organization, 1949. 51 pp.

Offers a description of the extension work of the *núcleos escolares campesinos* in Guatemala. Some educational activities of Jamaica's welfare program are also discussed, including the Community Education Campaign on Nutrition, mobile educational cinema units, and the Handcraft Programme (to instruct in local crafts).

1035. UNITED NATIONS. BUREAU OF SOCIAL AFFAIRS. *Social Progress Through Community Development*. Document E/CN.5/303/Rev. 1. New York: 1955. 120 pp.

Explores a myriad of community development projects, grouping them into local and national programs. Included are Jamaica Social Welfare Commission's program of village improvement which concentrates activities in the four main areas of cooperatives, community education, cottage industries, and mobile cinema units; Mexico's *ejido* system and its program of supervised agricultural credit; Puerto Rico's Community Education program which trains community leaders in community development techniques.

1036. VRIES, EGBERT DE, ed. *Social Research and Rural Life in Central America, Mexico and the Caribbean Region: Proceedings of a Seminar Organized by UNESCO in Cooperation with the United Nations Economic Commission for Latin America, Mexico City, 17-27 October 1962*. Technology and Society. Paris: United Nations Educational, Scientific, and Cultural Organization, 1966. 257 pp.

Basically deals with education and economic development in rural areas, recognizing the need for education beyond formal schooling. Includes discussion of community development programs, literacy campaigns, and agricultural and artisan cooperatives. The article on existing social and economic patterns and trends includes sections on education, health, and community development which use examples of nonformal programs to illustrate new approaches to education being developed, with particular reference to rural areas in the region. Programs discussed include: Mexico's Instituto Nacional Indigenista; Cuba's literacy campaign of 1961; University Extension Service in Costa Rica; Mexico's Ministry of Public Health and Social Welfare. Chapter 8 describes the newly instituted intensive university extension programs for rural communities in Costa Rica. Chapter 9 offers a general discussion of community development programs, their objectives, evaluation, administration, personnel requirements, and trends. Programs are classified into three types: integrative, adaptive, and project. Gives a number of examples of projects in operation to illustrate the discussion, such as the Division of Community Education in Puerto

Rico, Centros de Bienestar Rural in Mexico, Proyecto Piloto de Educación Fundamental in Río Coco, Nicaragua, the Pote Cole Project in Haiti, the Jamaica Social Welfare Society, and the Instituto Nacional Indigenista in Mexico. Chapter 10 elaborates on the programs developed by the Instituto Nacional Indigenista of Mexico.

1037. WILLIAMS COLLEGE. ROPER PUBLIC OPINION RESEARCH CENTER. *Use of Radiophonic Teaching in Fundamental Education.* Williamstown, Massachusetts: 1963. Various pagination.

Detailed account based on field study of the organization and administration of radio schools operated by Acción Cultural Popular in El Salvador and Honduras. Describes the programming and discusses some of the problems of the project.

1038. UNITED NATIONS. SECRETARIAT. *Report of the United Nations Study Tour on Community Development to Mexico, Costa Rica, Jamaica and Puerto Rico.* United Nations Series on Community Development, 30. New York: 1958. 43 pp.

Provides a general description of the administration and activities of the following community development agencies: (1) for Mexico: CREFAL, Cultural Missions, the Rural Social Welfare program of the Ministry of Public Health and Social Welfare, and the National Indian Institute; (2) for Costa Rica: the fundamental education program, National Institute of Housing and Urbanization, agricultural extension services, Nutrition Program, and the Inter-American Institute of Agricultural Sciences at Turrialba; (3) for Jamaica: the Jamaica Social Welfare Commission, Jamaica Agricultural Society, Sugar Industry Labour Welfare Board, and the National Program Coordination; (4) for Puerto Rico: the Division of Community Education and the Social Program Administration.

CONCEPTUALIZATION

1039. COMMONWEALTH CARIBBEAN REGIONAL YOUTH SEMINAR, PORT-OF-SPAIN, TRINIDAD AND TOBAGO, AUGUST, 1970. *Youth and Development in the Caribbean.* London: Commonwealth Secretariat, 1970. 257 pp.

Much of the discussion is directed toward the question of formal versus nonformal education. A section is included on expenditure priorities for in-school and out-of-school educational programs. Chapter 2 has several sections devoted to the need for more nonformal educational opportunities, particularly in the area of vocational training.

South America

MULTIFACETED PROGRAMS

1040. "Andean Indian Mission," *Industry and Labour*, 10:5 (September 1, 1953), 178-182.
> Outlines the antecedents to the program and its organization and makes recommendations for projects in each of the countries involved: Peru, Ecuador, and Bolivia.

1041. BEAGLEHOLE, ERNEST. "A Technical Assistance Mission in the Andes," *International Labour Review*, 67:6 (June, 1953), 520-534.
> Thoughtful analysis of techniques used, difficulties encountered, and lessons learned in carrying out Mission programs, which included developing cooperative organizations for agriculture, stockraising, and handicrafts; health education; practical training in handicrafts; and training of community leaders and teachers. The Mission was the joint operation of the ILO, OAS, UNESCO, FAO, and WHO and spanned the entire Andean plateau region of Ecuador, Peru, and Bolivia.

1042. "Guajira: Taming a Desert," *ILO Panorama*, 40 (January/February, 1970), 2-13.
> The project in the Guajira region of Colombia and Venezuela consists in part of resettlement programs in which settlers receive training in community development, home economics, hygiene, carpentry, and building construction. The program is administered by the ILO, but the UN, UNESCO, and FAO also participate.

1043. INTERNATIONAL LABOR OFFICE. *The Andean Programme: Human Beings Working Together*. Geneva: 1958. 103 pp.
> Optimistic account of the work of the ILO in the three-country program. Provides a good introduction to the program but offers little analysis. Presents information about some of the projects initiated and background to the creation of the program.

1044. INTERNATIONAL LABOR ORGANIZATION. PANEL OF CONSULTANTS ON INDIGENOUS AND TRIBAL POPULATIONS, 1ST SESSION, 1962. *Appraisal of the Achievements of the Andean Indian Programme*. Geneva: 1962. 108 pp. and supplements.
> Thorough discussion of the Andean Indian Program from its inception in 1954 to date. Describes work in the three countries, cooperating

efforts of other international agencies, and a summation of progress achieved in the fields of activity. Also comments on the formulation of the national integration plans for the indigenous populations which were a direct result of the Mission program.

1045. LOCKWOOD, AGNESE NELMS. "Indians of the Andes: Technical Assistance on the Altiplano," *International Conciliation*, 508 (May, 1956), 355-431.

Country-by-country account of projects undertaken at the various bases in Ecuador, Peru, and Bolivia, as well as sections on the background, administration, and financing of the program known as the Andean Mission. Gives some idea of difficulties encountered but does not offer any substantive analysis of the program or its impact.

1046. MÉTRAUX, ALFRED. " 'Land Hunger' on the Top of the Andes," *Courier*, 7:12 (May, 1955), 4-9.

General article describing problems encountered by the Andean Mission program.

1047. "La OIT y la Misión Andina," *Boletín Indigenista*, 21:2 (June, 1961), 90-95.

Very general description of the program and some comment on five proposed projects. Also comments on the types of problems with which the program is most concerned.

1048. "Programa indigenista andino: Evaluación de sus realizaciones," *Anuario Indigenista*, 23 (December, 1963), 43-68.

Reports on several areas developed by the Andean Mission program: community development, housing, social services, formal education, health and sanitation, and training of in-country personnel. Fairly detailed account, giving a good idea of the work undertaken and the location for particular projects.

1049. "Raising Standards of Living in the Andes Mountains," *United Nations Review*, 1:10 (April, 1955), 19-24.

General article on the Andean Mission program, concentrating on the Pilapi base in Bolivia, but also giving some idea of the overall administration of the program and the assistance rendered by international agencies and civil servants. Outlines activities in other countries.

1050. RENS, JEF. "The Andean Programme," *International Labour Review*, 84:6 (December, 1961), 423-461.

A thorough and well written description of the program with a very positive slant. Describes the historical background, basic aims, actual projects undertaken, results achieved, and financing of the Andean Mission program. A map of the local bases is included, and the appendix lists gifts to the program from various countries. The program is primarily concerned with improving agricultural methods and production conditions.

1051. RENS, JEF. "The Andes Programme: A Programme of International Aid for the Indians of the Andes," *Free Labour World*, 110 (August, 1959), 345-349.
Yet another article describing the basic aims of and projects undertaken by the Andean Mission program.

1052. RENS, JEF. "The Development of the Andean Programme and Its Future," *International Labour Review*, 88:6 (December, 1963), 547-563.
Update of the report made in 1961, marking the expansion of the program to other Andean countries (Colombia, Chile, Argentina, and Venezuela) and its tenth anniversary. Discusses the integration of the program into national development schemes, the increasing proliferation of action bases within each country, international assistance and support, the future of the program, and obstacles yet to be overcome.

*1053. RENS, JEF. "Una gran empresa internacional de ayuda técnica: El programa andino," *Mundo del Trabajo Libre*, 10:109 (July, 1959), 10-12.

1054. RENS, JEF. "Helping the Andean Indians," *American Federationist*, 65:4 (April, 1958), 16-19.
Describes the various educational aspects of the Andean Mission program.

1055. RENS, JEF. "Latin America and the International Labour Organisation: 40 Years of Collaboration 1919-1959," *International Labour Review*, 80:1 (July, 1959), 1-25.
Includes a summary of activities of the Andean Mission program, used as the supreme example of ILO technical assistance in Latin America.

1056. RENS, JEF. "El programa andino," *Informaciones Sociales*, 17:1 (January/March, 1962), 3-42.
Presents the background to the program, its objectives, and a detailed description of the bases established in each country and activities and programs undertaken there. An evaluation of results follows, in addition to sections on financing and conclusions.

1057. RENS, JEF. "A Programme of International Assistance for the Andean Indians," *Inter-Parliamentary Bulletin*, 39:1 (First Quarter, 1959), 15-21.
General article providing background information and some idea of projects initiated.

1058. "7 Million Forgotten Indians in the Land of the Incas," *Courier*, 12:11 (November, 1959), 21-26.

>Well written article (with illustrations) explaining the many facets of the Andean Mission program in Peru, Ecuador, and Bolivia, such as literacy work, vocational training, agricultural and health instruction, and home care and skill training. Largely devoted to providing background information about conditions of life in the Andes.

1059. "A Voice in Their Own Destiny," *Americas*, 14:7 (July, 1962), 36-38.

>Describes various aspects of work of the Andean Mission program: vocational training, training of community leaders, and nutrition education.

1060. WALKER, GUILD. "Andean Indians: Project of United Nations Andean Mission in Peru, Bolivia, Ecuador," *Peruvian Times*, 14:690 (March 12, 1954), 5-6.

>Provides some background information, describing personnel involved and financing. Offers a somewhat detailed explanation of the Peruvian pilot project in Tambopata-Puno area and the proposed training center at Muquiyauyu, Junín. Briefer comments on the programs just underway in Bolivia (at Pillapi and Cochabamba-Santa Cruz) and in Ecuador.

AGRICULTURAL TRAINING

1061. "Bolivia and Peru Begin Cooperative Educational Program," Pan American Union, *Bulletin*, 80:4 (April, 1946), 233.

>New program available to the entire community to stress teaching of practical agricultural skills.

*1062. FOOD AND AGRICULTURAL ORGANIZATION. *Informe del Centro Sudamericano de Extensión Agrícola*. Belo Horizonte, Brazil: 1959. 235 pp.

1063. HILL, REY M. *Agricultural Assistance Through Capital Investment*. Building a Better Hemisphere Series, 3. Washington: Technical Cooperation Administration, Inter-American Regional Office, Institute of Inter-American Affairs, 1952. 11 pp.

>Describes Point Four agricultural assistance in Peru and Paraguay.

BASIC EDUCATION/LITERACY

1064. "INDICEP y la educación popular en América Latina: grandes corrientes ideológicas," *Convergence*, 4:4 (1971), 45-54.
Offers a critique of a Colombian radio program called Educación Fundamental Integral of Educación de Base, which is similar to Radio Sutatenza. Discusses the impact of various educational radio programs in Bolivia and espouses "*dinamización cultural*" for Bolivia. The new popular education must, however, emanate from and be controlled by the community. Strongly critical of such labels as "*alfabetización funcional*" and "*mutación cultural*" and of the programs defined by such terms. Declares that cultural oppression is the definition of illiteracy. Praises the work of Paulo Freire and Ivan Illich.

1065. *Literacy 1969-1971: Progress Achieved in Literacy Throughout the World*. Paris: United Nations Educational, Scientific, and Cultural Organization, 1972. 128 pp.
Chapter 4 briefly describes projects in Brazil, Chile, and Ecuador. While there is mention of various programs and techniques throughout the document, it is a very general discussion, bringing together discursively a wide range of approaches. Touches occasionally on the Freire method, its uses and effectiveness. Relevant material, however, must be searched out, and there is no index to facilitate this procedure.

1066. "Mass Education in Brazil and Chile," *Foreign Education Digest*, 19:2 (October/December, 1954), 117-119.
Report on Brazil's literacy and adult education campaign during the late 1940s. Also discusses Chile's adult education programs begun in 1942 with the creation of the anti-illiteracy and adult education division of the Ministry of Education. Notes such projects as the library education programs, mobile cultural exhibits, and radio education programs.

1067. "Paulo Freire," *Convergence*, 3:3 (1970), 62-68.
Discusses Freire's method and activities in literacy education in Brazil's Movimento de Cultura Popular and Movimento de Educação de Base, and in Chile with the ICIRA.

1068. PEREIRA, EVALDO SIMAS. "E economia e educação," *O Observador Econômico e Financeiro*, 14:163 (August, 1949), 30-35, 97-98.
Touches on Brazil's literacy campaign and Mexico's Cultural Mission

program in an article prompted by the recent Latin American conference on literacy and adult education.

1069. SANDERS, THOMAS G. "The Paulo Freire Method: Literacy Training and *Conscientización*," American Universities Field Staff, Fieldstaff Reports, *West Coast South America Series*, 15:1 (1968), 17 pp.

Describes the method of literacy training devised and promoted by Paulo Freire in both Brazil and Chile. The impact of this system has been the critical factor in its acceptance by those in political power in the aforementioned countries.

HEALTH, HYGIENE, AND NUTRITION INSTRUCTION

1070. HESELTINE, MARJORIE M. "Nutrition Problems and Programs in Latin America in 1943," *Child*, 8:7 (January, 1944), 99-102.

Briefly notes nutrition education programs in Lima's maternal and child health center, in a low-income housing project in Buenos Aires, and in Montevideo's clinics of the Children's Council.

1071. HOERNER, LENA MAY, and AGNES JUNE LEITH. "Nutrition Work to the South of Us," *Journal of Home Economics*, 36:4 (April, 1944), 203-208.

Comments on nutrition courses given in the Gotas de Leche (milk distribution centers for low-income families) throughout Uruguay and on YWCA nutrition work in the slum areas of Montevideo. Also notes Brazil's nutrition education programs: training course for women in practical nutrition work sponsored in part by the Institute of Inter-American Affairs and home extension programs.

1072. ROMAÑA, CECILIO. *Urgencia de organizar centros de higiene en las escuelas rurales.* 2d. ed. Resistencia, Argentina: Instituto de Medicina Regional, Universidad Nacional del Nordeste, 1959. 40 pp.

Calls for the creation of health centers annexed to rural schools for the purpose of disseminating information to the community at large. Describes health center activities in Ica, Peru and Salta, Argentina.

VOCATIONAL SKILL TRAINING

1073. EBEL, KARL HEINRICH. *El aprendizaje en América Latina: Estudio sobre el aprendizaje para jóvenes en seis países.* Centro Inter-americano de Investigación y Documentación sobre Formación Profesional, Estudios y Monografías, 2. Montevideo: Organización Internacional del Trabajo/CINTERFOR, 1967. 85 pp.

Deals with programs in Argentina (CONET), Peru (SENATI), Colombia (SENA), Brazil (SENAI and SENAC), Venezuela (INCE), and Uruguay (Universidad del Trabajo). Covers such topics as apprenticeship in relation to the formal educational system, legal and administrative structures, financing, programming, supervision and assessment, selection of apprentices, and methods of training.

1074. "Economic Growth and Social Policy in Latin America: The Seventh Conference of American States Members of the I.L.O.," *International Labour Review*, 84:1/2 (July/August, 1961), 50-74.

Summary of the conference agenda, which includes a discussion of the role of the several national apprenticeship-vocational training programs in South America—SENAI/SENAC, SENA, SENATI, CONET, INCE, and the Chilean National Vocational Training Committee—in the broad context of educational policy and planning. Throughout the report reference is made to the need for vocational and agricultural training programs, particularly in rural areas.

1075. PAN AMERICAN UNION. DEPARTAMENTO DE ASUNTOS EDUCATIVOS. *Servicios de educación técnica y formación profesional en Argentina, Brasil, Colombia, Perú y Venezuela.* Washington: 1965. 82 pp.

With the exception of the report on SENATI in Peru, which was sadly lacking in comparison with the others, all are well-detailed studies of the organization and administration of the national vocational training services in South America: CONET (Consejo Nacional de Educación Técnica) in Argentina, SENAI and SENAC in Brazil, SENA in Colombia, SENATI in Peru, and INCE in Venezuela.

1076. RENS, JEF. "Vocational Training and the Establishment of Service Workshops in a Poor Rural Area: The Experience of the Andean Indian Programme," *International Labour Review*, 85:2 (February, 1962), 129-147.

Excellent report on the vocational training aspect of the program, the reasons for its inclusion and the projects initiated. Discusses the organization of the workshops in each country, their locations, types of training offered, and the courses offered. Even includes detailed lists of equipment and tools provided for each workshop. Offers a comprehensive analysis and critique of the workshop program.

MISCELLANEOUS

1077. AMERICAN INTERNATIONAL ASSOCIATION. "The Rural Development Programs of the American International Association for Economic and Social Development," in Robert King Hall, N. Hans, and J. A. Lauwerys, eds., *Year Book of Education 1954.* London: Evans Brothers, 1954, pp. 549-560.

Describes the work of the Consejo de Bienestar Rural (CBR) and the Consejo Informativo de Educación Alimenticia (CIDEA) of Venezuela and the Associação de Crédito e Assistência Rural (ACAR) of Brazil. CBR programs include supervised rural credit and agricultural education, machinery training centers, and community centers for instruction in domestic skills. CIDEA concentrates its efforts in a multi-media nutrition education campaign. ACAR (in Minas Gerais) focuses on supervised agricultural credit and home extension programs.

1078. CANNON, MARY M. *Social and Labor Problems of Peru and Uruguay: A Study in Contrasts.* Washington: Women's Bureau, U.S. Department of Labor, 1945. 22 pp.

Of particular interest is the section on women and social problems which outlines early efforts of a number of private organizations to provide basic domestic skill and literacy training for women in Peru, including Catholic Action and Acción Femenina Peruana. The corresponding section for Uruguay notes the radio station directed by women who conducted an educational program largely intended for women.

1079. CÉSPEDES, FRANCISCO S. "The Contemporary Education Scene in Latin America," in Comparative Education Society, Eastern Regional Conference, *Challenges and Achievements of Education in Latin America.* Washington: Department of Educational Affairs, Pan American Union, 1964. 94 pp.

Short section of the chapter is devoted to new institutions and services which include the national industrial apprenticeship and training systems of Brazil (SENAI), Peru (SENATI), Colombia (SENA), and Venezuela (INCE). Also discusses new programs of adult education, such as Venezuela's División Nacional de Educación de Adultos.

1080. "Educación industrial en América Latina," *Revista Interamericana de Educación,* 9:38/39 (July/August, 1950), 249-254.

Includes brief descriptions of Argentina's literacy campaign and Brazil's Serviço Nacional de Aprendizagem Industrial (SENAI).

1081. HERRERA, FELIPE. "Local Communities in the Development of Latin

America,'' *The Review of the River Plate,* 136:3545 (October 9, 1964), 25-26, 43-44.

Mentions funding and technical assistance given to large-scale community development programs in Bolivia and Ecuador.

1082. INTER-AMERICAN DEVELOPMENT BANK. *Community Development Theory and Practice: Round Table, Mexico City and Washington, April 1966.* Washington: 1967. 280 pp.

The chapter on experiences in the Andean region concentrates on the work of the Andean Mission program and a number of programs for the integration of indigenous populations (Sección Integración del Campesino a la Vida Nacional of Ecuador, Indian Institute of Peru, Commissions for Assistance to and Protection of Indigenous Populations of Colombia, etc.). Types of educational activities are outlined, which include agricultural and stockraising instruction, vocational training, handicrafts and small business training, health and nutrition education, home improvement courses, and literacy work. Also includes monetary investment figures and an analysis of the effectiveness of the programs. The chapter on Venezuela offers a very informative and detailed description of the organization, goals, financing, and activities of its Programa Nacional de Desarrollo Comunal, from the national to the local levels. Includes many charts and graphs and accounts of projects in La Julia-Jobo Dulce; Guanipa Mesa, Anzoategui; Burro Negro, Zulia; Magdaleno, Aragua; and the '23 de enero' *barrio* of Caracas.

1083. INTERNATIONAL LABOR CONFERENCE. 49TH, GENEVA, 1965. *Agrarian Reform, with Particular Reference to Employment and Social Aspects.* Reports, 6. Geneva: International Labor Office, 1964. 128 pp.

The chapter on problems of agrarian reform and measures to solve them touches on a number of programs, but references are somewhat vague and information minimal. It mentions, for example, the pilot land resettlement plan in Santo Domingo de los Colorados, Ecuador, which provided technical services for settlers; Andean Mission program efforts; the SUDENE resettlement program in Brazil's northeast. The section on marketing credit and communications notes the supervised credit programs in Brazil (ACAR) and Chile.

1084. JARA P., FERNANDO. "Experiencias de teleducación auxiliar en el canal 13," *Revista de Educación,* Santiago, 13 (December, 1968), 63-65.

The use of television in Puno and Arequipa, Peru, as part of literacy and *concientización* programs is described. Channel 13 in Chile, under the auspices of the Universidad Católica, is directed toward community development. *Teleclubs* have been formed to increase the viewing audience.

1085. McGinn, Noel F. *Problems of Human Development in Urban Latin America.* Occasional Papers in Education and Development, 6. Cambridge, Massachusetts: Center for Studies in Education and Development, Graduate School of Education, Harvard University, 1971. 72 pp.

Concluding section on education for a new urban society develops a plan of nonformal education, citing examples of existing programs such as ACCION in Venezuela, Acción Popular in Peru, Promoción Popular in Chile, and Capacitación Popular in Colombia, all of which are broadly based urban community development programs.

1086. Pan American Union. Departamento de Asuntos Educativos. *Programas para adultos y su integración con los planes nacionales de desarrollo económico y social, en el Ecuador, el Perú y Venezuela.* Washington: 1965. 164 pp.

Describes in great detail the adult education programs in three countries. The section on Ecuador reviews the literacy campaigns (Liga Alfabetizadora Ecuatoriana and the Unión Nacional de Periodistas), the Andean Mission program, the cultural missions, and the mobile libraries. The section on Peru deals with the literacy campaign, the Andean Mission program, SENATI, the Instituto de Educación Fundamental, the Summer Institute of Linguistics, and the Centro de Promoción Popular. The section on Venezuela describes the work of the División de Educación de Adultos, INCE, the Programa Nacional de Desarrollo de la Comunidad, and agricultural extension.

1087. Rubio Orbe, Gonzalo. "Anotaciones de carácter educativo," *Revista Ecuatoriana de Educación,* 2a. época, 1:1 (January/June, 1961), 134-163.

The first section deals with the problems and shortcomings of rural education in Bolivia, Peru, and Ecuador. The second section is devoted to a description of educational programs (formal and nonformal) in each country.

1088. Taylor, Sue H. *El centro comunal en la vida rural.* Serie sobre Organización de la Comunidad, 10. Washington: Sección de Servicio Social, División de Trabajo y Asuntos Sociales, Unión Panamericana, 1954. 17 pp.

Very general description of the role of community centers in community development schemes in Venezuela (Consejo de Bienestar Rural—CBR) and Brazil (Associação de Crédito Rural—ACAR). Centers

serve as community education and meeting places where home improvement courses in particular are usually offered.

1089. "UNDP Education Project in Colombia Provides for Training of Adult
Education Personnel," *Adult Education Information Notes,* 4
(October/November, 1973), 6.

> The United Nations Development Program is to provide six experts
> to work in a four-year demonstration project on education for rural
> development. Personnel to be trained will be working in community
> development and out-of-school educational programs. Also mentions a
> similar project in Ecuador.

1090. UNITED NATIONS EDUCATIONAL, SCIENTIFIC, AND CULTURAL OR-
GANIZATION. *Functional Literacy as a Factor in Development.*
International Education Year 1970, no. 1. Paris: [1970?]. 19 pp.

> Lists UNESCO literacy and development projects under such headings
> as land reform (Chile and Ecuador), development of cooperatives
> (Ecuador), agricultural settlement (Ecuador), improvements in voca-
> tional qualifications and the integration of workers into industry
> (Brazil), change-over from a subsistence to a market economy (Ecua-
> dor), modernization and mechanization of agricultural techniques
> (Venezuela), and modernization of handicraft techniques (Ecuador).
> Each project combines literacy work with specific socioeconomic
> objectives.

1091. VIOLICH, FRANCES, and JUAN B. ASTICA. *Community Development
and the Urban Planning Process in Latin America.* Latin American
Studies, 6. Los Angeles: Latin American Center, University of
California, 1967. 115 pp.

> Discusses the problems and concepts of community development with
> reference to Latin America. Describes programs in Colombia, Vene-
> zuela, Peru, and Chile, where urban community development was
> institutionalized at the national level in the late 1950s and early
> 1960s.

Latin America

AGRICULTURAL TRAINING

1092. CHAPMAN, DOROTHY E. "Agricultural Extension Project in the Other Americas," *Agriculture in the Americas,* 6:2 (February, 1946), 27-29, 38.
>Describes the circulars devised by the U.S. Department of Agriculture for distribution by agricultural extension agents in Peru, Ecuador, El Salvador, and Guatemala to deal with specific local problems.

*1093. FOOD AND AGRICULTURAL ORGANIZATION. *La extensión agrícola en la zona norte de América Latina: Informe del seminario celebrado en México del 10 al 19 de junio de 1963.* México: 1963. 244 pp.

1094. FOOD AND AGRICULTURAL ORGANIZATION. *Prospects for Agricultural Development in Latin America.* Rome: 1953. 146 pp.
>Brief outlines of national agricultural development plans including mention of expansion of extension services, resettlement programs, and supervised credit programs.

*1095. FOOD AND AGRICULTURAL ORGANIZATION. RURAL INSTITUTIONS DIVISION. *Rural Extension in Latin America and the Caribbean: Report of the Technical Conference on Agricultural Extension and Rural Youth, Chiclayo, Peru, 29 November-12 December 1970.* Document ESR-ERY/70/Report. Rome: 1971/1972. 154 pp.

1096. LOOMIS, CHARLES P. "Extension Work for Latin America," *Applied Anthropology,* 3:4 (September, 1944), 27-40.
>Section on extension services in Latin America enumerates work being done in most countries, such as by the Cultural Missions in Mexico, the National Federation of Coffee Growers in Colombia, and the YMCA in Tepoztlán, Mexico.

1097. LOOMIS, CHARLES P. "Extension Work in Latin America," in Edmund deS. Brunner, Irwin T. Sanders, and Douglas Ensminger, eds., *Farmers of the World: The Development of Agricultural Extension.* New York: Columbia University Press, 1945, pp. 117-137.
>General discussion of agricultural extension throughout the area. Includes brief notations of different types of programs, such as the

Cultural Mission program in Mexico, the National Federation of Coffee Growers in Colombia, the United Fruit Company, the Federation of Coffee Growers in El Salvador, demonstration farms, and church missions.

*1098. Peña Cortes, Delio Gerardo, ed. *Historia y antecedentes de organización de algunos servicios de extensión agrícola en la América Latina y el Caribe.* Turrialba, Costa Rica: Instituto Interamericano de Ciencias Agrícolas, 1967. 71 pp.

1099. Rice, Edward B. *Extension in the Andes: An Evaluation of Official U.S. Assistance to Agricultural Extension Services in Central and South America.* AID Evaluation Paper 3A. Washington: Agency for International Development, 1971. 552 pp.

> Evaluates U.S. involvement in agricultural extension for the period 1942-1970. Defines agricultural extension as "an organized process of extending agricultural information . . . through channels other than formal schooling system." Covers projects in twelve countries in various levels of detail: Guatemala, El Salvador, Honduras, Nicaragua, Costa Rica, Panama, Colombia, Ecuador, Peru, Bolivia, Chile, and Paraguay.

1100. Ruiz Camacho, Rubén. *La extensión rural en marcha.* Bogotá: 1965. 114 pp.

> General content, organization, and potential impact of extension programs are discussed. Provides a description of the rural extension service of the Ministry of Agriculture and a more detailed explanation of the pilot extension project of the Servicio Técnico Agrícola Colombiano Americano (STACA) from 1953-1959 in Colombia. Another section enumerates extension programs of various institutions in Colombia. A section is also included on extension programs in Costa Rica.

1101. Warren, Gertrude L. "4-H Clubs in the Americas," *Agriculture in the Americas,* 4:10 (October, 1944), 190-191.

> Brief descriptions of 4-H club activities in various Latin American countries, such as Venezuela, Brazil, Chile, Jamaica, and Cuba.

BASIC EDUCATION/LITERACY

1102. Barbieri, Sante Uberto. *Land of Eldorado.* New York: Friendship Press, 1961. 161 pp.

> Sections on the contribution to popular education and on attention to indigenous populations briefly mention religious (Protestant) efforts in

literacy training, particularly with regard to the indigenous populations.

1103. CORTRIGHT, RICHARD W. "Adult Basic Education in Latin America," *International Review of Education,* 12:2 (1966), 176-183.

Discusses a wide variety of literacy-adult education programs and attempts to grapple with the adult versus primary education problem. Concludes that educational planning must include adult education (i.e., nonformal) programs as well as expand primary education.

1104. ESPINOSA, FRANCISCO. "Educación de los adultos," *Cultura,* 41 (July/September, 1966), 123-127.

Discusses the pressing problem of illiteracy in Latin America and focuses on a few attempts to remedy the situation, such as Mexico's Cultural Missions, Radio Sutatenza programs in Colombia, the Dirección General de Desarrollo Socio-Educativo Rural of Guatemala, and the Departamento de Alfabetización y Educación de Adultos in El Salvador.

1105. LÓPEZ DE FILIPIS, HAYDÉE. "Alfabetización de adultos," *Revista de Educación,* Asunción, 2:5/6 (June/September, 1946). 51-56.

Briefly describes literacy campaigns in Mexico, Chile, Peru, Ecuador, Venezuela, Guatemala, Honduras, Dominican Republic, Haiti, and Colombia. A more detailed description of Paraguayan efforts is presented.

1106. LEAVITT, HOWARD B. "U.S. Technical Assistance to Latin American Education," *Phi Delta Kappan,* 45:4 (January, 1964), 220-225.

Provides an overview of U.S. dollar investment in Latin American education, including special programs for literacy and fundamental education. Figures are given in general categories and then broken down by country and type of program.

1107. MADDISON, JOHN. *Radio and Television in Literacy: A Survey of the Use of the Broadcasting Media in Combating Illiteracy among Adults.* Reports and Papers on Mass Communication, 62. Paris: Department of Mass Communication, United Nations Educational, Scientific, and Cultural Organization, 1971. 82 pp.

Covers specific programs in ten Latin American countries, the use of electronic media in countering illiteracy, and the future of radio and television in literacy campaigns.

1108. MEDARY, MARJORIE. *Each One Teach One: Frank Laubach, Friend to Millions.* New York: Longmans, Green, 1954. 227 pp.

Chapter 8 gives a brief account of Laubach literacy activities throughout Latin America.

1109. Seminario Iberoamericano de Alfabetización, 1er., Madrid, 1964. *Conclusiones y recomendaciones.* Serie 5: Seminarios y Reuniones Técnicas, 1. Madrid: Departamento de Información y Publicaciones, Oficina de Educación Iberoamericana, 1964. 36 pp.
  Provides general recommendations only, but a list of working documents contains several pieces on literacy campaigns in various Latin American countries.

1110. Torres, Luis F. "Campañas de alfabetización en America," *Revista Ecuatoriana de Educación*, 2:7/8 (July/December, 1949), 69-89.
  Covers literacy programs in Argentina, Mexico, Venezuela, Ecuador, and Bolivia.

CULTURAL EXTENSION

1111. Esman, Sherley Goodman, and Dorothy E. Greene. "Cultural Centers in the Other American Republics," U.S. Department of State, *Record*, 1:8 (October/December, 1945), 1-6.
  Reports on U.S. cultural centers in Latin America whose primary activity is teaching English and Spanish or Portuguese. These centers also maintain libraries which are open to the community at large and often offer series of lectures on topics of cultural interest.

HEALTH, HYGIENE, AND NUTRITION INSTRUCTION

*1112. Food and Agricultural Organization. *Home Management and Consumer Education in Rural Development Programmes: Latin America*, by V. Lattes de Casseres. Nutrition Information Documents Series, 5; Document ISN-IDS/72/5. Rome: 1972, 83 pp.

1113. O'Hara, Hazel. "For the Common Health," *Journal of Health, Physical Education, Recreation*, 22:1 (January, 1951), 26-27.
  General description of activities of the Servicio Cooperativo Interamericano de Salud Pública (SCISP) in a number of Latin American nations. Activities range from medical care to sanitation improvements to health instruction.

1114. U.S. Institute of Inter-American Affairs. Health and Sani-

TATION DIVISION. *Co-operative Health Programs of the U.S.A. and Latin America*. Washington: 1948. 20 pp.

> Briefly describes educational work of health centers administered as joint U.S.-Latin American projects. Among the programs are health counseling, nutrition projects, community meetings, and film programs on health.

LABOR UNION EDUCATION

1115. "Cuernavaca: The Fifteenth Advanced Instructor Training Course," *Labour Education*, 14 (October, 1968), 16-17.

> Brief outline of the seven-week course organized by the Organización Regional Interamericana de Trabajadores (ORIT) for high-level trade unionists in Latin America.

1116. INTER-AMERICAN REGIONAL ORGANIZATION OF WORKERS OF THE ICFTU. DEPARTMENT OF EDUCATION. *Trade Union Education Manual: Summary of Recent Experiences and Practical Methods Used to Strengthen the Ranks of Democratic Trade Unionism*. Mexico: International Confederation of Free Trade Unions/Organización Regional Interamericana de Trabajadores, 1960. 154 pp.

> Describes local trade union training institutes held in Latin America during 1958-1959 and short courses offered by them for local union leadership. Focuses on collective bargaining techniques and on aspects of strengthening the local union. Includes descriptions of study programs for each institute in Chile, Ecuador, Colombia, Trinidad, and Cuba.

1117. "A Step Forward in the IMF Training Programme for Latin American Trade Unionists," *Labour Education*, 22 (December, 1971), 14-16.

> Describes the International Metalworkers' Federation program of some two hundred seminars and short courses made available to its members in Argentina, Brazil, Colombia, Chile, Mexico, Peru, and Venezuela.

PROFESSIONAL/PARAPROFESSIONAL TRAINING

1118. MEEK, GEORGE. "Farms, Skills and Credit: OAS Programs Promote

Agricultural Development," *Americas,* 14:9 (September, 1962), 16-19.

Describes professional training courses offered in three programs of the Organization of American States (OAS). Technical Education for the Improvement of Agriculture and Rural Life, initiated in 1951, trains extension and home demonstration agents, with centers of instruction in San José, Costa Rica; Lima, Peru; and Montevideo, Uruguay. National courses are also given on request. The Center for Agricultural Credit in Mexico City is sponsored by the OAS Program of Technical Cooperation to provide advanced training for professionals active in supervised credit programs. The third course is the Training Course for Administers of Agrarian Reform Programs.

1119. PAN AMERICAN UNION. *Technical Cooperation for Economic Development: Programs of the OAS.* Washington: 1958. 10 pp.

Includes a brief description of the OAS Program of Technical Cooperation which offers training programs at advanced levels of technical education through regional centers in Latin America. Emphasis is on such fields as agriculture, rural education, housing, industrial production, social welfare, and nutrition.

1120. UNITED NATIONS. ECONOMIC AND SOCIAL COUNCIL. *Economic Commission for Latin America Annual Report 1952/53: Supplement No. 3.* Document E/CN.12/324; E/2405. New York: 1953. 56 pp.

Section included which describes a ten-month economic development training program for professional economists, organized by the Commission and the Technical Assistance Administration.

1121. UNITED NATIONS. ECONOMIC COMMISSION FOR LATIN AMERICA. *Report on the ECLA/TAA Economic Development Training Programme.* Document E/CN.12/376. New York: 1955. 9 pp.

Provides a description of the origin, nature, and results of the combined Economic Commission for Latin America (ECLA)/Technical Assistance Administration (TAA) professional training program for selected Latin American economists in the field of economic development.

1122. UNITED NATIONS. SECRETARIAT. *Experimentos en formación profesional para el desarrollo de la comunidad en los paises de América Latina.* United Nations Series on Community Organization and Development, 29; Document ST/SOA/Ser.0/29 (ST/TAA/Ser.D/29). New York: 1957. 81 pp.

Describes the organization of a wide variety of professional level training courses (usually short-term) generally offered within public service agencies and associated with community development programs. Reports on programs in Bolivia, Brazil, Colombia, Costa Rica, El Salvador, Guatemala, Haiti, Mexico, and Puerto Rico.

VOCATIONAL SKILL TRAINING

*1123. CENTRO INTERAMERICANO DE INVESTIGACIÓN Y DOCUMENTACIÓN SOBRE FORMACIÓN PROFESIONAL. *Formación profesional rural; reunión técnica sobre métodos y medios de formación profesional para el sector rural en América Latina.* Montevideo: 1967. 115 pp.

1124. INTER-AMERICAN SEMINAR ON VOCATIONAL EDUCATION, UNIVERSITY OF MARYLAND, 1952. *Summary Report (Tentative).* Washington: Division of Education, Department of Cultural Affairs, Pan American Union, 1952. Various pagination.
    Very general recommendations, but list of working documents includes several pieces relating to nonformal vocational training in Latin America (e.g., SENAI in Brazil, SCIDE in Bolivia).

1125. INTERNATIONAL LABOR OFFICE. *Vocational Training: Third Item on the Agenda.* Conference of the American States Members of the ILO, 7th, Buenos Aires, 1961. Geneva: 1961. 128 pp.
    Lengthy section on apprenticeship programs in Latin America discusses such innovations as SENAI and SENAC in Brazil, CNAOP in Argentina, SENA in Colombia, and INCE in Venezuela. Further section covers new developments in the training of adults in special centers and places of employment. The section on training in handicrafts talks about training programs within craft cooperatives and unions and gives examples of programs in Ecuador and El Salvador. Also covers work in the area of handicraft training by the Andean Mission program of the International Labor Organization.

1126. STALEY, EUGENE. *Planning Occupational Education and Training for Development.* Praeger Special Studies in International Economics and Development. New York: Praeger, 1971. 188 pp.
    Short section is devoted to comments on the organizational structure and financing of apprenticeship training programs in Brazil, Colombia, Venezuela, Chile, Argentina, Peru, Costa Rica, and Ecuador.

1127. "The Training of Human Resources in the Economic and Social Development of Latin America," *Economic Bulletin for Latin America,* 11:2 (October, 1966), 1-57.
    Includes a brief section on training facilities outside the formal educa-

tion system which concentrates on specialized national training services, such as SENAI in Brazil, SENATI in Peru, and SENA in Colombia. Table 11 lists the major training services, the sectors they serve, their organization, financing, and main programs. A discussion of the needs of rural education calls for a nonformal approach.

MISCELLANEOUS

1128. BEHRMAN, DANIEL. *When the Mountains Move: Technical Assistance and the Changing Face of Latin America.* Paris: United Nations Educational, Scientific, and Cultural Organization, 1954. 69 pp.
Focuses on three programs in Latin America. The UNESCO pilot fundamental education project in the Valle El General, Costa Rica, runs the gamut of educational activities typical of such projects: crop and livestock production training, health and nutrition education, literacy instruction, for example. Colombia's Radio Sutatenza is a program of adult education administered by the Catholic Acción Cultural Popular. The weaving school in San Pedro Sacatepéquez, Guatemala, offers apprenticeship in weaving as well as elementary instruction in business methods such as accounting and marketing.

1129. CARROLL, THOMAS F. "Peasant Co-operation in Latin America," in Thomas F. Carroll, et al., *A Review of Rural Cooperation in Developing Areas.* Rural Institutions and Planned Change, 1. Geneva: United Nations Research Institute for Social Development, 1969, pp. 1-94.
Many efforts are recorded here in training, supervised credit, and other educational programs of rural cooperatives throughout Latin America. Good overview of cooperative activities in the region.

1130. CENTRO INTERAMERICANO DE EDUCACIÓN RURAL. *Educación de la comunidad (apuntes de clase).* 2d. ed. Publicaciones del Centro Interamericano de Educación Rural, 7. Washington: Pan American Union, 1962. 105 pp.
First several chapters are devoted to conceptual discussions of community development and fundamental education. Final chapters are given to an exploration and evaluation of fundamental education—community development programs in Bolivia (*núcleos escolares*), Puerto Rico (División de Educación de la Comunidad), and Mexico (Cultural Missions).

1131. CHACÓN NARDI, RAFAELA. "Notas sobre la educación fundamental en América Latina,'' Cuba, Comisión Nacional de la UNESCO, *Boletín,* 3:4 (April, 1954), 1-2.

Notes on the progress of CREFAL in Mexico, the pilot project in the Marbial Valley of Haiti, and Brazil's Campanha Nacional de Educação Rural.

1132. COOMBS, PHILIP HALL, and MANZOOR AHMED. *Attacking Rural Poverty: How Nonformal Education Can Help.* Baltimore: Johns Hopkins University Press, 1974. 292 pp.

Comprehensive study, international in approach, of problems facing rural areas and possible solutions to those problems, prepared by the International Council for Educational Development (ICED) for the World Bank. Chapter 4 focuses on the rural mobile training program of the Servicio Nacional de Aprendizaje (SENA) in Colombia, which began in 1967. Provides information on objectives, target groups, structure, facilities, methods, content, and staffing, and offers an appraisal of the program, known as Promoción Profesional Popular-Rural. Objectives are to provide short-term, low cost skill training to farmers, farm laborers, rural artisans, and small entrepreneurs. Courses are varied, ranging from crop and livestock methods to construction, mechanics, and human relations. Chapter 6 reports on the work of Acción Cultural Popular (ACPO), also in Colombia, which began in 1947 as an educational radio station and which has since expanded into a multipurpose, multimedia educational system (radio, newspaper, textbooks, correspondence courses). ACPO concentrates on literacy, fundamental education, and formal primary school equivalency courses, but it also has regular educational campaigns in agricultural techniques, health, and nutrition. In addition, it runs training institutes for field staff. The appraisal of this program is very positive. Chapter 7 relates the work of the Puebla Project in Mexico administered by the International Maize and Wheat Improvement Center (CIMMYT—Centro Internacional del Mejoramiento de Maíz y Trigo) and funded by the Rockefeller Foundation. In essence, this is a program of supervised credit. Offers a good discussion of objectives, management, staff, content and methods, facilities, and performance. Note that discussion of these projects is not limited to the chapters designated, but also appears in other chapters covering various aspects of nonformal education in rural areas, such as the economics of nonformal education and planning, organization, management, and staffing.

1133. ''Desarrollo de la educación de adultos en América,'' *Educación,* Washington, 1:4 (October/December, 1956), 19-45.

Brief historical review of adult education activities in a number of countries: Argentina, Brazil, Cuba, Chile, El Salvador, Peru. Dominican Republic, Uruguay, and Venezuela. Many focus on literacy education but other types of programs are discussed as well.

1134. "La educación en América," *Educación,* Washington, 1:4 (October/December, 1956), 47-58.
Brief accounts of educational programs in Bolivia (Servicio Cooperativo Interamericano de Educación—SCIDE), Brazil (Centro Regional de Educación de Base in Espírito Santo), Ecuador (literacy campaign of the Unión Nacional de Periodistas, and the Andean Mission program), Puerto Rico (literacy campaign), and Mexico (Cultural Missions).

1135. "La educación fundamental en América," *Educación,* Washington, 1:3 (July/September, 1956), 26-50.
Reports on a number of fundamental education programs in Latin America: in Bolivia, the Proyecto 'Copiasi' de Educación Fundamental and the community program of the Warisata Normal School; in Brazil, the Campanha Nacional de Educação Rural (CNER); in Colombia, the Escuela Superior de Orientación Rural Femenina's integral community education program; in Costa Rica, the Proyectos Pilotos de Educación Fundamental; in Chile, the Plan de Educación Fundamental in Ancud, Chiloé; in El Salvador, the Campaña de Alfabetización y de Educación Fundamental and the Brigadas Culturales; in Haiti, the Proyecto Piloto del Valle del Marbial; in Honduras, the Misiones Rurales; in Mexico, the Cultural Missions, Nayarit Project, CREFAL, Centros Coordinadores de Educación Indígena, and the Centros de Bienestar Social Rural; in Peru, the *núcleos escolares campesinos,* Grupos Móviles, and Centros de Educación Fundamental.

1136. García Jiménez, Jesús. *Televisión educativa para América Latina.* Instituto Latinoamericano de la Comunicación Educativa. México: Editorial Porrúa, 1970. 358 pp.
Chapter on television and functional literacy briefly mentions television programs entitled "Escuelas de Padres" which are directed toward families and attempt to deal with modern parent-child problems and which have had some success in Argentina and Venezuela. This chapter also includes a section on a rural television program directed toward women in Chile which is under the direction of the Fundaciones de Vida Rural of the Catholic University of Chile. The final chapter has sections on a wide variety of programs in various Latin American countries (Argentina, Brazil, Chile, Guatemala, Peru, Venezuela) which are directed toward out-of-school audiences.

1137. Hall, J. Thomas. "Vocational Training of Conscripts in the Armed

Forces of Selected Latin American Nations,'' *Labor Developments Abroad,* 15:8 (August, 1970), 1-11.

Reports on industrial or agricultural vocational training provided by the armed forces in: Argentina (limited to conscripts serving in Patagonia); Brazil (often in conjunction with SENAI or SENAC); Chile; Colombia (by contract with SENA); Ecuador; Guatemala; Peru (with the largest and most comprehensive program); and Venezuela (operated by INCE). Also includes brief comments on programs in Bolivia, Dominican Republic, El Salvador, Honduras, Paraguay, and Uruguay.

1138. HALLE, LOUIS J. ''Co-operative Agricultural Programmes of the Institute of Inter-American Affairs,'' U.S. Department of State, *Bulletin,* 18:467 (June 13, 1948), 758-762.

The Servicio Técnico Interamericano de Cooperación Agrícola (STICA) participates in a supervised rural credit program in Paraguay wherein STICA personnel act as extension agents demonstrating new methods and techniques. STICA also has an extension program in home economics which works in conjunction with the supervised credit program and has established a demonstration farm colony. The cooperative agricultural program of the Institute of Inter-American Affairs in Haiti and the Servicio Cooperativo Inter-Americano de Producción de Alimientos (SCIPA) in Peru are described in less detail.

1139. HAUCH, CHARLES C. *The Current Situation in Latin American Education.* U.S. Office of Education, Bulletin 1963, no. 21. Washington: Government Printing Office, 1963. 30 pp.

Brief section on adult and community education mentions programs such as Radio Sutatenza in Colombia, the Cultural Missions in Mexico, SENAI in Brazil, and SENA in Colombia.

1140. HUIZER, GERRITT. ''Desarrollo de la comunidad y reforma agraria,'' *América Indígena,* 27:2 (April, 1967), 283-300.

Discussion of methodological problems in planning and implementing community development programs. To illustrate his point the author uses examples of what he views as successful (Vico in Peru, las Fincas de Beneficio Proporcional in El Salvador) and unsuccessful (*ejido* program in Comarca Lagunera, Mexico; Turrialba extension program in Costa Rica; community development program in the Valle de la Esperanza in El Salvador).

1141. ''Integral Local Development Programmes in Latin America,'' *Economic Bulletin for Latin America,* 13:2 (November, 1968), 49-75.

Excellent article with accompanying table detailing community development programs within each country. Best comprehensive listing of projects encountered providing information about sponsoring agencies, legal bases, coverage, administrative hierarchy, levels of planning, substantive complexity, and training media. Text of the article provides a general description of programs, analysis, and trends.

1142. INTER-AMERICAN CONFERENCE ON INDIAN LIFE, 5TH QUITO, 1964. *V Congreso Indigenista Interamericano.* Quito: Tall. Graf. Nacionales, 1965. 5 vols.

Volume 2, on the education and integration of indigenous groups, was the most valuable in terms of information included on nonformal educational programs. The article entitled "Educación Indígena" includes some description and statistics on out-of-school programs in Mexico. Those mentioned are literacy centers, cultural centers, Cultural Missions, Brigadas de Promoción Indígena, radio school programs, Centros Coordinadores of the Instituto Nacional Indigenista, and various community development programs. The article entitled "El Adiestramiento Universitario para el Desarrollo de la Comunidad" describes Peru's Cooperación Popular community development program, its goals and organization. One element of the program is the organization of volunteer university student groups who are dispersed to communities throughout the country to help implement the program. A third article on the use of social promoters in programs of indigenous integration describes the training of local leaders in the Programa Puno Tambopata of the Plan Nacional de Integración de la Población Aborigen (PNIPA) and the Andean Mission program, two community development programs in Peru.

1143. INTERNATIONAL LABOR OFFICE. *Indigenous Peoples: Living and Working Conditions of Aboriginal Populations in Independent Countries.* Studies and Reports, New Series, 35. Geneva: 1953. 628 pp.

Chapter 10 touches on a great many programs, both public and private, in the areas of vocational and handicraft training and basic education in Latin American countries. Included are Brazil's Service for the Protection of Indians, Ecuador's agricultural training and vocational apprenticeship in workshops of the Order of St. Joseph of Turin and workshops of Salesian monks, Mexico's Cultural Missions, Peru's Brigadas de Culturización Indígena, Mexico's textile workshop and training center in Ixmiquilpán, and Peru's system of handicraft retraining centers. Chapter 11 discusses measures taken by governments specifically for indigenous populations: literacy work by the Ecuadorean Literacy League and the Unión Nacional de Periodistas; Ecuador's mobile rural cultural extension service (SAREC); Ecuador's textile center at Otavalo; Guatemala's literacy campaign; Mexico's *ejido* supervised farm credit program; Mexico's Indian Betterment Brigades; and Mexico's Cultural Missions. Chapter 12 concentrates on

international action, including UNESCO's Pátzcuaro Center (CRE-
FAL), FAO participation in Ecuador's textile center at Otavalo, and the
Andean Mission program.

1144. INTERNATIONAL LABOR OFFICE. *Vocational Training*. Third Conference of American States Members of the International Labor
Organization, Mexico City, 1946, Report 2. Montreal: 1946.
134 pp.
    Chapter 2 includes sections which discuss a wide range of activities
    throughout Latin America, such as apprenticeship, in-plant training,
    supplementary part-time training, training for agricultural occupa-
    pations, and training and retraining of adult workers.

1145. INTERNATIONAL LABOR OFFICE. *Vocational Training in Latin America*.
Studies and Reports, New Series, 28. Geneva: 1951. 319 pp.
    Lengthy, though general, report of the state of vocational and agri-
    cultural training. Chapters 3 and 4 deal with nonformal as well as
    formal programs, such as SENAI in Brazil, the Cultural Missions in
    Mexico, various agricultural extension services, and SCIPA in Costa
    Rica, Paraguay, and Peru. Particularly valuable are the detailed
    country reports in Appendix 1 for Argentina, Bolivia, Brazil, Chile,
    Colombia, Costa Rica, Cuba, Ecuador, Guatemala, Mexico, Peru,
    Uruguay, and Venezuela.

1146. KEMPLER, HOMER. "Patterns of Adult Education in Latin America,"
Adult Education Journal, 9:1 (January, 1950), 13-18.
    General report breaking down adult education programs into types:
    (1) literacy programs; (2) cultural missions (Mexico); (3) special
    projects (nuclear schools of Bolivia, Peru, and Guatemala; Amazon
    health education campaign in Brazil; UNESCO fundamental educa-
    tion programs; Puerto Rico's Division of Community Education);
    (4) other public adult education (agricultural extension services and
    health and nutrition programs of the various Ministries of Health).

1147. MCANANY, EMILE G. "Radio Schools in Nonformal Education: An
Evaluation Perspective," in Thomas J. La Belle, ed., *Educational
Alternatives in Latin America: Social Change and Social Stratifi-
cation*. Latin American Studies Series, 30. Los Angeles: Latin
American Center, University of California, 1975, pp. 238-254.
    Evaluates the performance of radio schools on five criteria—effort,
    performance, adequacy, efficiency, and process—based on the litera-
    ture available. Those schools specifically mentioned include Colom-
    bia's Acción Cultural Popular (ACPO), Brazil's Movimento de Edu-
    cação de Base (MEB), Honduras' Acción Cultural Popular Hondureña
    (ACPH), and Mexico's Tarahumara project. Comments on the future

of radio school efforts in Latin America. Includes a table of radio school projects on a country-by-country basis in Latin America for 1973.

1148. MEEK, GEORGE. "Training for Future Farmers: OAS Program Seeks to Strengthen Rural Youth Clubs," *Americas*, 16:10 (October, 1964), 32-34.

Discusses the work and importance of rural youth clubs throughout Latin America. Focuses on the promotional and coordinating activities of the Inter-American Rural Youth Program sponsored by the Inter-American Institute of Agricultural Sciences in Turrialba, Costa Rica. The Program also trains technicians working in rural youth programs. These endeavors are viewed as a vital means of disseminating information to rural populations.

1149. MORIALDO DE ABADIE SORIANO, OFELIA. "Análisis y crítica de la llamada educación fundamental," *Enciclopedia de Educación*, 13:1 (January, 1953), 95-156.

Discusses the concepts of fundamental education, using the Marbial project in Haiti, Vianí in Colombia, CREFAL, Mexico's Cultural Missions, and the Brazilian literacy campaign to illustrate points.

1150. MOSHER, ARTHUR T. *Technical Co-operation in Latin American Agriculture*. National Planning Association, Studies of Technical Cooperation in Latin America. Chicago: University of Chicago Press, 1957. 443 pp.

Presents case studies of extension and agricultural assistance programs, offering an evaluation and critique of each. The Servicio Cooperativo Interamericano de Producción de Alimientos (SCIPA) in Peru emphasizes extension work, which represents about half of its annual expenditures. Also works to maintain livestock demonstration farms and machinery pools. The Service Coopératif Interaméricain de Production Agricole (SCIPA) of Haiti has similar functions to those of SCIPA in Peru, again with emphasis on extension services, including youth clubs, in-service training for extension agents, and home demonstration. Mexico's Oficina de Estudios Especiales (OEE) concentrates on agricultural research, but does offer a type of apprenticeship trainee program each year to graduates of agricultural colleges. The Cooperative Agricultural Commission in Cuba is similar to Mexico's OEE in scope and programs. The Associação de Crédito e Assistência Rural (ACAR) in Minas Gerais, Brazil, carries on a program of supervised credit, farm and home extension education, and rural health education. Project 39 of the OAS, which is hemispherical in scope, concentrates on professional training courses and demonstration areas for its three geographic zones.

1151. "Popular Participation and Principles of Community Development in Relation to the Acceleration of Economic and Social Development," *Economic Bulletin for Latin America,* 9:2 (November, 1964), 225-255.

> Part B is devoted to a discussion of the principles of community development and trends in community development programming. Several programs are used as examples to illustrate points.

1152. PRIETO FIGUEROA, LUIS BELTRÁN. *La colaboración privada con la educación popular americana.* Publicaciones de la Dirección de Cultura de la Universidad Central. Caracas: Universidad Central de Venezuela, 1959. 236 pp.

> Valuable historical account of compulsory and voluntary private participation in educational programs, from literacy campaigns to in-plant educational and training programs, to coordinated vocational training programs such as SENAI in Brazil. Chapters 3 and 4 are devoted to country-by-country descriptions, covering virtually every Latin American nation. Also includes a chapter on labor union educational activities.

1153. "Revolution in Latin America," *Times Educational Supplement,* 2602 (April 2, 1965), 998.

> Comments on radio and television efforts in fundamental education (e.g., the Maryknoll radio program in Puno which teaches literacy, farming, hygiene, and current affairs).

1154. RUBIO ORBE, GONZALO. "Educación e integración de grupos indígenas," *América Indígena,* 25:2 (April, 1965), 179-228.

> Details what he sees as basic needs of and approaches to indigenous education, and in the section on adult education describes many programs which have already been implemented in Latin America, such as the Mexican Cultural Missions, Peru-Cornell Project, Summer Institute of Linguistics work, and the Brigadas Culturales of Peru and El Salvador.

1155. RUBIO ORBE, GONZALO. "Educación e integración de grupos indígenas," Universidad Central del Ecuador, *Anales,* 93:348 (1964), 5-54.

> Uses community development programs in Bolivia (Huatajata and the Andean Mission program), Peru (Andean Mission), Ecuador (Andean Mission), and Mexico (Centros de Coordinación Indigenista) as examples of programs designed to integrate indigenous populations into national life. Also comments on CREFAL, *núcleos escolares,* and the Peru-Cornell Project. The term "education" is used in the broadest sense throughout the article.

1156. RUBIO ORBE, GONZALO. "Educación e integración económica y cultural de los grupos indígenas," Instituto Interamericano del Niño, *Boletín*, 36:1:140 (March, 1962), 79-94.

Discusses and offers an analysis of a variety of educational programs directed toward indigenous populations of Mexico, Guatemala, Ecuador, Peru, and Bolivia.

1157. RUBIO ORBE, GONZALO. *Promociones indígenas en América.* Quito: Editorial Casa de la Cultura Ecuatoriana, 1957. 404 pp.

Discusses in detail the following programs: in Mexico, the programs of the Instituto Nacional Indigenista, particularly the *comunidades de promoción indígena* and literacy work; the work of the nuclear school in Warisata, Bolivia; in Peru, the Peru-Cornell Project in Vicos and farm demonstration projects; in Ecuador, the textile center in Otavalo (under the sponsorship of the FAO and Point Four), work of the Servicio Ambulante Rural de Extensión Cultural (SAREC), and the activities of various religious groups, such as radio programs, health education, domestic improvement, and literacy training.

1158. SAVLOFF, GUILLERMO. *Educación de la comunidad.* Biblioteca Pedagogos de América. Buenos Aires: Bibliográfica Omeba, 1969. 206 pp.

The basic premise of this work is that the school must do much more than teach traditional courses to the young. It must *lead* the community in social transformation. Chapter 6 is devoted to types of programs possible, providing a lengthy discussion of methods of approach. Chapters 11 and 12 describe in detail two examples of community schools (open to all): (1) lists activities and describes the organization of the school in Berisso, province of Buenos Aires; and (2) the *núcleo rural* in La Mina, department of Cerro Largo, Uruguay. Chapter 13 talks about the Mexican Cultural Missions, and chapter 14 discusses adult education in Argentina. Appendix 4 details the Proyecto Piloto de Casa de Jóvenes, an institution of popular education in Argentina open to all, but which is primarily where young people can go in their free time to develop their own interests. Activities and services include library, workshops, theater-meeting room, photo lab, kitchen, and sports facilities.

1159. SEMINARIO REGIONAL DE ASUNTOS SOCIALES. *Informe final, Seminarios Regionales de Asuntos Sociales: Resumen de las discusiones de la mesa redonda.* Washington: Departamento de Asuntos Económicos y Sociales, Unión Panamericana, 1952. 4 vols.

Volume 2, on workers' education, mentions a number of varied projects of worker education in progress and proposes initiation of others—libraries at places of work or in workers' centers, *centros de educa-*

ción obrera, and *institutos de trabajo.* Programs of health and adult education in Guatemala and El Salvador are discussed. Volume 1, on cooperatives, devotes a section to the need for educational efforts within cooperatives (both practical and fundamental).

1160. "South American TV," *Times Educational Supplement,* 2685 (November 4, 1966), 1104.

Gives a brief overview of problems facing education in Latin America and proposes ways in which television could be used most effectively to overcome the deficit in formal schooling. Notes broadly based educational television programming in Brazil, El Salvador, and Peru.

1161. THOMSON, R. *Educational Aspects of Community Development.* South Pacific Commission, Technical Paper, 74. Noumea, New Caledonia: 1955. 89 pp.

Brief reference to the traveling "itinerant" school in Chile: a caravan drawn by a tractor containing movie projector, loud speakers, and sewing machine. Its staff teaches reading and writing, sewing, weaving, and other handicrafts, and domestic arts. Also includes a short discussion of the community development campaign in Jamaica with projects focusing on nutrition and agriculture organized by voluntary leaders.

1162. UNITED NATIONS. BUREAU OF SOCIAL AFFAIRS. *International Survey of Programmes of Social Development.* Document E/CN.5/301/ Rev. 1, ST/SOA/21. New York: 1955. 219 pp.

Very general and selective reporting on the Costa Rican nutrition education campaign through nutrition centers for pregnant and nursing women, Brazil's nationwide adult education campaign initiated in 1947, Colombia's Radio Sutatenza project which uses radio for fundamental educational programming, and the SCIPA agricultural and home extension programs in several Latin American countries.

1163. UNITED NATIONS. DEPARTMENT OF SOCIAL AFFAIRS. *Biennial Report on Community, Family and Child Welfare, 1949 and 1950.* Document ST/SOA/Ser.D/2. New York: 1953. Various pagination.

Reports mention various nonformal programs such as the parent education programs in Chile which are provided by organizations concerned with maternal and child welfare and through mothers' centers, adult education facilities in Cuba which concentrate on literacy and agricultural instruction, and the Misiones Ambulantes de Cultura Inicial and adult education (primarily literacy work) at the Universidad Popular in Guatemala.

1164. UNITED NATIONS. DEPARTMENT OF SOCIAL AFFAIRS. *Sample List of*

Community Welfare Centres and Community Development Projects. Document ST/SOA/10. New York: 1952. 38 pp.

Provides a geographical listing of centers and projects. Sections for Latin America cover: Costa Rica—Turrialba Rural Center; Haiti— Haiti pilot project in the Marbial Valley, Orientation Schools, Service Coopératif Inter-Américain de Santé Publique (SCISP) and Service Coopératif Inter-Américain de Production Agricole (SCIPA); Mexico—*ejido* programs, Cultural Missions, CREFAL, Camohmila rural demonstration center, Nayarit pilot project; Jamaica—Jamaica Social Welfare Commission, Jamaica Agricultural Society; Trinidad and Tobago—Education Extension Service; Puerto Rico—Division of Community Education, Land Authority demonstration farms, Housing Authority; Brazil—rural missions for adult education; Colombia— Vianí project; Ecuador—medical centers and social missions, Reconstruction Board for Tungurahua, Otavalo Community Development; Paraguay—Capiatá Domestic Work Center; Peru—Cultural Brigades; Venezuela—American International Association (AIA) program.

1165. UNITED NATIONS. ECONOMIC COMMISSION FOR LATIN AMERICA. *Education, Human Resources and Development in Latin America.* Document E/CN.12/800. New York: 1968. 269 pp.

Chapter 2, section A, presents a picture of the present education system, which is divided into two parts: formal education system and nonformal instruction. The latter discusses the many and varied approaches, from training in the industrial sector through banks, public services, armed forces, trade unions, and cultural associations. Gives a good historical summary of nonformal programs. Table 8 presents a systematic breakdown of the kinds of institutions involved, principle training methods used, and the types of programs undertaken. Table 9 contains information on the main specialized training services in Latin America: SENA, SENAC, SENAI, SENATI, SCT (Servicio de Cooperación Técnica—Chile), INCE, CONET, and UT (Universidad de Trabajo—Uruguay). Chapter 2, section B, talks about expansion requirements with respect to educational and training facilities. It tackles the question of formal versus nonformal education and concludes that the two must coexist, but with closer ties. In chapter 3, the section on rural education again debates the formal/nonformal problem. Table 19 provides a country-by-country overview of the educational targets embodied in national plans; one category is technical training outside the formal education system.

1166. UNITED NATIONS. ECONOMIC COMMISSION FOR LATIN AMERICA. *Social Trends and Programmes in Latin America.* Document E/CN.12/645. New York: 1963. 59 pp.

While focusing primarily on agrarian-land distribution reform, some discussion of community development programs (e.g., Andean Mission program) and supervised credit (Mexico's Banco de Crédito Ejidal and Brazil's Associação de Crédito e Assistência Rural) is included.

1167. UNITED NATIONS EDUCATIONAL, SCIENTIFIC, AND CULTURAL ORGANIZATION. DEPARTMENT OF EDUCATION. *Report on the Study and Information Seminar for Leaders of Youth Movements in Latin America, Ceiba del Agua, Havana, Cuba, 5-26 October 1954.* Document ED/140. Paris: 1955. 22 pp.
Includes a section on youth organizations and fundamental education. Points out that youth organizations have carried out activities in literacy campaigns, hygiene and nutrition education, and the provision of practical information to the general population.

1168. U. S. OFFICE OF INTERNATIONAL HEALTH. *Health, Population and Nutrition Activities.* Washington: 1971. 405 pp.
Provides brief descriptions of health and nutrition education (Panama and Nicaragua rural mobile health units) and family planning programs (Chile, Costa Rica, Guatemala, Jamaica, El Salvador, Nicaragua, Panama, Paraguay, Venezuela) funded by Agency for International Development grants in 1969-1970.

1169. "Youth and Work in Latin America II: Youth Employment Prospects," *International Labour Review*, 90:2 (August, 1964), 150-179.
Good article offering some discussion of SENAI/SENAC, SENA, and CONET policies of vocational information, selection, counseling, and placement. The section dealing with vocational training acknowledges systematic in-plant training programs in Colombia and Chile. Devotes sections to apprenticeship programs and vocational training for women, noting particularly those of SENAI/SENAC, SENA, and SENATI. The section on elementary vocational training touches on a number of interesting nonformal programs such as: the new (1962) Mexican vocational training program; Dom Bosco schools, which provide skilled apprenticeship training; Andean Mission program; special literacy and skill training offered to conscripts in the military services of Colombia and Peru; Rural Extension Service efforts in Brazil; and the Rural Education Institute training program for rural promoters.

Conceptualization

1170. ABADIE SORIANO, ROBERTO. "Finalidades de la educación de adultos," *Anales de Instrucción Primaria*, 2a. época, 13:1 (January, 1950), 3-10.

Proposes a working definition of adult education and methods for its implementation. Adult education must be nonformal, out-of-school, and should be realized through a variety of approaches.

1171. ALTOBERRO, MARÍA CELIA, ROBERTO ABADIE SORIANO, and AFREDO RAVERA. "El Seminario Interamericano de Alfabetización y Educación de Adultos celebrado en Petrópolis, Brasil, bajo los auspicios de la UNESCO y la Unión de los Estados Americanos," *Anales de Instrucción Primaria*, 2a. época, 13:6 (June, 1950), 5-73.

Report of the literacy and adult education seminar held in Petrópolis in 1949. Delegates recognize the importance of fundamental education and call for programs of adult education through university extension, cooperatives, labor union, cultural missions, popular libraries, public health services, agricultural extension, religious and military institutions, and radio and television programming, as well as through the school system.

1172. AMAYA DE ORTIZ, MYRTHA N. *Educación de adultos: Teoría y práctica*. Buenos Aires: Librería de las Naciones, 1968. 119 pp.

School cannot meet all educational needs: other institutions must also be involved. Presents a philosophy of adult education, suggesting bases for the programming of adult education and methods and techniques. Includes a chapter on *ciclos culturales* as educational forums.

1173. AZUAJE, JOSÉ. "Reportaje sobre el seminario regional de educación de América Latina: Cinco semanas en pro de América," *Educación*, Caracas, 9:56 (August/September, 1948), 3-27; 10:57 (October, 1948/January, 1949), 18-39.

Résumé of discussions and recommendations of the Latin American education seminar. Topics reported on include literacy programs, adult and fundamental education, and rural education.

1174. BARRACLOUGH, SOLON L. "Training for Land Reform and Cooperatives," in Food and Agricultural Organization, Rural Institutions

Division, *Information on Land Reform, Land Settlement and Co-operatives*. Number 2. Rome: 1967, pp. 26-30.
Calls for systematic training on all levels, from professional to peasant, in order to implement agrarian reform. Based on experience with the Agrarian Reform Training and Research Institute (ICIRA) in Chile.

1175. BUITRÓN, ANÍBAL. *Cómo llegó el progreso a Huagrapampa: Guía práctica para los trabajadores del desarrollo de la comunidad.* Instituto Indigenista Interamericano, Serie Antropología Social, 4. México: Instituto Indigenista Interamericano, 1966. 121 pp.
Fictionalized conception of a community development project, based on experiences at Kuyo Chico and Vicos in Peru and at Pátzcuaro, Mexico while the author was serving as assistant director.

1176. BUITRÓN, ANÍBAL. "Integrated Action and Community Development," *Adult Leadership*, 14:2 (June, 1965), 52-54, 77.
Critique of the concept and praxis of community development programs: too much is attempted at once. Cites lack of organization, scope, authority, and finances as reasons for failure. Uses an unnamed program in Peru as an example. Advocates following a "logical order of priorities" rather than doing everything at once. See also: "La acción integral y desarrollo de la comunidad," *América Indígena*, 25:1 (January, 1965), 27-34.

1177. CARIBBEAN NUTRITION SEMINAR, SAN JUAN, PUERTO RICO, 1961. *Report*. FAO Nutrition Special Reports, 1. Rome: Food and Agricultural Organization, 1962. 61 pp.
Takes account of the need for health education programs out of the school and calls on rural extension services to provide information to the population. Also notes the role that rural youth clubs can play in the dissemination of health and nutrition information. Emphasizes the importance of health educators in community development programs. Recommends the use of mobile cinema units, puppet shows, lectures, and a variety of other means to reach people.

1178. CENTRO REGIONAL DE EDUCACIÓN FUNDAMENTAL PARA LA AMÉRICA LATINA. "Literacy and Adult Education," in Egbert de Vries, ed., *Social Research and Rural Life in Central America, Mexico and the Caribbean Region: Proceedings of a Seminar Organized by UNESCO in Cooperation with the United Nations Economic Commission for Latin America, Mexico City, 17-27 October 1962.* Technology and Society Series. Paris: United Nations Educational, Scientific, and Cultural Organization, 1966, pp. 219-229.
Proposes the creation of Literacy and Adult Education Departments

which must formulate broadly based programs covering community education, functional literacy campaigns, extension services, vocational training, and youth activities. Also encourages the creation of national community development training centers for training social promoters and other necessary personnel.

1179. CHAPARRO, ALVARO. "Education and Training for Agricultural Development," in Raymond F. Lyons, ed., *Problems and Strategies of Educational Planning: Lessons from Latin America*. Paris: International Institute for Educational Planning, United Nations Educational, Scientific, and Cultural Organization, 1966, pp. 76-81.
Deals with out-of-school agricultural training and the social benefits which can be derived from it.

1180. CHONCHOL, JACQUES. *El desarrollo de América Latina y la reforma agraria*. 2d. ed. Santiago: Editorial del Pacífico, 1965. 112 pp.
Chapter 6.3 on peasant education and training calls for the development of intensive systems of agricultural extension to reach the masses of illiterate rural farmers. Those with technical expertise should train lower level people to do basic extension work in the field in an effort to get around the problem of a shortage of qualified agronomists.

1181. CIUDAD, MARIO. "Las universidades latinoamericanas y la educación de adultos," Universidad de Chile, *Anales,* 124:140 (October/ December, 1966), 227-238.
Discusses the role of university extension in the broad context of adult education; the university should be at more advanced levels of non-formal instruction. Nonformal education should range from fundamental education programs to university extension, with each level carefully directed to a particular portion of the adult population. The author feels, for instance, that a literacy program directed by the University at Concepción (Chile), while of social value, should not have been undertaken by the university, but rather should have been left to its proper *"tarea"* in the basic education level.

1182. CLERCK, M. DE. "Social Research and Education for Rural Development in a Traditional Environment," in Egbert de Vries, ed., *Social Research and Rural Life in Central America, Mexico and the Caribbean Region: Proceedings of a Seminar Organized by UNESCO in Cooperation with the United Nations Economic Commission for Latin America, Mexico City, 17-27 October 1962.* Technology and Society Series. Paris: United Nations Educational, Scientific, and Cultural Organization, 1966, pp. 205-217.
Devotes some attention to the question of education for rural commun-

ity development, which has been largely of a nonformal nature. Declares that "classical" education is not sufficient to meet the requirements for technological and social change.

1183. "Conference on Education and Economic and Social Development in Latin America, Santiago, Chile, 1962," *Economic Bulletin for Latin America,* 7:2 (October, 1962), 193-213.

Recommendations include active promotion of nonformal programs essential to broadening the educated base of Latin American societies. Specifically recommends literacy programs, extension courses, community development programs, vocational training, and cultural extension. Further recommendations can be found in the sections on literacy campaigns and adult education, vocational training, and technical education. See also: "Conferencia sobre educación y desarrollo económico y social en América Latina," *Educación,* Washington, 7:25/26 (January/June, 1962), 59-103; and UNITED NATIONS. ECONOMIC COMMISSION FOR LATIN AMERICA. *Provisional Report of the Conference on Education and Economic and Social Development in Latin America.* Document E/CN.12/639. New York: 1963. 401 pp.

1184. COOMBS, PHILIP H. *The World Educational Crisis: A Systems Analysis.* New York: Oxford University Press, 1968. 241 pp.

Includes a section on the needs of developing nations with regard to nonformal education with specific reference to Latin America.

1185. "La educación extraescolar: Conclusiones a que llegó el Primer Congreso Mexicano de Educación Rural," *Revista del Maestro,* 4:11/12 (October, 1948/March, 1949), 68-72.

Early recognition of the insufficiency of formal schooling to meet educational needs and demands and the need for planned programs of nonformal education. Includes a general discussion of methods for the dissemination of information.

1186. FALS BORDA, ORLANDO. *Cooperatives and Rural Development in Latin America: An Analytic Report.* Rural Institutions and Planned Change, 3. Geneva: United Nations Research Institute for Social Development, 1971. 147 pp.

The chapter on the organization of cooperatives devotes a section to a description of educational campaigns on cooperative principles and methods directed toward peasants to promote the idea of cooperatives and to gain the acceptance of the peasants. These campaigns have subsequently been judged "irrelevant" to the success of a cooperative venture. However, training provided by the cooperative in administration and accounting was found to be useful.

1187. FREIRE, PAULO. "Adult Literacy Process as Cultural Action for Freedom," *Harvard Educational Review,* 40:2 (May, 1970), 205-225.

Freire discusses his theories on illiteracy and his approach (*conscientización*) to literacy training in the context of Latin America.

1188. FREIRE, PAULO. "Cultural Action and Conscientization," *Harvard Educational Review*, 40:3 (August, 1970), 452-477.
Further consideration of Freire's philosophy and social context of his thought. Dwells on concept of cultural action for cultural freedom.

*1189. FREIRE, PAULO. *Cultural Action for Freedom*. Monograph Series, 1. Cambridge, Massachusetts: Harvard Educational Review, 1970. 55 pp.

1190. FREIRE, PAULO. *Educação como prática da liberdade*. Série Ecumenismo e Humanismo, 5. Rio de Janeiro: Editôra Paz e Terra, 1967. 150 pp.
Freire's concepts further elaborated, with an introduction to the man and his thought by Francisco C. Weffort. See also his: *La educación como práctica de la libertad*. Lima: Fondo de Cultura Universitaria, 1970. 80 pp.

1191. FREIRE, PAULO. *Pedagogy of the Oppressed*. Translated by Myra Bergman Ramos. New York: Herder and Herder, 1970. 186 pp.
Freire expands on his concepts of *conscientización* as the means for awakening the consciousness of the peasants during a process of literacy training. See also his: *Pedagogía del oprimido*. Lima: 1971. 250 pp.; and *Conciencia, crítica y liberación: pedagogía del oprimido*. Bogotá: Ediciones 'Camilo', 1971. 237 pp.

1192. FREIRE, PAULO. *Sobre la acción cultural*. Lima: Fondo de Cultura Magisterial, 1972. 116 pp.
Series of papers written by Freire while he was working for the Instituto de Capacitación e Investigación en Reforma Agraria (ICIRA) in Chile. Presents his educational methodology, which is radically opposed to the formal school system. His pedagogy calls for the cultural milieu to act as the locus for free and creative educational processes. An expansion of his views expressed in *Pedagogy of the Oppressed*.

1193. GONZÁLEZ RIVERA, MANUEL. "La función social del radio como agencia de cultura colectiva, especialmente en el ramo de la educación higiénica popular," *Salubridad y Asistencia*, 7:2 (March/April, 1947), 175-182.
Discusses the importance of radio in health education in underdeveloped nations because of the broad base it can cover and because there is no need to cope with illiteracy. Calls for greatly extending the present use of radio in the field of health education.

1194. HAUSER, PHILLIP M., ed. *Urbanization in Latin America: Proceedings of a Seminar Jointly Sponsored by the Bureau of Social Affairs of the United Nations, the Economic Commission for Latin America and UNESCO (in Co-operation with the International Labor Organization and the Organization of American States), Santiago (Chile), 6-18 July 1959.* Technology and Society Series. Paris: United Nations Educational, Scientific, and Cultural Organization, 1961. 331 pp.
    Briefly deals with the question of formal and nonformal education as related to the problems of urbanization. Only one of many areas of concern discussed with regard to urbanization.

1195. ILLICH, IVAN. "False Ideology of Schooling," *Saturday Review,* 53:42 (October 17, 1970), 56-58, 68.
    Discusses psychological and financial reasons why obligatory schooling is a failure in terms of society as a whole in Latin America.

1196. ILLICH, IVAN. "The Futility of Schooling in Latin America," *Saturday Review,* 51:16 (April 20, 1968), 57-59, 74-75.
    Psychological and financial drawbacks to compulsory, universal schooling in Latin America.

1197. JONES, EARL. "An Analysis of Inter-American Adult Education Programs," *Phi Delta Kappan,* 45:4 (January, 1964), 189-192.
    Offers a critique and analysis of the apparent failures of post World War II adult education–community development programs in Latin America, such as CREFAL, Brazil's rural education campaign, and Vicos in Peru. Believes that programs have never been soundly based, lacking a clear-cut expression of the philosophy behind the programming.

1198. LA BELLE, THOMAS J. "The Impact of Nonformal Education on Income in Industry: Ciudad Guyana, Venezuela," in Thomas J. La Belle, ed., *Educational Alternatives in Latin America: Social Change and Social Stratification.* Latin American Studies Series, 30. Los Angeles: Latin American Center, University of California, 1975, pp. 257-292.
    Reports on a survey designed to assess the impact of nonformal education on income earning potential in industry. Results indicate that out-of-school education may do little to foster greater access to economic resources.

1199. LA BELLE, THOMAS J., and ROBERT E. VERHINE. "Education, Social Change, and Social Stratification," in Thomas J. La Belle, ed., *Educational Alternatives in Latin America: Social Change and Social Stratification.* Latin American Studies Series, 30. Los

Angeles: Latin American Center, University of California, 1975, pp. 3-71.

Introduction to the concepts of nonformal education, relating those concepts to recent developments in Latin America. Expounds on the increasing attention being paid to educational alternatives in the region and elsewhere and analyzes them from the standpoint of social change and social stratification.

1200. LAGOS ORBETA, GASTÓN. *Una revolución educacional: Enseñanza de adultos y educación post-escolar.* Talca, Chile: Librería e Impr. 'Torre', 1948. 226 pp.

Calls for the creation of a system of educational facilities and programs to be made available to the adult public as a whole, with programs ranging from apprenticeship and health centers to mobile libraries and radio schools.

*1201. LLOYD, A. S. "Freire, Conscientization, and Adult Education," *Adult Education,* 23 (Fall, 1972), 3-20.

1202. LOURENÇO, MANOEL BERGSTRÖM. "Review of the Rio Seminar," *Fundamental Education,* 2:1 (January, 1950), 16-19.

Recognizes the failure of schools in Latin America to provide cultural relevancy. There must be new and broader approaches to education in order to reach the people. Sees this aim being accomplished through adult fundamental education programs. Schools in Latin America only answer the needs of a few people and, as designed, cannot serve as satisfactory institutions of mass education until certain levels of political, social, and economic development have been reached.

1203. MANRIQUE DE LARA, JUANA. "La biblioteca pública y la educación de los adultos," México, Biblioteca Nacional, *Boletín,* 1:2 (April/June, 1950), 16-27.

Calls for public libraries to take an active and direct part in adult education, both as an adjunct to formal schools and as initiators of courses for adults, particularly in Latin America where schooling is not readily available to all.

1204. MARTIN, D'ARCY. "Pedagogía y política: La educación de adultos en América Latina," *Convergence,* 4:1 (1971), 54-60.

Radical analysis of adult education in Latin America, dismissing the notion of political neutrality in educational planning. Calls for the Freire approach to adult education—to awaken social consciousness and introduce praxis into the learning process.

1205. MORALES BENÍTEZ, OTTO. "Extensión agrícola y desarrollo rural," *Arco,* 16 (September/October, 1961), 328-332.

Stresses the importance of agricultural extension in adult education
and rural development. Sees the necessity for nonformal, out-of-school
educational resources to reach the adult population. Rural extension is
referred to as a new type of education.

1206. MOREIRA, JOÃO ROBERTO. "Educação elementar em face do planejamento econômico," *Revista Brasileira de Estudos Pedagógicos,*
28:67 (July/September, 1957), 155-168.
Section on emergency instruction deals with the need for short-term
intensive instruction, particularly in the areas of literacy and vocational training, in order to reach those who are unable, for whatever
reason, to participate in the formal primary school system.

1207. MOREIRA, JOÃO ROBERTO. "Educação rural e educação de base,"
Revista Brasileira de Estudos Pedagógicos, 28:67 (July/September,
1957), 87-143.
In a lengthy exposition on rural education, Moreira discusses the need
for basic, suppletive educational programs to meet the special needs
of rural areas. Focuses on the role of basic education in the rural
setting.

1208. MURILLO REVALOS, JOSÉ ANTONIO. "Definición conceptual de educación extra-escolar," Morelia, México, Universidad Michoacana
de San Nicolas de Hidalgo, *Boletín Mensual,* 38 (June, 1960),
13-14.
Offers a brief definition of *educación extra-escolar,* which the author
ties to the UNESCO concept of fundamental education. Not a particularly valuable contribution to the conceptual formation of nonformal
education.

1209. NANNETTI CÁRDENAS, GUILLERMO. "Concepto y alcanze de la educación fundamental," *Educación,* Washington, 1:3 (July/Septem-
ber, 1956), 2-12.
Concepts based on UNESCO definitions, applied to Latin America,
with particular reference to CREFAL. Elaborates on training of personnel, planning, organization, administration, function of the rural
school, and fundamental education in the urban setting.

1210. NANNETTI CÁRDENAS, GUILLERMO. "Un nuevo tipo de biblioteca
popular," *Educación,* Washington, 1:3 (July/September, 1956),
20-21.
Calls for a new type of library to take an active part in the fundamental
education process to fill in the gap where formal schools are lacking.

1211. NELSON, LINDA. "Analysis of Home Economics Extension Programmes in the Latin American Region," *Nutrition Newsletter,*
8:4 (October/December, 1970), 30-37.

Analysis of the current status of home economics extension. Directs comments primarily toward problems facing home economics extension in the hemisphere. The author feels extension must be viewed as an essential part of community development programs.

1212. NELSON, LINDA. "Home Economics in Agrarian Reform," *Nutrition Newsletter*, 10:1 (January/March, 1972), 10-16.

Detailed proposal for home economics education in conjunction with agrarian reform programs designed to reach the campesino in his environment. Includes the suggested components for such a program, as well as organizational possibilities and the means of dissemination of information. Components include nutrition education, basic understanding of the potentials for human growth, home management, interpersonal communication, civic and community participation, preparation and preservation of foods, and basic upkeep, maintenance, and repair of houses and community buildings.

1213. ORGANIZATION FOR ECONOMIC COOPERATION AND DEVELOPMENT. *Problems of Human Resources Planning in Latin America and in the Mediterranean Regional Project Countries: Long-Term Forecasts of Manpower Requirements and Educational Policies (Report on the Seminar Held at Lima in March 1965 and Complementary Documents)*. Paris: 1967. 279 pp.

General discussion dealing with the need for coordinating educational planning on formal and nonformal levels.

1214. PAN AMERICAN UNION. DEPARTAMENTO DE ASUNTOS ECONÓMICOS Y SOCIALES. DIVISIÓN DE TRABAJO Y ASUNTOS SOCIALES. *Seminarios regionales de asuntos sociales: Educación obrera; informe final; resumen de las discusiones de Mesa Redonda de Educación Obrera, Quito, Ecuador, mayo de 1950, San Salvador, El Salvador, noviembre de 1950, Pôrto Alegre, Brasil, mayo de 1951.* Washington: 1952. 77 pp.

Discussion includes a general description of educational efforts on behalf of workers in various institutional settings throughout Latin America, such as in trade unions, cultural centers, evening classes for workers, cooperatives, and university extension.

1215. PARAISO, VIRGINIA A. "Social Service in Latin America: Functions and Relationships to Development," *Economic Bulletin for Latin America*, 11:1 (April, 1966), 71-105.

Comprehensive article on the meaning of social service in Latin America, how it functions at present, its role in development policy, and the future role of social services. Social services often take on the task of providing educational services, such as education for family life and home management, social education, and nutrition and health education. See also: UNITED NATIONS. ECONOMIC COMMISSION FOR LATIN AMERICA. *Social Service in Latin America: Functions and Relationships to Development.* Document E/CN.12/L.9. New York: 1965. 62 pp.

1216. PENNA, CARLOS VICTOR. "La biblioteca y la educación fundamental," *Revista Lyceum,* 8:31 (August, 1952), 39-45.

Comments on the necessity for new approaches in education to reach those who do not attain formal schooling. Calls for active library participation in fundamental education by means of mobile units, lending services, offering lecture series, serving as a community center, and complementing existing community programs.

1217. PEREIRA, EVALDO SIMAS. "A economia e a educação," *O Observador Econômico e Financeiro,* 14:163 (August, 1949), 30-35, 97-98.

Focuses on the need for a more broadly based concept of education as discussed by the delegates to the Rio seminar on adult education. Primarily concerned with literacy, but also comments on the need to provide further educational opportunities for adults so they can begin to contribute to society more fully. Recognizes the enormous economic obstacles in the path of an expanding formal education system in Latin America.

*1218. RAVERA, ALFREDO. "Análisis y crítica de la educación fundamental," *Enciclopedia de Educación,* 13:1 (January, 1953), 3-94.

*1219. REIMER, EVERETT W. *An Essay on Alternatives in Education.* 2d. ed., revised and amplified. CIDOC Cuaderno, 58. Cuernavaca, México: Centro Intercultural de Documentación, 1971. Various pagination.

1220. RIO, FERNANDO DEL. "Agricultural Education in Latin America and Its Promise for the Future," *Phi Delta Kappan,* 45:4 (January, 1964), 202-207.

The section on informal teaching of agriculture comments on agricultural extension services, rural youth clubs, and recent developments in the field. Advocates strengthening nonformal as well as formal programs.

1221. ROBERTS, LYDIA J. "First Caribbean Conference on Home Economics and Education in Nutrition," U.S. Department of State, *Bulletin,* 27:694 (October 13, 1952), 576-579.

Talks about the need to develop home extension programs more fully in conjunction with existing agricultural extension services. Extension agents are viewed as important educational assets in rural areas.

1222. ROMERO LOZANO, SIMÓN, and SEBASTIÁN FERRER MARTÍN. *El planeamiento de la educación.* Cuadernos, Serie 2: Anticipos de Investigación, 7. Santiago: Instituto Latinoamericano de Planificación Económica y Social, 1968. 148 pp.

> Chapter 10 devotes a section to a discussion of nonformal education in the context of educational planning and national development. Recognizes the growing awareness of the insufficiency of the formal school system and states that a complementary system must be created to satisfy the demands of developing nations for maximum utilization of human resources.

1223. SANTA CRUZ ERRÁRURIZ, GONZALO. *El mejoramiento de los trabajadores agrícolas y la sindicalización campesina.* Santiago: Imprenta 'Cervantes', 1941. 98 pp.

> Comments on the importance of educational activities within trade union organizations.

1224. SEMINARIO INTERAMERICANO DE ALFABETIZACIÓN Y EDUCACIÓN DE ADULTOS, PETRÓPOLIS, BRASIL, 1949. DELEGACIÓN DE HONDURAS. *Informes del Seminario Interamericano de Alfabetización y Educación de Adultos y de la I Reunión Panamericana de Consulta sobre Geografía, celebrados en Petrópolis, Rio de Janeiro, Brasil, del 27 de julio al 2 de septiembre y del 12 al 24 de septiembre de 1949, respectivamente.* Tegucigalpa: 1950. 81 pp.

> Offers recommendations for action in adult education in Latin America. Recognizes the need for involvement by many institutions outside the school.

1225. TEJADA, CARMELA. *Inter-American Seminar on Literacy and Adult Education, Rio de Janeiro.* Washington: Department of Cultural Affairs, Division of Education, Pan American Union, 1950. 48 pp.

> Section 5 on literacy and adult education discusses educational activities of "primary social groups" within the community and their role in adult education. Calls for the coordinated action of all institutions involved in the educational process, from cooperatives to public health services.

1226. TOUBES, AMANDA. "Un enfoque de la educación de adultos," Universidad de Buenos Aires, *Revista,* quinta época, 6:4 (October/December, 1961), 743-752.

> Essay calls for new approaches to educational problems that the school system cannot solve. The concept of adult education, or permanent education, means making readily available avenues of general and specific learning. Theorizes on the need to single out natural leaders of a group who will then act as agents of change. Theories of small

group behavior should be implemented to transmit information, stimulate interest, and generally encourage awareness of individual surroundings.

1227. UNITED NATIONS. ECONOMIC COMMISSION FOR LATIN AMERICA. *Social Change and Social Development Policy in Latin America.* Document E/CN.12/826. New York: 1970. 318 pp.

Chapter 12 states at the outset that "for purposes of policy formulation 'education' should include the whole range of alternative or complementary means by which knowledge, values and specialized skills are transmitted." The discussion evolves from that point.

1228. UNITED NATIONS EDUCATIONAL, SCIENTIFIC, AND CULTURAL ORGANIZATION. "Plan de educación de adultos en América," Instituto Interamericano del Niño, *Boletín*, 34:2 (June, 1960), 164-175.

Offers a basic working definition of adult education for Latin America and suggests possibilities for programs through university extension, popular universities, workers' education in labor unions and industry, cultural centers, and special interest clubs. Outlines various methods of instruction (audio-visual presentations, lectures, group discussion).

1229. URIONA FERNÁNDEZ, CASTO. *Educación cooperativa y desarrollo de la comunidad.* La Paz: 1964. 185 pp.

Presents a philosophy of cooperative education and its role in community development and adult education. Several chapters are devoted to group dynamics and the psychology and sociology of education.

1230. VALENZUELA, DAVID. *Servicio voluntario: Una necesidad vital en América Latina; un estudio sobre el papel del voluntario en la realización de los planes de desarrollo nacional.* Informe Analítico, 4. Washington: Secretaria Internacional para el Servicio Voluntario, 1968. 45 pp.

Discusses the need for volunteers in community development programs in Latin America. Specifically calls for the use of trained volunteer corps in literacy and fundamental education, health education, and agricultural extension projects.

Index

Cited by entry number

Abadie Soriano, Roberto, 954, 955, 1170, 1171
Abreu, Jayme, 174
Ação Comunitária do Brasil, 245
Ação Popular, Brazil, 246
Acción Comunal, Colombia, 328, 389
Acción Cultural Popular, Colombia, 313, 315, 319, 321, 324, 329, 332-334, 336, 337, 339, 341, 388, 390, 1128, 1132, 1147
Acción Cultural Popular, El Salvador, 1037
Acción Cultural Popular Hondureña, 558, 559, 1037, 1147
Acción en Venezuela, 963, 1008, 1011, 1085
Acción Femenina Peruana, 1078
Acción Popular, Peru, 900, 1085
Acción Social Católica, Colombia, 367
Actualidad Agrícola (radio program), Puerto Rico, 935
Adam, Félix, 977, 1007
Adams, Richard N., 807
Adiestramiento Rápido de la Mano-de-Obra, Mexico, 601, 737, 746
Adult Education Program, Trinidad and Tobago, 951
Adult Education Training Seminar, Mexico, 735
Agency for International Development, 95, 245, 484, 687, 1017, 1168
Agency for International Development, Human Resources Office, Brazil, 245
Agnes Erskine College, 110, 245
Agnes Erskine Foundation. See Agnes Erskine College
Agrarian Reform Corporation, Chile. See Corporación de Reforma Agraria, Chile
Agricultural Credit Bank, Colombia, 388
Agricultural Development Bank, Peru, 863
Agricultural Enterprise Promotion Program, Ecuador, 484
Agricultural Missions, Inc., 563
Aguilera Dorantes, Mario, 576-578
Aguilar Paz, Jesús, 565

Ahmed, Manzoor, 1132
AID Evaluation Paper, Agency for International Development, 1099
Alba, Víctor, 737
Alberti S., Agustín, 295
Albertus, Ursula, 471
Albornoz, Miguel, 472
Alcan Jamaica Ltd., 569
Alers Montalvo, Manuel, 401, 863
Alexander, Angela, 429
Alianza Popular Revolucionaria Americana, Peru, 900
Allen, D., 579
Alonso Sánchez, Hilario, 414
Altoberro, María Celia, 1171
Alvarado, Rafael, 490
Alvarez A., José, 488
Alvarez Ahumada, Zelanda, 42
Amalfi, Delia Cecilia, 18
Amas de Casa, Ecuador, 494, 496
Amaya, Susana, 314
Amaya de Ortiz, Myrtha N., 1172
American Anthropological Association, Memoir, 531
American Friends Service Committee, 617, 667, 672, 1030
American International Association for Economic and Social Development, 1013, 1077, 1164
Andean Indian Mission. See Andean Mission Program
Andean Indian Program. See Andean Mission Program
Andean Mission Program, 48, 66, 76, 93, 447, 449, 450, 456, 465, 488, 491, 493, 498, 826, 842, 854, 886, 892, 899, 909, 916, 918, 1040, 1041, 1043-1060, 1076, 1082, 1083, 1086, 1125, 1134, 1142, 1143, 1155, 1166, 1169
Anderson, Ann, 568
Andreani, Juan, 43
Animação Popular, 145

Antuña, Santiago E., 677
Anzola Gómez, Gabriel, 580
Aparicio Vega, Guillermo, 792
APRA, Peru. *See* Alianza Popular Revolucionaria Americana, Peru
Arce, Antonio M., 504, 505
Argentina, Comisión Nacional de Alfabetización y Edificación Escolar, 7, 44
Argentina, Comisión Nacional de Alfabetización y Educación de Adultos, 8
Argentina, Comisión Nacional de Aprendizaje y Orientación Profesional, 26, 32, 37, 1125
Argentina, Consejo Nacional de Educación, 9, 10
Argentina, Dirección de Desarrollo Comunal, 42
Argentina, Dirección General de Aprendizaje, 27
Argentina, Junta Nacional de Administración, 11
Argentina, Ministerio de Educación y Justicia, 12, 26
Argentina, National Apprenticeship and Vocational Guidance Committee. *See* Argentina, Comisión Nacional de Aprendizaje y Orientación Profesional
Argentina, Secretaría de Estado de Comunicaciones, 4
Arguedas, José María, 899
Armstrong, O. K., 862
Arroyave C., Julio César, 360
Arze Loureiro, Eduardo, 351
Arze Quintanilla, Oscar, 88
Asociación Colombiana de Facultades de Medecina, 363
Asociación de Ligas Peruanas Agrarias de Campesinos de Avanzada, 900
Asociación de Servicios Artesanales y Rurales, Bolivia, 92
Asociación Pro-Bienestar de la Familia Colombiana, 363
Associação Brasileira de Crédito e Assistência Rural. *See* Associação de Crédito e Assistência Rural, Brazil
Associação de Crédito y Assistência Rural, Brazil, 112, 126, 131, 238, 245, 1077, 1083, 1088, 1150, 1166
Associação Nordestina de Crédito e Assistência Rural, Brazil, 239, 241
Astete Maravi, Leopoldo, 793
Astica, Juan B., 1091
Atkinson, Carroll, 940
Avala, V. O., 1022, 1024
Avalos Davidson, Beatrice, 308

Avila Camacho, Manuel, 690, 693, 702, 713, 722, 725-727, 748, 760, 766
Avila Garibay, José, 581
Azuaje, José, 1173

Baez Camargo, G., 690
Baez Soler, Osvaldo, 440
Baeza Goñi, Arturo, 291
Bailey, Bernardine, 582
Bairon, Max A., 47
Ballestaedt G., Alfredo, 73, 343
Bamberger, Michael, 1008
Banco Agropecuario, Peru, 903
Banco Cafetero, Colombia, 388
Banco de Crédito Ejidal, Mexico, 1166
Banco de México, 763
Banco Nacional de Crédito Ejidal, Mexico, 689
Bandeira, Marina, 134
Banks, Marjorie, 842
Baracco Gandolfo, Carlos, 864
Barber, Fred W., 127
Barbieri, Sante Uberto, 1102
Bardales B., Rafael, 565
Bardi, P. M., 163
Barraclough, Solon L., 1174
Barrantes, Emilio, 920
Barrera Vásquez, Alfredo, 691, 692
Barrientos Salas, Robinsón, 277
Barriga Vázquez, Benjamín, 583
Barry, Marion, 893
Baum, John A., 794
Bausch, Thomas A., 1008
Bazán, Juan Francisco, 880
Beaglehole, Ernest, 1041
Bebbington, Peter C., 795
Bechara, Miguel, 128
Beeck, Rodolfo, 894
Behrman, Daniel, 315, 393, 529, 1128
Beisiegel, Celso de Rui, 135
Bellegarde, Dantés, 553
Benjamin, Georgia K., 533
Bereday, George Z. F., 334
Bernard, Joseph C., 541
Bethencourt R., Omar J., 961
Biblioteca 'Almafuerte,' Escuela Experimental No. 24, La Matanza, Argentina, 18
Biblioteca de Autores Contemporáneos, Ministerio de Educación Nacional, Mexico, 580
Biblioteca del Maestro Veracruzano, 759
Biblioteca Pedagógica de Perfeccionamiento Profesional, Instituto Federal de Capacitación del Magisterio, Mexico, 742

Biblioteca Pedagogos de América, 1158
Björnberg, Arne, 48
Bolanos, V. L., 465
Bolívar López, Luis, 952
Bolivia, Consejo Nacional de Educación, 49, 50
Bolivia, Department of Culture, 58
Bolivia, Ministerio de Salud Pública, 51
Bolivia, Ministry of Education, 58
Bolivia, National Plan of Rural Development, 91
Bolton Caro, J., 348
Bologna, Italo, 176, 177
Bond, D'Este, 97
Bonilla, Manuel, 565
Bonilla y Segura, Guillermo, 585-587
Books for the People Fund, 352, 358
Botch, Henry K., 80
Bourne, Dorothy Dulles, 944
Bourne, James R., 944
Bourque, Susan Carolyn, 900
Brady, Jerry, 963
Bravo, Raúl, 52
Brazil, Departamento de Ensino Complementar, 245
Brazil, Departamento Nacional de Educação, 139
Brazil, Diretoria do Ensino Agrícola, 232
Brazil, Ministério da Educação e Cultura, 98, 114, 137, 153, 245
Brazil, Ministério da Educação e Saúde, 138, 139, 158
Brazil, Ministério do Planejamento e Coordenação Geral, 232
Brazil, Ministério Extraordinário para a Coordenação dos Organismos Regionais, 140
Brembeck, Cole S., 371, 912, 1032
Brenes Mesén, Roberto, 406
Briceno, R., 468, 777
Brigada Cultural de Asuntos Indígenas, Mexico, 755
Brigadas Culturales, El Salvador, 512, 1135, 1154
Brigadas Culturales, Peru, 1154, 1164
Brigadas de Culturización Indígena, Peru, 902, 905, 915, 919, 1143
Brigadas de Mejoramiento Indígena, 627, 753
Brigadas de Promoción de Agricultura y Agropecuaria, Mexico, 745, 746
Brigadas de Promoción Indígena, Mexico, 1142, 1143
Brigadas Indígenas, Mexico, 747
Brigadas Móviles de Promoción Agropecuaria, Mexico, 753

Brister, William C., 796
British Volunteer Programme, 776
Brooker Sugar Estates, Guyana, 539
Brown, Marion R., 272
Brownstone, Paul L., 316
Bruner, Richard, 678
Brunner, Edmund de S., 1097
Bruno, James E., 1014
Building a Better Hemisphere Series, Technical Cooperation Administration, Institute of Inter-American Affairs, 169, 231, 403, 404, 503, 507, 790, 860, 872, 1063
Buitrón, Aníbal, 499, 588, 1175, 1176
Bunster, Martin, 309
Burbano Martínez, Héctor, 491, 739
Burke, Malcolm K., 797, 890
Burnet, Mary, 317
Burns, Brenda, 542

Cadernos de Ciências Sociais, Instituto de Ciências Sociais, Universidade do Brasil, 208
Caja Agraria, Colombia, 388
Calderón Cuentas, Juan de la C., 74
Calm, Lillian, 254
Camarinha, José, 142
Camohmila Rural Demonstration Center, Mexico, 1164. *See also* Young Men's Christian Association, Mexico
Camp, John R., 972
Campaña de Alfabetización, Ecuador, 490
Campaña de Alfabetización y Cultura Popular, Venezuela, 982
Campaña de Alfabetización y Educación Fundamental, El Salvador, 1135
Campaña Nacional de Alfabetización, Peru, 885
Campaña para la Reforma Eficaz de las Comunidades Escolares de la República, Peru. *See* Crecer Project, Peru
Campanha de Educação de Adultos, Brazil, 239
Campanha de Educação de Adultos, *Publicação*, 139
Campanha Nacional de Alfabetização de Adultos, Brazil, 135
Campanha Nacional de Educação Rural, Brazil, 98, 102-104, 109, 113, 117, 244, 1131, 1135
Campanha Nacional de Erradicação do Analfabetismo, Brazil, 153, 239
Campi Avançados, 245
Cannon, Mary M., 1078
Cano, Celerino, 740

Capa, Cornell, 812
Capacitación Popular, Colombia, 1085
Capiatá Domestic Work Center, Paraguay. *See* Centros de Trabajos Dómesticos, Paraguay
Capó, Carmelina, 318
Cardona, Rafael, 534
Cardoso, Fernando Henrique, 195
Caribbean Conference on Home Economics and Education in Nutrition, 1221
Caribbean Nutrition Seminar, 1177
Caro Aguirre, Horacio, 368
Carrasco, Rosa, 298
Carroll, Thomas F., 1129
Carruthers, Ben Frederic, 978
Carvalho, Manuel Marques de, 196
Casa de Cultura Ecuatoriana, 489
Casa de la Asegurada, Mexico, 604
Casa del Estudiante Indígena, Mexico, 745
Casabon Sánchez, Luis, 415
Caseres Arandi, Alicia, 458
Casswell, Harold D., 803
Castañón Pasquel, J., 78
Castillo, Ignacio M. del, 697
Castillo, Isidro, 578
Castillo Ledón, Amalia, 741
Castillo Trujillo, Sonia, 975
Castro, Angélica, 589
Castro de la Fuente, Angélica, 589, 590
Castro Harrison, Jorge, 907
Castro Rivas, M. A., 129
Catholic Action, Peru, 1078
Catholic University of Chile. *See* Universidad Católica, Chile
Cattaneo Díaz, M., 27
Cebellero, Angeles, 941
Centennial Youth Column, Cuba, 1032
Center for Agricultural Credit, 1118
Central School, Monymusk, Jamaica, 574
Centro de Adiestramiento de Operadores, Mexico, 738
Centro de Aprendizaje Agrícola Don Bosco, Venezuela, 1010
Centro de Artes Manuales, Ecuador, 493
Centro de Bienestar Social, Mexico, 767
Centro de Capacitación Rural, Venezuela, 998, 999
Centro de Coordinación Indigenista, Venezuela, 1010
Centro de Cultura Social, Colombia, 387
Centro de Educación Fundamental, Ancud, Chile, 264
Centro de Estudios de Territorios Nacionales, Universidad Nacional de Colombia, 359
Centro de Estudios Nacionales, Mexico, 698

Centro de Formación Agropecuaria, Venezuela, 1010
Centro de Investigación y Acción Social, Nicaragua, 776
Centro de Misiones Sociopedagógicas de Artigas, Uruguay, 952
Centro de Motivación y Asesoria, Ecuador, 444
Centro de Promoción Popular, Peru, 1086
Centro de Rehabilitación Campesina del Altiplano de Bolivia, 94
Centro Experimental de Asistencia Médico Social, Chile, 291
Centro Experimental de Salud San Joaquín, Chile, 269
Centro Interamericano de Educación Rural, 997, 1130
Centro Interamericano de Educación Rural, *Publicaciones,* 1130
Centro Interamericano de Investigación y Documentación sobre Formación Profesional, 1123
Centro Internacional de Mejoramiento de Maiz y Trigo, 678, 679, 1132
Centro Nacional de Agronomía, El Salvador, 506
Centro para el Desarrollo de la Educación No-Formal, Colombia, 392
Centro para el Desarrollo Social y Económico, Bolivia, 92
Centro Piloto de la Sierra de Puebla, Mexico, 662
Centro Regional de Educação de Base, Brazil, 1134
Centro Regional de 'Educación, Paraguay, 786
Centro Regional de Educación Fundamental para la América Latina, 264, 580, 582, 588, 591-598, 600, 602, 608, 613, 624, 625, 628, 629, 633, 635, 646, 649, 650, 656, 658, 660, 662-666, 669, 670, 673, 675-677, 680, 681, 686, 688, 704, 732, 744, 748, 763, 764, 773, 776, 1027, 1033, 1038, 1131, 1135, 1143, 1155, 1175, 1178, 1197, 1209
Centro Rural Universitário de Treinamento e Ação Comunitária, Brazil, 245
Centro Urbano-Nueva Parroquia Project, Lanús, Argentina, 2
Centros Coordinadores, Mexico, 614, 615, 619, 652, 1135, 1142
Centros de Bienestar Social Rural, Mexico, 1135
Centros de Capacitación Indígena, Mexico, 753

Centros de Capacitación para el Trabajo Industrial, Mexico, 737, 746
Centros de Capacitación para el Trabajo Rural, Mexico, 740, 745, 746
Centros de Coordinación Indigenista, Mexico, 1155
Centros de Educación Extra-Escolar, Mexico, 753
Centros de Educación Fundamental, Peru, 1135
Centros de Educación y Desarrollo de la Comunidad, Venezuela, 961
Centros de Enseñanza Agropecuaria Fundamental, Mexico, 745, 753
Centros de Seguridad Social para el Bienestar Familiar, Mexico, 604, 641
Centros de Trabajos Domésticos, Paraguay, 787, 788, 1164
Centros Nacionales de Capacitación, Mexico, 753, 754
Centros Nacionales de Formación de Instructores, Colombia, 373
Centros y Talleres Artesanales, Peru, 904
Céspedes, Aurelio, 369
Céspedes, Francisco S., 1079
Chacón Nardi, Rafaela, 279, 599, 1026, 1131
Chang, L., 409
Chaparro G., Alvaro, 345, 1179
Chapin, Barbara, 600
Chapman, Dorothy E., 1092
Chartier, R. A., 2
Chavarría Flores, Manuel, 523
Cháves Esquivel, O., 394
Chávez, Ignacio, 1027
Chesterfield, Ray A., 964
Children's Council, Uruguay, 1070
Chile, Department of Agricultural Extension, 272
Chile, Department of Social Welfare, 292
Chile, Departamento de Extensión Cultural, 267
Chile, Dirección de Asuntos Indígenas, 255
Chile, Dirección General de Educación Primaria, 280, 288
Chile, División de Acción Comunal, 388
Chile, Literacy and Fundamental Education Section, 388
Chile, Ministerio de Educación, 279, 297, 298, 301, 303, 305, 1066
Chile, Ministerio de Educación Pública, 309
Chile, Ministerio de Trabajo y Previsión Social, 305
Chile, Ministry of Agriculture, 272, 303
Chile, Ministry of Education. *See* Chile, Ministerio de Educación

Chile, National Health Service, 272, 293, 298, 303
Chile, Sección Cultura y Publicaciones, 309
Chile, Sección de Alfabetización y Educación de Adultos, 279
Chile, Sección Educación de Adultos, 280
Chonchol Chait, Jacques, 310, 1180
Chueca Sotomayor, Carlos, 798
Church, Clarence, 524
CIDOC Cuaderno, Centro Intercultural de Documentación, 1219
Cisneros Cisneros, César, 500
Ciudad, Mario, 1181
Clark, John M., 445, 446
Clauro Montaño, Toribio, 53
Clerck, M. de, 1182
Clifford, Roy A., 346, 561
Club de Cantineros de la República de Cuba, 414
Clubes Agrarios Juveniles, Uruguay, 953
Clubs Agrícolas Juveniles Perú, 836, 838
Cobos, Bernardo, 601
Coleção Forum Roberto Simonsen, Centro e Federação das Indústrias do Estado de São Paulo, 201
Colección Agramante, Editorial Palestra, 42
Colección de Antropología Social, Instituto Nacional Indigenista, Mexico, 744
Colección de Testimonios, Documentos, Acuerdos, Decretos y Leyes Importantes para la Historia de un Régimen, 698
Colegio Félix Olivares, Panama, 784
Colombia, Commission for Assistance to Indigenous Populations, 1082
Colombia, Commission for Protection of Indigenous Populations, 1082
Colombia, Departamento de Extensión Cultural y Bellas Artes, 355
Colombia, Ministerio de Educación Nacional, 344, 353-355, 361, 385, 387, 388, 390, 391
Colombia, Ministry of Agriculture, 1100
Colombia, Ministry of Public Health, 363
Colorado, Eugenio, 367
Comas, Juan, 447, 1028
Comisión Nacional Cubana de la UNESCO, 431
Comisión Nacional de Aprendizaje y Orientación Profesional, Argentina. *See* Argentina, Comisión Nacional de Aprendizaje y Orientación Profesional
Commissão Brasileira-Americana de Educação Industrial, 231
Commonwealth Caribbean Regional Youth Seminar, 1039

Community Centers, Trinidad and Tobago, 951
Community Education Campaign on Nutrition, Jamaica, 1034
Community Education Centers, Trinidad and Tobago, 951
Community Education Program, Puerto Rico. *See* Programa de Educación de la Comunidad, Puerto Rico
Compañía Administradora del Guano, Peru, 903
Comparative Education Conference, 306
Comparative Education Society, Eastern Regional Conference, 1079
Comunidades de Promoción Indígena, Mexico, 599
Conceição, Diamantina Costa, 104
Conceição, Diógenes, 197
Confederação Nacional da Indústria, Brazil, 120
Confederación de Trabajadores Mexicanos, 601
Confederación Latinoamericana para la Educación Fundamental Integral, 332
Confederación Nacional de Estudiantes de México, 735
Confederación Universitaria Boliviana, 83, 84, 86
Confederation of Colombian Workers, 366
Conference of American States Members of the International Labor Organization, *Report*, 627, 1125, 1144
Conference on Agricultural Extension and Rural Youth, 1095
Conference on Education and Economic and Social Development in Latin America, 430, 509, 535, 1183
Conferencia Interamericana sobre Desarrollo de la Comunidad, 305
Conferencia Plenaria, United Nations Educational, Scientific, and Cultural Organization, 668
Conferencia sobre Educación y Desarrollo Económico y Social en América Latina. *See* Conference on Education and Economic and Social Development in Latin America
Congreso Indigenista Interamericano, 1142
Congreso Mexicano de Educación Rural, 1185
Congresso Brasileiro de Educação, 233
Congresso Nacional de Educação de Adultos, Brazil, 234
Consejería de Promoción Popular, Chile, 305
Consejo de Bienestar Rural, Venezuela, 962, 969, 970, 1011, 1013, 1077, 1088

Consejo de Lenguas Indígenas, 692
Consejo General de Trabajadores, 39
Consejo Informativo de Educación Alimenticia, Venezuela, 1077
Consejo Nacional de Educación Técnica, Argentina, 1073-1075, 1165, 1169
Consejo Venezolano del Niño, 961
Considine, John J., 319
Cook, Katherine M., 603
Coombs, Philip Hall, 1132, 1184
Cooperación Popular, Peru, 818, 1142
Cooperativa José Cardijn, 268
Cooperativa Victoria R.L., Costa Rica, 407
Cooperative Agricultural Commission, Cuba, 1150
Coordinated Services for Indian Communities, Mexico, 651
Coordinating Secretariat of National Unions of Students, 81, 735
Cornehls, James V., 921
Cornell-Peru Project. *See* Peru-Cornell Project
Cornely, Seno A., 235
Corona M., Enrique, 742
Corporación de Reforma Agraria, Chile, 306
Corporación de Vivienda, Chile, 298
Correa, Arlindo López, 144
Corredor Rodríguez, Berta, 339
Cortés Carabantes, Waldemar, 256, 281, 299
Cortés E., Valente, 733
Cortright, Richard W., 1103
Costa Rica, Ministerio de Trabajo, 408
Costa Rica, Oficina de Capacitación y Aprendizaje, 408
Costa Rica, Secretaría de Trabajo y Previsión Social, 410
Cotton Institute, Colombia, 388
Coutiño Ruiz, Oralia, 604
Crafts Development Agency, Jamaica, 568
Crecer Project, Peru, 910, 911
Crédito Agrícola Supervisado, Guatemala, 534
Creole Foundation, 986, 999
Croy, Otto C., 973
Cruzada ABC, Brazil, 106, 110, 245
Cuadernos de Asistencia Social, 172
Cuba, Comisión Nacional de la UNESCO. *See* Comisión Nacional Cubana de la UNESCO
Cuba, Ministerio de Educación, 416, 418
Cuéllar, Hernán, 54
Cuerpo de Extensión de Servicios, Bolivia, 93
Cuerpos Cívicos de Alfabetización Popular, Chile, 265, 266, 280, 302
Cullell, Inés, 320
Cultural Missions, Mexico. *See* Misiones Culturales, Mexico

Cummings, Richard L., 437
Curso de Seguimiento, Cuba, 431, 435
Cursos para Campesinos Adultos, Colombia, 344, 390

Dale, George A., 554
Dannemann, Robert N., 198, 247
Darío Utria, Rubén, 1011
Dartique, Maurice, 556
Davie, Alberto G., 45
Davignon, Charles A., 799
Dávila, Carlos, 199
Davis, Russell G., 1015
De Kadt, Emanuel, 145
Delegación Boliviana al Seminario de Trabajo sobre Desarrollo de la Comunidad, 91
Délmez, Albert Juares, 606
Demartini, Pedro Paulo, 146, 147
Dennison, Edward S., 75
Department of Inter-American Technical Cooperation in Agriculture, 272
Díaz, Angel, 1000
Di Franco, Joseph, 346, 402, 504, 505, 561, 562
Dino, P. H., 730
Dissertation Series, Latin American Studies Program, Cornell University, 823, 900
Dobyns, Henry F., 801-803
Dolff, Helmuth, 1020
Dom Bosco Schools, 1010, 1169. *See also* Método Dom Bosco
Dominican Republic, Department of Agriculture, 443, 1025
Donoso Loero, Teresa, 289
Doughty, Paul L., 803
Drucker, Manuel, 967
Dryden Professional Books in Education, 657
D'Ugard, Carlos, 853
Duque Villegas, A., 347

Ebaugh, Cameron D., 300, 902
Ebel, Karl Heinrich, 1073
Economic Commission for Latin America, 1120, 1121, 1165, 1166, 1194, 1215, 1227
Ecuador, Department of Adult Education. *See* Ecuador, Departamento de Educación de Adultos
Ecuador, Departamento de Educación de Adultos, 492, 495
Ecuador, Ministerio de Educación Pública, 474, 492, 495
Ecuador, Ministerio del Trabajo y Bienestar Social, 448
Ecuador, Ministry of Education. *See* Ecuador, Ministerio de Educación Pública

Ecuador, Sección Integración del Campesino a la Vida Nacional, 1082
Ecuadoran Development Corporation, 445, 446
Edfelt, Ralph, 236
Ediciones ODEA, Oficina de Educación de Adultos, Venezuela, 1007
Educación Básica Laboral, Peru, 833
Education Extension Service, Trinidad and Tobago, 1164
Educational Studies and Documents, United Nations Educational, Scientific, and Cultural Organization, 38, 1029
Edwards, Agustín, 296
Egginton, Everett, 322
Eguino, Carlos A., 96
El Salvador, Departamento de Alfabetización y Educación de Adultos, 512, 1104
El Salvador, Departamento de Educación Fundamental, 510
El Salvador, Ministerio de Cultura Popular, 512
El Salvador, Ministerio de Educación, 509, 510
El Salvador, Ministerio de Trabajo y Previsión Social, 511
El Salvador, Sección de Educación Obrera, 511
Elson, Benjamin F., 607
Ensminger, Douglas, 1097
Equipos de Educación Fundamental, Bolivia, 65
Escuela Complementaria de Especialización Artística, Colombia, 385
Escuela de Artes y Oficios, Panama, 784
Escuela de Servicio Social, Peru, 858
Escuela del Aire, Argentina, 17, 24
Escuela del Aire de Puerto Rico, 940
Escuela Experimental de Cultura Popular 'Pedro Aguirre Cerda,' Chile, 257, 271, 302
Escuela Nacional de Servicio Social, Bolivia, 91
Escuela Popular de Adultos, Costa Rica, 406
Escuela Práctica de Agricultura, Venezuela, 972
Escuela Profesional, Panama, 784
Escuela Superior de Orientación Rural Femenina, Colombia, 1135
Escuela Vespertina, Costa Rica, 406
Escuelas Artesanales de Producción, Venezuela, 1012
Escuelas de Cristo, 62
Escuelas de Emergencia, Dominican Republic, 440
Escuelas de Orientación, Haiti, 541, 1033, 1164

Escuelas de Padres (television program), Argentina, 1136

Escuelas de Padres (television program), Venezuela, 1136

Escuelas Radiofónicas, Peru. *See* Maryknoll Radio School, Peru

Escuelas Radiofónicas Populares, Ecuador, 464

Esman, Sherley Goodman, 1111

El Espectador, Colombia, 365

Espinosa, Francisco, 1104

Estación Experimental Agropecuaria Pergamino, *Boletín de Divulgación,* 6

Estación Experimental Agropecuaria Sáenz Peña, *Publicación,* 5

Estación Experimental, Pergamino, Argentina, 6

Estrella Gutiérrez, Fermín, 29

Estudios de Comunidades y Regiones, Instituto de Educación, Universidad de Chile, 269

Estudios del Valle del Urubamba, Instituto de Estudios Peruanos, 825

Estudios Sociológicos Latino-Americanos, Oficina Internacional de Investigaciones Sociales de FERES, 456

Estudios y Documentos de Educación, United Nations Educational, Scientific, and Cultural Organization, 155

Estudios y Monografías, Centro Interamericano de Investigación y Documentación sobre Formación Profesional, 1073

Estudios y Monografías, Department of Social Affairs, Pan American Union, 268, 407

Estupiñan Tello, Julio, 451

Etling, Arlen, 55

Evans, David R., 452

Evans, Luther H., 608

Fabian Research Series, Fabian Society, 434

Fabila, Alfonso, 609

Fagen, Richard R., 419, 433

Fals Borda, Orlando, 1186

Family Planning Association, Puerto Rico, 933

FAO Nutrition Special Reports, Food and Agricultural Organization, 1177

Farías, Luis M., 743

Farmer Nucleo School, Guatemala, 536

Faust, Augustus F., 237

Fe y Alegría, Peru, 910, 911

Federación Agraria Argentina, 41

Federación Argentina del Personal de Gas del Estado, 39

Federación de Estudiantes de Chile, 263

Federación Nacional de Cafeteros, Colombia, 351, 388, 1097

Federación Nacional de Campesinos del Perú, 900

Federación Nacional de Cooperativas Arroceras, Ecuador, 484

Federation of Coffee Growers, Colombia. *See* Federación Nacional de Cafeteros, Colombia

Federation of Coffee Growers, El Salvador, 1097

Fernández Ballesteros, Alberto, 543

Fernández Serna, Gabino, 700

Fernández y Fernández, Ramón, 750

Ferreira, Manoel José, 168

Ferrer Martín, Sebastián, 323, 1222

Fibras Químicas, S.A., 736

Figueroa Ortiz, José, 610

Fincas de Beneficio Proporcional, El Salvador, 1140

Fischlowitz, Estanislau, 203

Fisher, Glen H., 611, 612

Fleming, Philip B., 403

Fogel, Gerardo, 786

Folletos, Dirección General de Alfabetización y Educación Extraescolar, Mexico, 709

Fonseca, Celso Suckow da, 204

Fonseca, Edson Nery da, 248

Fontoura, Amaral, 249

Food and Agricultural Organization, 76-78, 129, 130, 273, 276, 348, 364, 465-468, 485, 486, 522, 681, 682, 730, 763, 777, 867, 868, 903, 1023, 1041, 1042, 1062, 1093-1095, 1112, 1157, 1174

Food and Agricultural Organization, Rural Institutions Division, 682, 1095, 1174

Food and Agricultural Organization, Technical Working Party on Cocoa Production and Protection, 130

Ford Foundation, 683

Forero Nogués, Marion, 361

FORMO, Brazil, 236

Fornaciari, Dora, 13

Forni, Floreal H., 5

Fornoza de Rincón, Mercedes, 975

Foster, George M., 613

Foundation for Community Development and Municipal Improvement, Venezuela, 1011

Franck, Peter G., 836

Freeburger, Adela R., 301, 904

Freire, Paulo, 13, 135, 152, 282, 285-286, 475, 1064, 1067, 1069, 1187-1192, 1201, 1204

Freitas, Honorato de, 105

Freitas, M. A. Teixeira de, 250
Fuente, Julio de la, 614, 615, 744
Fuentes Roldán, Alfredo, 493
Fuenzalida, J. B., 616
Fulton, David C., 617
Fundação Movimento Brasileiro de Alfabetização, 136
Fundación de Vida Rural, Chile, 289, 307, 1136
Fundación de Viviendas y Asistencia Social, Chile, 298
Fundaciones de Desarrollo Rural Brethren & Unida, Ecuador, 453
Fundamental Education Movement, Brazil, 148
Furbay, John H., 387, 395
Furtado, Jorge Alberto, 205

Gaete Pequeño, Dora, 258
Gaines, Carolyn L., 396, 404
Galat Noumer, José, 357
Gale, Laurence, 388
Galecio Gómez, Juan, 274, 467
Galván, Luis Enrique, 905
García Jiménez, Jesús, 1136
García Vieyra, Alberto, 30
Gardner, Clinton Harvey, 701
Garrison, Ray L., 895
Genovesi, Luis José, 14
Georgi, A. A., 702
Gerbracht, Carl, 206
Gibson, Raymond C., 804
Gill, C. H. S., 569
Gill, Clark C., 745
Gillen, John, 618
Gillette, Arthur, 259, 260, 434, 805
Gingerich, Garland E., 563
Giordano, Luis, 25
Gluckstadt, Ilse, 619
Godall, Harold L., 806
Godfrey, Erwina E., 238
Goes, Joaquim Faria, 207-209
Goetz, Delia, 1009
González de Dávila, Cecelia, 949
González Díaz Lombardo, Francisco, 768
González M., Guillermo, 261
González Rivera, Manuel, 1193
González Salazar, Gloria, 620, 746
Gotas de Leche, Uruguay, 1071
Graham, Alva W., 525
Gray, W. S., 703
Greene, Dorothy E., 1111
Grim, George, 883
Groenewegen, Adriano, 5
Grossman, William L., 210

Grupos Móviles, Peru, 1135
Guajira Project, Venezuela. *See* Proyecto La Guajira, Venezuela
Guardia M., Luis, 79
Guatemala, Dirección de Educación de Adultos, 535
Guatemala, Dirección General de Asuntos Agrarios, 534
Guatemala, Dirección General de Desarrollo Socioeducativo Rural, 514, 535, 536, 1104
Guatemala, Ministerio de Trabajo y Previsión Social, 530
Guerrero Amaya, Ezequiel, 590
Guevara, Luis Alfredo, 869
Guillén, Carlos, 508
Guzmán Cruz, Vicenta, 747

Haiti, Department of Agriculture, 556
Haiti, Division of Agricultural Extension, 556
Haiti, Division of Rural Education, 556
Hall, J. Thomas, 1137
Hall, Robert King, 21, 209, 211, 212, 275, 1077
Halle, Louis J., 1138
Hallett, Robert M., 503
Handcraft Programme, Jamaica, 1034
Hans, N., 209, 1077
Harbison, Frederick, 371
Harrison, Steve, 896
Hart, Donn V., 544
Hart, Thomas A., 56
Harvard Educational Review, *Monograph Series*, 1189
Harvey, W. E., 506
Hatch, D. Spencer, 621-623
Hauch, Charles C., 301, 904, 1139
Hauser, Phillip M., 1194
Havighurst, Robert J., 239
Herrera, Felipe, 1081
Herrera, Javier, 281
Herudek, Joachim, 494
Herzog, William A., 106
Heseltine, Marjorie M., 1070
Hildebrand, John R., 516
Hildebrand, Norbert, 507
Hill, Rey M., 1063
Himes, James R., 870
Hispanic-American Studies, University of Miami Press, 498
Hoerner, Lena May, 1071
Hollanda, Hortensia de, 168
Holmberg, Allan R., 807-811
Holmes, Lula Thomas, 748
Holsinger, Justus G., 926

Honduras, Consejo Nacional de Alfabetización, 566
Honduras, Ministerio de Educación Pública, 566
Hooper, Ofelia, 780
Hoover Institution Studies, Hoover Institution on War, Revolution, and Peace, 433
Houtart, François, 324
Howes, H. W., 1029
Hsin-Pao, Yang, 251
Huarizata Normal School, Bolivia. *See* Warisata Normal School, Bolivia
Hughes, Lloyd H., 57, 58, 624-626
Hugill, J. A. C., 574
Huizer, Gerrit, 1140
Hurtado, Osvaldo, 475, 494
Huxley, Matthew, 812

Ianni, Otávio, 195
Illich, Ivan, 1064, 1195, 1196
Indian Betterment Brigades, Mexico. *See* Brigadas de Mejoramiento Indígena, Mexico
INDICEP, 1064
Industrial Productivity Center, Mexico, 757
Industrial Social Service, Brazil. *See* Serviço Social da Indústria, Brazil
Industrial Training Centers, Mexico. *See* Centros de Capacitación Industrial, Mexico
Informe Analítico, Secretaria Internacional para el Servicio Voluntario, 1230
Informe Técnico, International Labor Organization, 411, 412
Institute for Agricultural Development, Chile. *See* Instituto de Desarrollo Agropecuario, Chile
Institute of Ethnological Research, University of the Atlantic, Colombia, 370
Institute of Inter-American Affairs, 60, 71, 816, 836, 852, 865, 878, 1071, 1114, 1138
Institute of Inter-American Affairs, Food Supply Division, 878
Institute of Inter-American Affairs, Health and Sanitation Division, 1114
Institute of International Education, 963
Institute of Rural Education, Chile. *See* Instituto de Educación Rural, Chile
Instituto Campesino de Educación, Bolivia, 92
Instituto Centroamericano de Extensión de la Cultura, 1020
Instituto Colombiano de Bienestar Familiar, 325-327
Instituto Colombiano de Reforma Agraria, 322
Instituto Ecuatoriano de Antropología y Geografía, 489

Instituto Ecuatoriano de Investigaciones para Educación de Adultos, 497
Instituto de Alfabetización en Lenguas Indígenas, Mexico, 692
Instituto de Alfabetización para Indígenas Monolingües, Mexico, 589
Instituto de Bienestar Rural, Paraguay, 791
Instituto de Capacitación, Investigación y Reforma Agraria, Chile, 276, 1067, 1174, 1192
Instituto de Capacitación y Productividad, Guatemala, 530
Instituto de Cultura Popular, Argentina, 16
Instituto de Desarrollo Agropecuario, Chile, 305, 306
Instituto de Desarrollo Comunitario, Chile, 256, 299
Instituto de Educación Fundamental, Peru, 1086
Instituto de Educación Rural, Chile, 262, 270, 298, 301, 303, 306, 307
Instituto de Educación Rural, Peru, 900
Instituto de Estudios Sindicales de Centro América, 1031
Instituto de Información Campesina, Chile, 275
Instituto de Orientación Campesina, Chile, 304
Instituto del Inquilino, Chile, 258, 261
Instituto Indigenista Interamericano, 662
Instituto Indigenista Nacional, Guatemala, 538
Instituto Indigenista Peruano, 853, 1082
Instituto Interamericano de Ciencias Agrícolas. *See* Inter-American Institute of Agricultural Sciences
Instituto Interamericano de Ciencias Agrícolas, Publicación Miscelánea, 1019
Instituto Latinoamericano de la Comunicación Educativa, 1136
Instituto Latinoamericano de Planificación Económica y Social, *Cuadernos, Serie 2: Anticipos de Investigación,* 1222
Instituto Lingüístico de Verano. *See* Summer Institute of Linguistics
Instituto Mexicano del Seguro Social, 604, 641, 746
Instituto Nacional de Agricultura, Panama, 784
Instituto Nacional de Antropología y Historia, Mexico, 767
Instituto Nacional de Aprendizaje, Costa Rica, 409, 411, 412
Instituto Nacional de Capacitación, Chile, 295, 299

Instituto Nacional de Cinema Educativo, Brazil, 158
Instituto Nacional de Cooperación Educativa, Venezuela, 976, 988, 1000-1004, 1007, 1008, 1010-1012, 1015, 1073-1075, 1079, 1086, 1125, 1137, 1165
Instituto Nacional de Estudos Pedagógicos, Brazil, 156
Instituto Nacional de la Juventud Mexicana, 752, 753
Instituto Nacional de Nutrición, Colombia, 364
Instituto Nacional Indigenista, Mexico, 614, 615, 619, 652, 715, 744, 753, 1027, 1036, 1038, 1142, 1157
Instituto Rural Evangélico, 238
Instituto Técnico de Inmigración y Colonización, Venezuela, 1016
Instituto Tecnológico y de Estudios Superiores de Monterrey, Departamento de Relaciones Industriales, *Serie: Monográficos, Cuadernos*, 733
Instituto Venezolano de Acción Comunitaria, 1008, 1011
Institutos Campesinos de Sutatenza, Colombia, 334
Instructivo Interno de Extensión, División de Extensión, Federación Nacional de Cafeteros, Colombia, 351
Inter-American Committee for Agricultural Development, 469
Inter-American Conference on Indian Life, 72, 1142
Inter-American Cooperative Public Health Service. *See* Servicio Cooperativo Interamericano de Salud Pública
Inter-American Development Bank, 1082
Inter-American Education Foundation, 57
Inter-American Institute of Agricultural Sciences, 397, 401, 1018, 1038, 1140, 1148, 1164
Inter-American Program for Rural Youth, 397
Inter-American Program for Training Personnel in Indian Community Development, 91
Inter-American Regional Organization of Workers. *See* Organización Regional Interamericana de Trabajadores
Inter-American Rural Youth Program, 1148
Inter-American Seminar on Literacy and Adult Education. *See* Seminario Interamericano de Alfabetización y Educación de Adultos
Inter-American Seminar on Vocational Education, 1124
International Bank for Reconstruction and Development, 903

International Conference of Social Work, 244
International Council for Educational Development, 1132
International Development Corporation, 900
International Education Year 1970, 1090
International Labor Conference, 1083
International Labor Office, 3, 389, 575, 627, 791, 1010, 1043, 1125, 1142-1145
International Labor Organization, 48, 66, 93, 199, 214, 372, 374, 384, 389, 411, 412, 454, 737, 763, 842, 897, 916, 1041-1044, 1055, 1073, 1125, 1194
International Maize and Wheat Improvement Center. *See* Centro Internacional de Mejoramiento de Maiz y Trigo
International Marketing Institute, 687
International Metalworkers' Federation, 1117
Investigaciones Sociales, Serie: Monografías Andinas, Editorial Estudios Andinos, 888
Isales, Carmen, 927
Ixmiquilpán Textile Workshop, Mexico, 1143

Jamaica, Ministry of Youth and Community Development, 572
Jamaica, Social Development Commission, 572
Jamaica Agricultural Society, 571, 1038, 1164
Jamaica Social Welfare Commission, 570, 1029, 1035, 1036, 1038, 1164
Jamaica Welfare Ltd., 1033
Jamaica Youth Corps, 1032
Jara P., Fernando, 1084
Jara Támara, Abraham F., 906
Jessel, Camilla, 15
Jesualdo, 420
Jickling, David L., 518
Jiménez Castellanos, Juan, 454
Jiménez Malaret, René, 945
Jiménez Sánchez, Leobardo, 684
João Baptista do Amaral Foundation, 245
Joint Center for Urban Studies of the Massachusetts Institute of Technology and Harvard University, *Publication*, 1015
Jolly, Richard, 435
Jones, Earl, 402, 405, 1197
Jornadas Bibliotecarias Chilenas, 311
Juan Domingo Perón Textile Apprenticeship School, 37
Junta de Exportación Agrícola, Chile, 275
Juventud de Acción Católica Cubana, 415

Karsen, Sonja, 398
Kasdon, Lawrence M., 705
Kasdon, Nora S., 705

Kelley, Joseph B., 328
Kempler, Homer, 1146
Key, Harold, 82
Kidd, J. R., 946
King, Clarence, 1030
Kirberg, Enrique, 427
Kirkaldy, John, 573
Knight, Mabel, 628, 706
Knox, John, 240
Koenig, Werner, 375
Kuyo Chico Project, Peru, 825, 826, 1175

La Belle, Thomas J., 106, 236, 322, 378, 452, 951, 964, 1014, 1147, 1198, 1199
Labor Institute, El Salvador, 508
Labor Studies Centers, Peru, 912
Laboy, María Justina, 1019
Lafayette Cooperative Sugar Association, Puerto Rico, 939
Lagos Orbeta, Gastón, 1200
Laguerre Vélez, Enrique A., 629
Lamberto Moreno, J., 630
Lane, Layle, 631
Langrod, Witold, 749
Latin American Congress of Radiophonic Schools, 332
Latin American Studies Series, Latin American Center, University of California, 106, 236, 322, 378, 452, 951, 964, 1014, 1091, 1147, 1198, 1199
Latorre Salamanca, Gonzalo, 302
Lattes de Casseres, V., 1112
Laubach, Frank, 476, 480, 690, 725, 726
Laubach Literacy Inc., 358
Lauwerys, Joseph A., 174, 209, 334, 539, 569, 1000, 1077
Lavalle Urbina, Eduardo L., 695
League for Instructing Illiterate Laborers, Haiti, 552
Lear, John, 817
Leavitt, Howard B., 1106
Legião Brasileira de Assistência, 243
Leith, Agnes June, 1071
Lemke, Donald A., 437
Lenz, Frank B., 632
León de la Barra, Bernabé, 624
León Palacios, O. de, 536
Leonard, Olen E., 93
Lepage Barreto, Ramón, 974
Lewis, Alfred E., 107
Lewis, Mary Gunnell, 995
Levy, Gustavo, 263
'Libertad', 294
Liga Alfabetizadora Ecuatoriana, 1086, 1143

Liga de Enseñanza de Alfabetización, Ecuador, 476, 483
Lima, Francisco da Gama, 215
Lima, Vicente Ferrer Correia, 109
Lind, Lards, 545
Linke, Lilo, 476
Lira López, Salvador, 750
Llerandi, Felipe, 998
Llosa Larrabure, Jaime, 818
Llovera Ll., B., 981
Lloyd, A. S., 1201
Lôbo, Maria Regina, 115
Lockwood, Agnese Nelms, 1045
Lombardo Toledano, Vicente, 762
Loomis, Charles P., 871, 1096, 1097
Lopes, Stênio, 216
López de Filipis, Haydée, 1105
López Ricoy, Luis, 634
Lorenzetto, Anna, 439
Lourenço, Manoel Bergström, 149-151, 240, 1202
Lowry, Dennis T., 708
Lube, Catalina, 941
La Lucha Fundamental Education Project, Costa Rica, 393, 398
Lugo de Sendra, Clara, 939
Lundy, Howard W., 168
Lyle, Jack, 559, 819
Lyon, Norman, 110
Lyons, Raymond F., 1179

Macedo, Luiz Antonio, 164
Mack, Mary D., 635
Maddison, John, 1107
Maes, Ernest E., 52
Mahlman, Harold E., 790
Maitland, John, 636
Management and Productivity Center, Trinidad and Tobago, 951
Manrique de Lara, Juana, 769, 1203
Mantovani, Juan, 31
Manzanilla, Víctor Hugo, 1003
Manzano, Matilde, 422
Marbial Fundamental Education Project, Haiti, 542-551, 557, 1027-1029, 1033, 1131, 1135, 1149, 1164
Mardones Guíñez, Irene, 303
Marier, Roger, 570
Marshall, Kendric N., 546
Martin, D'Arcy, 1204
Martins Pereira, José, 294
Martínez Salas, Antonio, 975
Martínez Tono, Rodolfo, 376, 377
Mary Loretta, Sister, 111

Maryknoll Radio School, Peru, 67, 70, 844, 850, 904, 917, 1153
Mathias, R., 455
Matos, A., 130
Mauck, Wilfred, 59, 60
Mauna, Nelson Severino, 264
McAnany, Emile G., 1147
McConnell, H. Ormonde, 557
McEvoy, J. P., 637
McGinn, Noel F., 1015, 1085
McKay, Alberto, 781
Medary, Marjorie, 1108
Medellín Pilot Public Library, Colombia, 340, 360, 362
Medina, José Ramón, 982
Meek, George, 1118, 1148
Mejía Castro, Arístides, 1031
Melo, Almeri Bezerra de, 152
Mencías Chávez, Jorge, 456
Mende, Tibor, 547
Mendoza, Angélica, 61
Mendoza Gutiérrez, Alfredo, 776
Mendoza R., Samuel, 820
Mennonite Church, 926
Método Dom Bosco, 245. *See also* Dom Bosco Schools
Métraux, Alfred, 1046
Mexico, Consejo Nacional Técnico de la Educación, 754
Mexico, Department of Labor, 731
Mexico, Department of Public Health, 731
Mexico, Department of Public Health and Welfare, 610
Mexico, Dirección General de Alfabetización y Educación Extraescolar, 638-639, 709, 711, 712, 751
Mexico, Dirección General de Asuntos Indígenas, 640, 745
Mexico, Dirección General para el Desarrollo de la Comunidad Rural, 746
Mexico, Ministry of Communications and Public Operations, 738
Mexico, Ministry of Public Health and Social Welfare, 1036, 1038
Mexico, Secretaría de Educación, 642, 729
Mexico, Secretaría de Educación Pública, 643-645, 671, 708, 710-712, 753, 754, 770
Mexico, Secretaría de Recursos Hidráulicos, 755
Mexico, Secretariat of Agriculture and Livestock, 683
Mexico (State), Dirección de Agricultura y Ganadería, 685, 734

Meyer, Walter Lanford, 527
Michaels, Leila, 646
Miller, Raymond W., 872
Miñano García, Max H., 399, 772
Misión Andina. *See* Andean Mission Program
Misión de Educación Rural, Chile, 298
Misión 'Economía y Humanismo', 390
Misiones Ambulantes de Cultura Inicial, Guatemala, 1161
Misiones Culturales, Mexico, 117, 451, 579, 581, 583, 585-587, 603, 605, 606, 609, 611, 616, 626, 630, 631, 634, 638, 639, 642-645, 647, 655, 657, 659, 661, 709, 739-742, 744, 745, 747-751, 753, 755, 757-761, 764, 766, 1026, 1028, 1029, 1033, 1038, 1068, 1097, 1104, 1130, 1134, 1135, 1139, 1142, 1143, 1145, 1149, 1154, 1158, 1164
Misiones de Cultura Campesina, Chile, 304
Misiones Educativas, Cuba, 432
Misiones Evangélicas Brethren & Unida Andina Indígena, Ecuador, 453
Misiones Rurales, Honduras, 1135
Misiones Sociales, Ecuador, 451, 490
Misiones Sociales, Haiti, 541
Moehlman, Arthur Henry, 657
Mohr, Hermann J., 329
Molina Córdova, Armando, 735
Moll Briones, Luis, 265, 266, 284
Monge Medrano, Carlos, 801, 802, 808, 821
Mongrut Muñoz, Octavio, 822
Monographs on Fundamental Education, United Nations Educational, Scientific, and Cultural Organization, 549, 570, 626, 667
Montalvo, Abner Selim, 823, 824
Montalvo, Efraín, 907
Montenegro B., Raúl, 349
Montesinos, Roberto, 983
Montojos, Francisco, 217
Montoya Medinacely, Víctor, 62, 63
Moosai Maharji, S., 950
Morales Benítez, Otto, 1205
Morales de los Rios, Adolfo, 218
Morales y del Campo, Ofelia, 436
Moreira, João Roberto, 153, 239, 241, 1206, 1207
Morialdo de Abadie Soriano, Ofelia, 1149
Morin, Renee, 756
Mosher, Arthur T., 112, 1150
Movimento Brasileiro de Alfabetização, 136, 141, 155, 242, 245
Movimento de Cultura Popular, Brazil, 1067
Movimento de Educação de Base, Brazil, 134,

145, 146, 154, 239, 242, 244, 245, 1067, 1147
Movimento Universitário de Desenvolvimento Econômico e Social, Brazil, 245
Movimiento de la Juventud Agraria, Uruguay, 953
Murgueytio, Reinaldo, 477
Murillo, José, 423
Murillo Revalos, José Antonio, 1208
Museo Nacional de Higiene, Mexico, 767
Museo Social Argentino, 41
Museu de Arte, São Paulo, Brazil, 163
Mutal, Silvio, 83, 84
Myers, Charles Nash, 757
Myren, Delbert T., 684

Nannetti Cárdenas, Guillermo, 330, 1209, 1210
Nash, Manning, 531
National Agrarian Institute, Venezuela, 1011
National Federation of Coffee Growers, Colombia. *See* Federación Nacional de Cafeteros, Colombia
National Institute of Housing and Urbanization, Costa Rica, 1038
National Program Coordenation, Jamaica, 1038
National Union of Colombian Workers, 366
National Vocational Training Committee, Chile, 1074
National Vocational Training Service for Industry, Mexico. *See* Adiestramiento Rápido de la Mano-de-Obra, Mexico
Navea Acevedo, Daniel, 304
Nayarit Fundamental Education Project, Mexico, 576-578, 584, 611, 612, 617, 618, 636, 642, 644, 648, 654, 667, 668, 672, 748, 1026, 1135, 1164
Negrín, Julio, 428
Nelson, Linda, 1211, 1212
Netherlands Universities Foundation for International Cooperation, *Publications*, 836
Neves e Silva, Maria Helena, 165
Neys, Karel, 439
Nicaragua, Ministerio de Educación Pública, 773, 774
Nichols, Andrew J., 873
Nicoletta Solinas, T. S., 961
Niilus, L., 2
Nitsch, Manfred, 332
Noel, John Vayasour, 716
Nogales Castro, Fernando, 85
Nogues, André, 32
Nordin, June Leith, 173
Norman, James, 649

Núcleo Educativo Comunal, Peru, 805
Núcleo Selvícola de Moré, Bolivia, 54
Núcleos Escolares, Colombia, 388
Núcleos Escolares Campesinos, Bolivia, 47, 50, 52, 57, 60, 63, 67, 68, 71, 1130, 1146
Núcleos Escolares Campesinos, Guatemala, 1034, 1146
Núcleos Escolares Campesinos, Peru, 792-794, 804, 841, 851, 852, 907, 910, 911, 919, 1135, 1146
Nuevo Mundo (radio station), Colombia, 365
Núñez del Prado C., Oscar, 825, 826
Nutrition Information Documents Series, Food and Agricultural Organization, 1112
Nutrition Program, Costa Rica, 1038

Occasional Papers in Education, United Nations Educational, Scientific, and Cultural Organization, 318, 338, 931, 942
Occasional Papers in Education and Development, Center for Studies in Education and Development, Harvard University, 1085
Oficina de Educación Iberoamericana, 985
Oficina de Estudios Especiales, Mexico, 1150
Oficina Regional de Educación de la UNESCO para América Latina y el Caribe, 155
Ogden, Horace G., 650, 686
O'Hara, Hazel, 64, 457, 827, 1113
Olazcoaya, Quintín, 750
Olivé, Rodolfo, 39
Opper, C. G., 922
ORDEC, Venezuela, 1008
Order of St. Joseph of Turin, 1143
Ordóñez, María Victoria de, 537
Organización Internacional del Trabajo. *See* International Labor Organization
Organización Regional Interamericana de Trabajadores, 1031, 1115, 1116
Organizaciones de Base Campesinos, Bolivia, 92
Organizadores de Acción Comunal, Venezuela. *See* Acción en Venezuela
Organization for Economic Cooperation and Development, 40, 1213
Organization for Rehabilitation Through Training, Brazil, 238
Organization of American States, 4, 22, 114, 242, 305, 333, 458, 651, 662, 1041, 1118, 1119, 1149, 1151, 1194
Organization of American States, Comisión Interamericana de Telecomunicaciones, 4, 22, 114, 242, 333

Organization of American States, Comité Interamericano de Desarrollo Agrícola, 874

Organization of American States, Committee for Cultural Action, 651

Organization of American States, Consejo Interamericano Económico y Social, 4, 22, 114, 242, 333

Organization of American States, Inter-American Cultural Council, 651

Orientation Schools, Haiti. *See* Escuelas de Orientación, Haiti

Orlandí, J., 252

Ortiz, V. G., 485

Ortiz Benítez, Lucas, 624

Osorio, José, 908

Ospina Restrepo, Gabriel, 458

Otavalo Textile Center, Ecuador, 1157, 1164

Otero, Jorge, 943

Oxford Committee for Famine Relief, 55

Ozaeta, Pablo M., 334

Pacheco, S., 522

Pacheco Cruz, Santiago, 717

Pacific Science Association, 293

Padre Anchieta Foundation, 146, 147

Padrón, Hiram, 1002

Paez Formoso, Miguel A., 960

Palacios Herrera, Oscar, 1003

Palacios R., Julián, 828

Palmer, David Scott, 909

Pan American Union, 34, 253, 784, 874, 1075, 1086, 1119, 1214

Pan American Union, Department of Cultural Affairs, 784

Pan American Union, Departamento de Asuntos Económicos y Sociales, 1214

Pan American Union, Departamento de Asuntos Educativos, 1075, 1086

Pan American Union, División de Trabajo y Asuntos Sociales, 1214

Pan American Union, Division of Education, 253, 784

Panama, Department of Agriculture, 780

Panama, Departamento de Salud Pública, 782

Panama, Ministerio de Salud, 781

Panama, Ministerio de Trabajo, Previsión Social y Salud Pública, 782

Panama, Ministry of Education, 783

Panama, Sección de Bioestadística y Educación Sanitaria, 782

Panel of Consultants on Indigenous and Tribal Populations, 1044

Paraiso, Virginia A., 1215

Parra Pradenas, Ortelio, 267

Partido Agrario, Uruguay, 960

Pasquale, Carlos, 220

Patch, Richard Wilbur, 829

Paulston, Rolland G., 437, 910-913, 1032

Peace Corps, 358, 496, 568, 829, 909

Pearse, Andrew C., 1033

Pellegrini, Maria, 115

Peña Cortés, Delio Gerardo, 1098

Penna, Carlos Víctor, 1216

Peraza Medina, Francisco, 718

Pereira, Evaldo Simas, 1068, 1217

Perera, Hilda, 417

Pérez Salinas, Pedro B., 1003

Pérez Yacomotti, Nélida, 928

Perlaza Saavedra, F., 77, 868

Peru, Dirección de Asuntos Indígenas, 869

Peru, Dirección de Educación Común, 884, 885

Peru, Dirección de Educación Primaria y del Adulto, 914

Peru, Ministerio de Educación Pública, 912, 914, 915

Peru, Ministerio de Fomento y Obras Públicas, 915

Peru, Ministerio de Salud Pública, Trabajo y Previsión Social, 915

Peru, Ministry of Agriculture, 857, 912

Peru, Ministry of Labor and Communities, 912

Peru, Presidente, 915

Peru-Cornell Project, 798, 800-803, 807-811, 813, 814, 817, 821, 823-827, 829, 835, 846, 855, 856, 870, 877, 888, 899, 901, 908-910, 916, 918, 1140, 1154-1157, 1175, 1197

Pijoan, Michel, 779

Pindorama Educational Center, Brazil, 116

Pinto, Luis Emilio, 732

Pinto, Zilma Coelho, 160

Plan de Educación Fundamental, Chile, 1135

Plan de Escuelas Populares, Cuba, 427

Plan de Mejoramiento Integral de Tactic, Guatemala, 528

Plan del Mínimo Técnico, Cuba, 427, 430, 431, 435, 437

Plan Nacional de Alfabetización de Adultos, Ecuador, 475, 478

Plan Nacional de Integración de la Población Aborigen, Peru, 825, 830-832, 908, 909, 1142

Planning Pamphlet, National Planning Association, 948

Platt, William James, 306, 307

Point Four Program, 503, 507, 790, 862, 872, 1063, 1157

Polyvalent Educational Center '5 de Septiembre', Cuba, 428
Population Council, Trinidad and Tobago, 951
Pote Cole Project, Haiti, 1036
Pou de Mejia, Margarita, 442
Pozzi, Jorge Tomás, 46
Practical Agricultural Schools, Mexico, 1025
Practical Agriculture and Demonstration Center, Venezuela, 1009
Practical School of Skilled Workers in the Cultivation of Coffee, Venezuela, 1006
Praeger Special Studies in International Economics and Development, 944, 1126
Prieto Figueroa, Luis Beltrán, 1152
Primera Escuela Sindical Argentina, 39
Pritt, D. N., 424
Program of Technical Cooperation, Organization of American States, 1118, 1119
Programa Andino. *See* Andean Mission Program
Programa de Alimentación y Educación Nutricional, Paraguay, 791
Programa de Crédito Agrícola Supervisado, Peru, 908
Programa de Educación de la Comunidad, Puerto Rico, 927-932, 944, 947, 1035
Programa de las Naciones Unidas para el Desarrollo, Sector Cooperación Técnica, 791, 1010
Programa de Promoción Agrícola, Honduras, 558
Programa Educacional Cooperativo, Bolivia, 52
Programa Intensivo de Preparação da Mão-de-Obra, Brazil, 205, 232, 236, 245
Programa Nacional de Desarrollo Comunal, Venezuela, 1011, 1082
Programa Nacional de Desarrollo de la Comunidad, Guatemala, 520
Programa Nacional de Desarrollo de la Comunidad, Venezuela, 1086
Programa Nacional Intensivo de Alfabetización y Educación de Adultos, Argentina, 7-8, 11, 44
Programa Puno-Tambopata, Peru, 826, 853, 854, 899, 908, 916, 1142
Project 39, Organization of American States, 1150
Projeto Rondon, Brazil, 245
Promoción Popular, Chile, 1085
Promoción Profesional Popular-Rural, Colombia, 1132
Proyecto Capiasi de Educación Fundamental, Bolivia, 1135

Proyecto de Antropología Aplicada, Peru, 916
Proyecto La Guajira, Venezuela, 966-968, 1010, 1042
Proyecto Piloto de Alfabetización de Adultos, Ecuador, 475
Proyecto Piloto de Casa de Jóvenes, Argentina, 1158
Proyecto Tarasco, Mexico, 692, 697
Puebla Project, Mexico, 678, 679, 684, 1132
Puerto Rico, Administración del Hogar del Agricultor, 947
Puerto Rico, Commission for Improvement of Isolated Communities, 944
Puerto Rico, Commonwealth Board for Vocational Education, 934
Puerto Rico, Congreso, Cámara de Representantes, 929
Puerto Rico, Department of Education, 942
Puerto Rico, Department of Public Instruction, 928
Puerto Rico, Departamento de Agricultura y Comercio, 939, 947
Puerto Rico, Departamento de Trabajo, 947
Puerto Rico, División de Educación de la Comunidad, 927-932, 942, 1029, 1030, 1033, 1036, 1038, 1130, 1146, 1164
Puerto Rico, División de Instrucción Vocacional, 943
Puerto Rico, Division of Community Education. *See* Puerto Rico, División de Educación de la Comunidad
Puerto Rico, Economic Development Administration, 948
Puerto Rico, Housing Authority, 1164
Puerto Rico, Land Authority, 939, 1164
Puerto Rico, Oficina de Salud, 947
Puerto Rico, Social Programs Administration, 939, 1038
Puerto Rico Reconstruction Administration, 936, 945
Puga, Mario, 652
Puig, José Pedro, 956
Puryear, Jeffrey M., 378

Quesada, A., 76
Quirno Costa, José A., 35

Radio Escuela, Uruguay, 957
Radio Escuela Experimental, Chile, 302
Radio Sutatenza, Colombia, 313-317, 319-321, 332-337, 339, 341, 365, 388, 390, 464, 559, 1064, 1104, 1128, 1139, 1162
Radvanyi, Laszlo, 654
Ramos, Myra Bergman, 1191
Ravera, Alfredo, 1171, 1218

Ravndal, Christian M., 460
Reconstruction Board for Tungurahua, Ecuador, 1164
Redfield, Robert, 655
Reimer, Everett W., 1219
Rens, Jef, 1050-1057, 1076
Reports and Papers on Mass Communication, United Nations Educational, Scientific, and Cultural Organization, 1107
Research Report Series, Industrial Relations Section, Department of Economics, Princeton University, 757
Reyes Rosales, José Jerónimo, 759
Reyes Salcido, Edgardo, 736
Ribeiro, Adalberto Mário, 170
Rice, Edward B., 1099
Richter, Willi, 116
Rio, Fernando del, 1220
Rio Coco Fundamental Education Project, Nicaragua, 772, 773, 775, 1036
Rio Piedras Agricultural Experiment Station, Puerto Rico, *Bulletin*, 936
Ríos, José Arthur, 117
Ríos Castro, Rigoberto, 293
Riske, Roger, 951
Rivera Ramírez, Alejandro, 886
Robbins, Jerry H., 223
Roberts, Lydia J., 1221
Robles, Optulio de, 36
Rockefeller Foundation, 238, 272, 678, 1132
Rodríguez Bou, Ismael, 947
Rojas, F., 867
Rolfo, Federico, 953
Romaña, Cecilio, 1072
Romaña, José M. de, 917
Romero, Fernando, 555, 834
Romero Lozano, Simón, 1222
Romero O., Eddie J., 966, 967
Romero P., Fernando, 898, 923
Roper Public Opinion Research Center, 1037
Rosado, Humberto, 1019
Rossi, Adriano, 268
Rosten, Frank, 835
Roucek, Joseph S., 425, 657
Rubio Orbe, Gonzalo, 65, 94, 1087, 1154-1158
Ruddle, Kenneth R., 964
Ruhl, J. Mark, 322
Ruiz, Rodrigo, 407
Ruiz Camacho, Rubén, 1100
Ruiz Franco, Arcadio, 538
Ruopp, Phillips, 618
Rural Cultural Service, Bolivia. *See* Servicio Cultural Rural, Bolivia
Rural Extension Service, Brazil, 1169

Rural Institutions and Planned Change, United Nations Research Institute for Social Development, 1129, 1186
Rural Social Service, Brazil, 99
Rural Social Welfare Program, Mexico, 1038
Rural Teacher Training Center, Venezuela. *See* Centro de Capacitación Rural, Venezuela
Rural Welfare Service, Brazil, 118
Rust, Val D., 951

Saavedra E., Enrique, 269, 312
Sabanes, C. M., 2
Saco, Alfredo, 924
Sahagún Torres, J., 996
Salas S., Irma, 269, 312
Salas Populares de Lectura, Mexico, 760
Salazar, Segundo Miguel, 461, 462
Salbado, Dilke, 157
Salcedo, José Joaquín, 315, 319, 337
Salgado, Alvaro de Faria, 24, 166
Salles, Eugenio de Araujo, 244
Salud y Bienestar (radio program), Panama, 782
Sampaio, Rogerio, 119
Samper Ortega, Daniel, 391
Sánchez, George I., 657, 1004
Sánchez, Patricio S., 338
Sandelmann, John C., 836
Sanders, Irwin T., 1097
Sanders, Thomas Griffin, 285, 286, 363, 1069
Sanginés Uriarte, Marcelo, 95
Santa Catalina Center, Llavallol, Argentina, 3
Santa Cruz Erráruriz, Gonzalo, 1223
Santa María University, Chile, 296
Savloff, Guillermo, 1158
Sayre, Mrs. Raymond, 658
Scanlon, David G., 174, 539, 569, 1000
Schick, Rene, 775
Schneider, Robert G., 837
Scholes, Walter V., 659
School of Inter-American Studies, University of Florida, *Publications Series 1*, 1033
School of Popular Learning, Mexico, 674
Schools of Christ, 62
Schools of Orientation, Haiti. *See* Escuelas de Orientación, Haiti
Scully, Michael, 722
Schweng, Lorand D., 66
Seers, Dudley, 435
Seltzer, George, 371
Seminar for Leaders of Youth Movements in Latin America, 1167
Seminario de Trabajo sobre Desarrollo de la Comunidad, 91

Seminario Iberoamericano de Alfabetización, 1109

Seminario Interamericano de Alfabetización y Educación de Adultos, 1171, 1173, 1224, 1225

Seminario Interamericano de Líderes de Juventudes Rurales, 397

Seminário Internacional sôbre 'Resistências á Mudança—Fatôres que Impedem ou Dificultam o Desenvolvimento', 224

Seminario Regional de Asuntos Sociales, 1159

Seminario Suramericano de Extensión Agrícola, 343

Seminarios y Reuniones Técnicas, Oficina de Educación Iberoamericana, 1109

Serie Antropología Social, Instituto Indigenista Interamericano, 93, 1175

Serie Didáctica, Programa Nacional Intensivo de Alfabetización y Educación de Adultos, Argentina, 8, 44

Série Ecumanismo e Humanismo, 1190

Serie Estudios y Documentos, Centro de Documentación e Información Educativa, Tucumán, Argentina, 13

Série Estudos Brasileiros, Serviço de Informação Agrícola, Brazil, 99

Serie Informativa, Programa Nacional Intensivo de Alfabetización y Educación de Adultos, Argentina, 7, 11

Serie Planes, Programas y Orientaciones Técnicas, Dirección General de Alfabetización y Educación Extraescolar, Mexico, 711, 712

Serie sobre Educación Social del Trabajador, División de Trabajo y Asuntos Sociales, Pan American Union, 511

Serie sobre Organización de la Comunidad, División de Trabajo y Asuntos Sociales, Pan American Union, 367, 458, 932, 1088

Serie Socio-Económica, Centro de Investigaciones Sociales, Oficina Internacional de Investigaciones Sociales de FERES, 339

Series N on Vocational Education, Division of Education, Pan American Union, 555, 784

Service Coopératif Interaméricain de Production Agricole, Haiti, 1150, 1164

Service Coopératif Interaméricain de Santé Publique, Haiti, 1164

Service for the Protection of Indians, Brazil, 1143

Servicio Agricultura Interamericano, 70

Servicio Ambulante Rural de Extensión Cultural, Ecuador, 454, 461, 462, 483, 490, 1143, 1157

Servicio Cooperativo Interamericano de Educación, Bolivia, 56, 60, 64, 67, 68, 71, 90, 1124, 1134

Servicio Cooperativo Interamericano de Educación, Guatemala, 535

Servicio Cooperativo Interamericano de Educación, Panama, 783

Servicio Cooperativo Interamericano de Educación, *Publicaciones Serie A*, 783

Servicio Cooperativo Interamericano de Producción de Alimentos, 1162

Servicio Cooperativo Interamericano de Producción de Alimentos, Costa Rica, 1145

Servicio Cooperativo Interamericano de Producción de Alimentos, Paraguay, 1145

Servicio Cooperativo Interamericano de Producción de Alimentos, Peru, 796, 797, 816, 836, 838, 861, 862, 875, 876, 878, 901, 903, 1138, 1145, 1150

Servicio Cooperativo Interamericano de Producción de Alimentos, Venezuela, 972, 995

Servicio Cooperativo Interamericano de Salud Pública, 62, 1113

Servicio Cooperativo Interamericano de Salud Pública, Peru, 839, 840, 890, 891

Servicio Cooperativo Peruano Norteamericano de Educación, 841, 886, 918

Servicio Cultural Rural, Bolivia, 57, 58, 69

Servicio de Cooperación Técnica, Chile, 306, 307, 1165

Servicio de Cultura del Ejército, Cuba, 432

Servicio de Demonstración del Hogar Campesino, Venezuela, 995

Servicio de Educación Fundamental, Bolivia, 91

Servicio de Extensión Agrícola, Chile, 274

Servicio de Extensión Agrícola Rural, Peru, 864, 866, 908

Servicio de Fomento de la Economía Indígena, Guatemala, 518, 521

Servicio de Investigación y Promoción Agraria, Peru, 874

Servicio Ecuatoriano de Capacitación Profesional, 448

Servicio Ecuatoriano de Voluntarios, 463

Servicio Extensivo de Educación Agrícola, Mexico, 642

Servicio Nacional de Aprendizaje, Colombia, 350, 369, 371-384, 389, 1073-1075, 1079, 1125, 1127, 1132, 1137, 1139, 1165, 1169

Servicio Nacional de Aprendizaje, Colombia, Seccional Cundinamarca, 381

Servicio Nacional de Aprendizaje, Colombia, Seccional de Antioquía, 382, 383

Servicio Nacional de Aprendizaje y Trabajo

Industrial, Peru, 894-898, 904, 912, 913, 921, 1073-1075, 1086, 1127, 1165, 1169
Servicio Nacional de Extensión Agrícola, Ecuador, 469
Servicio Oficial de Radiodifusión, Argentina, 4
Servicio Técnico Agrícola Colombiano Americano, 1100
Servicio Técnico Interamericano de Cooperación Agrícola, Costa Rica, 396, 400, 404
Servicio Técnico Interamericano de Cooperación Agrícola, Paraguay, 789, 791, 1138
Serviço de Ação Comunitária, Brazil. *See* Universidade Católica de Pernambuco, Serviço de Ação Comunitária
Serviço de Alimentação da Previdência Social, Brazil, 170, 173
Serviço de Assistência Rural, Brazil, 244
Serviço de Educação de Adultos, Brazil, 245
Serviço de Extensão Cultural. *See* University of Recife, Serviço de Extensão Cultural
Serviço de Informação Agrícola, Brazil, 99
Serviço de Radiodifusão Educativa, Brazil, 114, 158
Serviço Especial de Saúde Pública, Brazil, 111, 168, 169
Serviço Nacional de Aprendizagem Comercial, Brazil, 178, 196, 198, 203, 208, 215, 219, 224, 234, 237, 240, 243, 245, 1073-1075, 1125, 1137, 1165, 1169
Serviço Nacional de Aprendizagem Industrial, Brazil, 100, 174, 176, 177, 179-192, 194, 195, 197-204, 206, 208-212, 214, 216, 217, 220, 222-227, 229-231, 234, 236, 237, 240, 243, 245, 369, 1073-1075, 1079, 1080, 1124, 1125, 1127, 1137, 1139, 1145, 1152, 1165, 1169
Serviço Nacional de Aprendizagem Industrial, Brazil, Administração Regional no Estado da Guanabara, 182
Serviço Nacional de Aprendizagem Industrial, Brazil, Departamento Nacional, 183
Serviço Nacional de Aprendizagem Industrial, Brazil, Departamento Regional de Sergipe, 192
Serviço Nacional de Aprendizagem Industrial, Brazil, Departamento Regional de São Paulo, 187-191
Serviço Nacional de Aprendizagem Industrial, Brazil, Departamento Regional do Espírito Santo, 184
Serviço Nacional de Aprendizagem Industrial, Brazil, Departamento Regional do Rio Grande do Sul, 185, 186

Serviço Social da Indústria, Brazil, 101, 107, 108, 119-124, 203, 236, 243
Serviço Social do Comércio, Brazil, 161, 243
Sheats, Paul Henry, 660
Shell Oil Company, 1010
Shannon, Lyle W., 927
Shellaby, Robert K., 876
Shepard, Marietta Daniels, 358
Silva, José Carlos N. da, 146
Silveira, Horácio, 227
Simmons, John L., 687
Sindicato de Luz y Fuerza, Argentina, 39
Sindicato General de Matarifes, El Salvador, 511
Sínodo Evangélico de Guatemala, 537
Sistema Socio-Educativo Rural, Guatemala, 535
Smith, Henry Lester, 661
Smith, Lucille, 842
Smith, Marinobel, 760
Smith, Thomas Lynn, 131
Smith, William C., 688
Social Anthropological Series, Publications in Anthropology, University of Chicago, 655
Sociedad Nacional Agraria, Peru, 903
Sodi M., Demetrio, 662
Soinit, Albert, 843
South Pacific Commission, *Technical Paper*, 1161
Souza, Fernando Tude de, 158
Spangen, Berthe, 86
SRI Project, Stanford Research Institute, 307
St. Clair, David, 845
Staley, Eugene, 1126
Stanley, Ruth Hoffman, 689
Stanton, Margaret Gwenllian, 275
Status Report, Pan American Union, 352
Stead, William H., 948
Stein, William W., 877
Stenton, Jean E., 663
Stevenson, Gordon K., 999
Stowe, Leland, 846
Studies and Reports, New Series, International Labor Office, 1143, 1145
Studies in Comparative Education, Division of International Education, U. S. Office of Education, 804
Studies in Comparative Education, University of Pittsburgh Press, 239
Studies of Technical Cooperation in Latin America, National Planning Association, 1150
Studies on Compulsory Education, United Nations Educational, Scientific, and Cultural Organization, 483

Suárez S., Alberto, 351
Sugar Industry Labour Welfare Board, Jamaica, 1038
Summer Institute of Linguistics, 82, 95, 159, 460, 524, 528, 535, 537, 607, 692, 724, 795, 806, 812, 820, 837, 843, 845, 847, 848, 859, 883, 886, 911, 1021, 1086, 1154
Superación de la Mujer, Cuba, 416, 431
Superación Obrera-Campesina, Cuba, 431, 433, 435
Superintendência do Desenvolvimento do Nordeste, Brazil, 100, 140, 193, 1083

Tabbush, Yvonne, 160
Tannenbaum, Frank, 761
Tanner, Louise Brantley, 848
Tarahumara Project, Mexico, 1147
Tarasco Project, Mexico. See Proyecto Tarasco, Mexico
Tardío Maida, Alberto, 70
Tarso Santos, Paulo de, 276
Tavares, José Nilo, 161
Taylor, Carl Cleveland, 41
Taylor, Sue H., 1088
Teaf, Howard M., Jr., 836
Teatro Cultural, Colombia, 387
Technical Education for the Improvement of Agriculture and Rural Life, 1118
Technical Meeting on Agricultural Extension, 1034
Technology and Society, United Nations Educational, Scientific, and Cultural Organization, 394, 1036, 1178, 1182, 1194
Tejada, Carmela, 1225
Telescuela Popular Americana, Peru, 819, 849
Theodorou, N. T., 273, 466
Thomasson, F. H., 539
Thompson, Adia, 762
Thompson, Timothy J., 371, 912, 1032
Thomson, R., 1161
Thornton, Basil, 986
Tidone, Jorge Federico, 17
The Times, London, 850
Tinageros Goizueta, Nicanor, 851
Tingo María Agricultural Experiment Station, Peru, 857, 860, 871
Tirado Benedi, Domingo, 162
Tobacco Development Institute, Colombia, 388
Tobacco Marketing Association, Puerto Rico, 939
Tobar, Julio, 501
Tonkin, Joseph D., 935
Toral Viteri, Miguel, 487
Torres, Luis F., 1110

Torres Bodet, Jaime, 706, 716, 722, 725, 760, 766
Torres Restrepo, Camilo, 339
Toubes, Amanda, 1226
Trail, JoAnn S., 496
Training Course for Administers of Agrarian Reform Programs, 1118
Trinidad and Tobago Telephone Company, 951
Tulane University, Middle American Research Institute, Publication, 612
Turosienski, Severin K., 438
TV2 Cultura, Brazil, 133

Unidad Sanitaria, Catia, Venezuela, 994
Unidad Sanitaria, Santa Teresa del Tuy, Venezuela, 996
Unidades Móviles de Educación Fundamental, Peru, 886
Unión de Federaciones Universitarias de Chile, 259, 260, 287
Unión de Trabajadores de Colombia, 367
Unión Nacional de Periodistas, Ecuador, 455, 472, 473, 476, 477, 479-483, 493, 497, 498, 1086, 1134, 1143
United Fruit Company, 1097
United Methodist Committee for Overseas Relief, 55
United Nations, 521, 763, 842, 893, 925, 1011, 1035, 1038, 1042, 1060, 1089, 1120-1123, 1162-1166, 1215, 1227
United Nations, Bureau of Social Affairs, 1035, 1162, 1194
United Nations, Commissioner for Technical Assistance, 1011
United Nations, Department of Economic and Social Affairs, 1011
United Nations, Department of Social Affairs, 1163, 1164
United Nations, Economic and Social Council, 1120
United Nations, Economic Commission for Latin America. See Economic Commission for Latin America
United Nations, Office of Public Information, 763
United Nations, Technical Assistance Administration, 521, 925, 1120, 1121
United Nations Children's Fund, 364
United Nations Development Program, 1089
United Nations Educational, Scientific, and Cultural Organization, 84, 154, 316, 330, 338, 340, 342, 362, 393, 394, 398, 426, 439, 454, 471, 529, 543-546, 549-551, 557, 576, 608, 617, 618, 628, 654, 660,

664-670, 673, 675, 692, 748, 772, 954, 1029, 1041, 1042, 1090, 1128, 1143, 1146, 1167, 1171, 1194, 1208, 1209, 1228
United Nations Educational, Scientific, and Cultural Organization, Department of Cultural Activities, 340, 362
United Nations Educational, Scientific, and Cultural Organization, Department of Education, 1167
United Nations Series on Community Organization and Development, 1122
United Nations Technical Assistance Program, 540
U.S., Department of Agriculture, 1092
U.S., Department of Health, Education and Welfare, 918
U.S., Office of Education, *Bulletin*, 237, 300, 301, 387, 395, 438, 554, 587, 650, 902, 904, 931, 1004, 1009, 1139
U.S., Office of International Health, 1168
U.S. Technical Assistance Program, 738
Universidad Católica, Chile, 289, 298, 1084, 1136
Universidad Central, Venezuela, Dirección de Cultura, *Publicaciones*, 1152
Universidad Centroamericana, Nicaragua, 776
Universidad de Puerto Rico, Consejo Superior de Enseñanza, *Publicaciones Pedagógicas, Serie 2*, 947
Universidad del Trabajo, Uruguay, 1073, 1165
Universidad Nacional de Colombia, 359
Universidad Obrera, Mexico, 762
Universidad Popular, Guatemala, 535, 537, 1163
Universidad San Cristóbal de Huamanga, Peru, 834, 904
Universidad Católica de Pernambuco, Serviço de Ação Comunitária, 125
Universidad Federal, Rio Grande do Norte, Brazil, 245
University Extension Service, Costa Rica, 1036
University of Concepción, Chile, 1181
University of Costa Rica, 394
University of Puerto Rico, 1022
University of Recife, Serviço de Extensão Cultural, 152
University of Tarija, Bolivia, 86
University of the Atlantic, Colombia, 370
Uriona Fernández, Casto, 1229
Urtubia L., Olga, 271
Uruguay, National Council of Hygiene, 959
Uruguay, Office of Health Education, 959
Uzcátegui, Emilio, 483

Valenzuela, David, 1230
Valenzuela Kunckel de Sánchez, María, 671
Valle, Armando J., 564
Valle de la Esperanza Fundamental Education Project, El Salvador, 1140
Valle El General Fundamental Education Project, Costa Rica, 393, 398, 1128, 1135
Vanderbilt, Amy, 725
Vane, Erik, 726
Vannoy, Joellene, 365
Van Zeyl, Cornelis J., 1014
Varela Recéndez, Salvador, 764
Vargas de Adams, Emily, 392
Vásquez, Emilio, 919
Vásquez, Mario C., 801, 802, 810, 821, 888
Vásquez, Pedro Tomás, 1007
Vázquez Calcerrada, P. B., 936
Vega, Antonio, 407
Vela, José Manuel, 512
Velandia B., Wilson, 392
Velasco, Adolfo, 72
Velasco Núñez, Manuel D., 853
Veloz, Rubén, 464
Venezuela, Bureau of Literacy and Popular Culture. *See* Venezuela, Oficina Nacional de Alfabetización y Cultura Popular
Venezuela, Comisión Indigenista, 854, 968
Venezuela, División Nacional de Educación de Adultos, 1079, 1086
Venezuela, Embassy, 987
Venezuela, Ministerio de Educación, 1005
Venezuela, Ministerio de Educación Nacional, 989
Venezuela, Ministry of Agriculture, 1011
Venezuela, Ministry of Health and Welfare, 1011
Venezuela, Oficina de Alfabetización y Cultura Popular del Estado de Aragua, 990
Venezuela, Oficina de Alfabetización y Cultura Popular del Estado de Nueva Esparta, 991
Venezuela, Oficina de Alfabetización y Cultura Popular del Estado Yaracuy, 992
Venezuela, Oficina de Educación de Adultos, 993
Venezuela, Oficina Nacional de Alfabetización y Cultura Popular, 980, 987, 989
Venezuela, Patronato Nacional de Alfabetización, 980
Venezuela, Presidente, 1012
Verhine, Robert E., 1199
Vezzani, A. A., 738
Vianí Fundamental Education Project, Colombia, 318, 330, 338, 342, 1149, 1164
Vicens, Juan, 771

Vicos Project, Peru. *See* Peru-Cornell Project
Vieira, Alvaro, 299
Villanueva Pinillos, Alfonso, 889
Villaronga, Mariano, 938
Vintinner, Frederick J., 1017
Violich, Frances, 1091
Vocational Education, Series N, Pan American Union. *See Series N on Vocational Education,* Division of Education, Pan American Union
Volkshockschulen-Verband, 1020
Voluntary School Service, Colombia, 356
La Voz de los Andes (radio station), Ecuador, 457
Vries, Egbert de, 394, 1036, 1178, 1182

Waggoner, Barbara Ashton, 513
Waggoner, George R., 513
Wakefield, A. J., 571
Wale, Fred G., 927, 931
Walker, Florence G., 856, 857
Walker, Guild, 1060
Walls, Forest Wesley, 673
Walsh, Thomas E., 413
Ware, Caroline F., 858, 932, 1011
Warisata Normal School, Bolivia, 56, 61, 64, 71, 72, 1135, 1157
Warren, Gertrude L., 1101
Watson, Goodwin, 765
Weaver, Anthony John, 776
Weffort, Francisco C., 1190
Wendell, Margarita, 528
Wharton, Clifton R., Jr., 1013
Whetten, Nathan L., 766

White, John W., 171
White, Robert A., 560
Wilgus, A. Curtis, 608, 741, 1033
Williams College, Roper Public Opinion Research Center, 1037
Wilson, Edmund, 551
Wilson, Jacques M. P., 498
Wise, Mary Ruth, 859
Wise, Sidney, 674
Wojcicki, Antoni, 1011
Women's Civic League, Bolivia, 87
Woolley, George A., 860
Woolsey, Wallace, 675, 676
World Bank, 1132
World Health Organization, 364, 1041
Wright, J. C., 231

Yahn, Mario, 172
Yáñez, Agustín, 728
Ygobone, Aquiles D., 38
Young Men's Christian Association, Mexico, 621-623, 632, 637, 766
Young Women's Christian Association, Uruguay, 1071
Youngstrom, C. O., 470

Zalduondo, Celestina, 933
Zalvidea R., Edmundo, 861
Zarrilli, Humberto, 956
Zetterberg, Hans L., 767
Zubryn, Emil, 729
Zuna Rico, Jorge, 80
Zúñiga, Eduardo, 287